Big Dan

Photo credit: *Rio Grande*

BIG DAN

The Story of a Colorful Railroader

by

FRANK CUNNINGHAM

THE DESERET NEWS PRESS
SALT LAKE CITY, UTAH
1946

BOOKS BY FRANK CUNNINGHAM

SKY MASTER—*The Story of Donald Douglas*

BIG DAN—*The Story of a Colorful Railroader*

COPYRIGHT 1946

BY

FRANK CUNNINGHAM

*To the men of America's railroads
and especially those pioneers of
High Iron who threw rails
across the Rockies.*

Foreword

*R*AILROADS have been the life lines of America over the years. This country, so vast and wide, has been solidified by communication. Over a goodly part of our history that communication has been through transportation, and that transportation in large degree has been by rail.

There are no dialects in America such as may be found in other much smaller and less travelled countries. Neither do our customs and daily habits greatly vary. The reason is that Americans get around. They do their business from coast to coast with no barriers to intervene. They work together, study together, attend sports events together, vacation together, and they travel the whole country over to do it.

One great factor stands out in all this, and that is that it has been through the operation of the Iron Horse that Americans have been able to do all these things. The railroads therefore, have been among the great builders of what we have come to call "our way of life."

As the rails have been extended in a vast network over this country, the nation has grown. Think of America back in 1826 when the first railroad began its operation, running on crude wooden tracks. Contrast that with America of today. Read the thrilling story of the laying of the rails from the Atlantic to the Pacific, and you read the epic drama of westward colonization. With each advancing step of the rail lines, education was promoted, industry established and developed, cities were built, farmers broke new land because the rails offered a way to market their crops, churches enlarged their congregations, prosperity spread abroad. So the story of the rails is the story of the nation. Through the onward march of the Iron Horse, the country opened by the sweat and blisters of the men who laid the pathway of High Iron has become the ultimate realization of our nation's High Hopes. The once phantom dreams of our American pioneers have been brought to life by the clang of the locomotive bell, the roar of fast moving trains, and the conductor's thrilling cry of "All Abroad."

But what are railroads without the men who operate them? They are but inanimate things, waiting for the master hands to move them. It takes brain, and brawn, and human understanding to operate those trains; it takes a skillful hand, a steady eye, unerring judgment, a love for fellow men and devotion to service; it takes a deep sense of responsibility for the lives and property of the public.

America has had many great railroaders in its day. One of those great ones, typical of them all, is Big Dan. Daniel G. Cunningham, after whom this book is named, knows the railroads from the ground up. He has been part of the railroad industry of this country all his adult life, and the railroad industry has been part of him. He has lived it and breathed it, and sweat over it and loved it. And in response, the railroads have loved him, the men who labored with him adored him, would have sacrificed anything for him. In this respect Big Dan is a composite of so many clear headed railroad executives, and because these men were like Dan, the railroads were able to operate, and serve the land.

Dan started railroading at 18 years of age as a machinist apprentice. He worked 10 hours a day and got 6 cents an hour. When he became a full fledged machinist, he was paid the top wage of that time, 23 cents an hour, and was glad to get it. But big men move on. Dan became general foreman on the Norfolk and Western, general foreman for the Santa Fe at Needles, Superintendent of Shops for the Denver & Rio Grande Western at Salt Lake, Superintendent of Motive Power for the Denver & Salt Lake; and Master Mechanic of the Salt Lake Division of the Rio Grande.

His life is a life of service. His work, a labor of love. He is big in body and big in soul. His heart embraced the whole operation of the road; it took in the community. So well did the people of Salt Lake come to know him through his service in the municipality, so well did they understand his ability to make things go, that they called upon him to serve as a community leader in modernizing their city Fire Department, and named the largest truck in the department *Big*

Dan after "D. C." himself. When he was retired from active service on the railroad, he was honored by the railroad, the families of the employes, the city and the state.

It is fitting that he and the American railroads have been made co-subjects of this book. They belong together, they grew together. This volume is a tribute to the railroad industry; it is also a tribute to the men of that industry, through a most worthy representative, Big Dan Cunningham. His nephew Frank, has done America a great service in writing this volume.

MARK E. PETERSEN,
General Manager, *The Deseret News*

ACKNOWLEDGMENTS

Acknowledgment is given material gathered by the Association of American Railroads, Transportation Bldg., Washington D. C.

Several of the poetry quotations are from *Poems of James Ryder Randall* edited by Matthew Page Andrews.

Front cover jacket picture is a Currier & Ives lithograph of an Atlantic, Mississippi and Ohio train, courtesy of the Norfolk and Western.

Back cover jacket picture is courtesy of Glen Fishback, Sacramento, Calif.

End sheets picture is the Rio Grande *Scenic Limited* gliding over Tennessee Pass, the highest main line standard gauge crossing of the Continental Divide.

Special acknowledgment is given for the generous cooperation of Mr. George F. Dodge, Director of Public Relations, Denver and Rio Grande Western; Mr. Ken Lightburn, Director of News Bureau, Denver and Rio Grande Western; and Mr. R. R. Horner, Manager of the Advertising and Magazine Department, Norfolk and Western.

LIST OF ILLUSTRATIONS

Big Dan ....Frontispiece
Captain George Cunningham 27
Three Little Confederates 27
Virginia and Tennessee Train 28
"The Pocahontas" 28
Victorious Southerners 61
The Mighty "Dictator" 61
General Herman Haupt 61
Railroad Fighting in Virginia 62
Five Locomotives Built at Vicksburg 62
1838—City Point Railroad 83
General William Mahone 83
The Old "Dick Thomson" 84
An A. M. & O. Passenger Locomotive 84
Locomotive Used by the Shenandoah Valley 84
Big Dan and Classmate 129
Inez Eley Cunningham 129
Norfolk and Western Family 130
The Famed "Shou-wa-no" 227
First Standard Gauge Rio Grande Western Train 227
General William Jackson Palmer 228
Poster Proclaiming the Conquest of the Rockies 228
Marshall Pass 237
Five Car Freight on the Slopes of Marshall Pass 238
When Wood was King 238
The Royal Gorge Conquered 255
One of the Scenic Wonders of American Railroading 256
Action on the Moffat when Big Dan was Superintendent 281
Roaring Across the Top of the West 281
David H. Moffat 282
Engine Designed by Big Dan 282
"Teakettle" Narrow Gauge Locomotives 299
A Rio Grande Narrow Gauge Stock Train 299
Power in the Mountains 300
Moffat's Railroad Carries On 300

A Heavy Rio Grande Locomotive Thunders
    Through Glenwood Canyon _____309
A Norfolk and Western Coal Train _____310
Giants of the Rails _____310
"Let Her Roll, Let Her Roll, Mr. Engineer" _____319
It's not Always Fair Weather on the Rio Grande _____319
Frank H. Cunningham _____319
Means of Transportation _____320
Judge Wilson McCarthy _____329
Henry Swan _____329
W. H. Sagstetter _____329
W. B. Hall _____329
H. S. Wall _____330
Frank Haymond _____330
R. G. Henley _____330
J. D. Loftis _____330
L. C. Sprague _____330
Julian Bamberger _____330
President Heber J. Grant and Big Dan _____335
Famous American Legion Engine _____336

BIG DAN • The Story of a Colorful Railroader

CHAPTER I

"GET a rope and string the big bastard up!"

The crowd of angry railroad men moved in on the tall young man pinned against the wall of the Norfolk and Western railroad boiler shop at Roanoke, Virginia. Some of the workers, carrying a rope, pushed through the milling group.

"Dan Cunningham, you damned tin soldier, try dancing on the end of this!" The shouting worker lifted the rope before the eyes of the young man, who stood calmly as the incensed throng faced him. If ever Dan had been called on to get out of a tight spot in his twenty years of life, this was it.

When Dan Cunningham had joined the Roanoke Light Infantry, he hadn't anticipated having to fire on his fellow citizens. He had felt honored at having been taken into the ranks, as the militia had a long waiting list and, unless the applicant was of high character, he was not allowed to enlist. It had been fun to put on the dress uniform with its gray coat, blue trousers, and spiked helmet and have the pretty girls of Roanoke admire you even as their mothers had esteemed the Confederate gray uniformed fighters of Lee, Jackson and Stuart.

Once a week the militia drilled in the third floor armory at the old Bridgewater Carriage House. In firing practice with the state furnished rifles, the guardsmen would get bruised shoulders from the kick of the Springfields which were single shot weapons. Put in a shell, fire, eject the shell, open up the latch, put in another bullet, and fire again; such was the slow procedure. The militia actually never expected to shoot at anything but paper targets and this required no rapidity of fire.

Then one somber day in 1893 a negro had gone berserk, assaulted a white woman and beaten her unconscious. The red lust of vengeance began to color the thoughts of white men and it grew and whirled and rose in their minds until it spilled its volcanic outburst over the edge of man's reason.

"Lynch him! Lynch him! Lynch him!"

Between that cry of the mob and the negro in jail was the barrier of a line of fifty-seven uniformed young men standing as stoutly as if they were "the thin red line of England" maintaining the dream of empire. But charging against the troops were no heathen Fuzzy-Wuzzies nor Afghans tumbling out of Khyber Pass. These infuriated men, crazed with vengeance, were friends, neighbors, fellow tradespeople. Men who had broken open hardware stores, seized rifles and ammunition and were now bearing down on their own soldiers, pledged to uphold the laws of the state of Virginia.

Dan stood in the military formation pale, scared and yet defiant. With his companions he fired over the mob's head. The empty shell hopped out of the Springfield and he put in another bullet and fired again, aiming well over the civilians. The volleys of bullets were not enough to stop the advance of several hundred rioters. Instead, the citizens, themselves, commenced shooting and some of them fired not above the caps of the young militiamen but into the ranks.

Several troops dropped their rifles, fell to the ground. Bullets lanced holes in Dan's jacket. The order came to fire into the mob. Men died and were wounded because they could not wait for the law to hang a criminal.

Dan's mind was a blur of gun fire and wounded men crying out in their agony. He felt his rifle flying out of his hands. Bullets had torn it from his grasp. Around him the militiamen were falling back as they had no real heart for shooting down their own people. But they continued to fire as the mob swept forward. Then, outnumbered five to one, the state troops broke, fled for their lives from the conflict.

The unimpeded host engulfed the jail. . . .

Several days later Dan and his brother, George, also one of the militia, had reached safety in the North Carolina hills. Resentment against the troops had run so high in Roanoke, many of the soldiers had taken refuge in the mountains. The two Virginia troopers sat beside a liquor still and talked to the moonshiner who had taken them in. The hillsman had almost accomplished what the mob hadn't as, when Dan and George first approached his still, he had fired on them, believing from their uniforms they were government men searching for illicit liquor makers.

But when the young men explained that "although we are really the law, we are hiding from the lawless," the moonshiner saw the irony in the situation and made them welcome. For nearly two weeks the fugitives from injustice lived with the tarheel moonshiner and helped him turn out applejack. Finally Dan rebelled at the idea of hiding out as a result of trying to carry out the duty he had vowed to uphold. He reasoned he and his fellow militiamen had tried to stop the mob by firing over its head and certainly, when the rioters shot into the troops, there was no recourse but to shoot back, if the law was to be enforced.

Dan turned to George, said, "I'm going back home."

"Don't be an utter fool, Dan. You know they'll hang you as soon as they see you."

Nevertheless, Dan left the hospitable moonshiner, who made him a gift of half a gallon of applejack, and he and George started back to Roanoke. The brothers slipped into their home after nightfall. As George had his own business, he could remain inside the house until tempers had calmed down. But Dan worked for the Norfolk and Western railroad. The following morning Dan returned to his job as machinist apprentice at the Roanoke shop. No sooner had he entered the boiler shop than the workmen dropped their tools and rushed at him with a roar which reminded Dan of the lynch-crazed mob. Somebody shouted, "Get a rope and string the big bastard up!" The enraged men pressed Dan against the shop wall.

Dan shook off the hands seeking to seize him and said, "Fellows, I am a soldier; a member of the Roanoke Light Infantry. I was only obeying orders and doing my duty as a member of the Virginia militia. You know the troops did not start the riot, but it was their duty to try to stop it. Now I'm a long drawn out guy, six feet four so go ahead and hang me if you want to. Just do me one favor. Pick out a high tree where my feet won't drag the ground!"

One of the men in the crowd was a good friend of Dan's. This friend jumped atop a work bench and shouted, "Stop this God damned foolishness! Dan Cunningham is right. He is a Virginia soldier. What he did against the mob, any one of us would have done, if he had real blood. Cunningham is a damned good soldier and a damned good man. Besides any person who comes back to face the wrath of a bunch like us deserves to live!"

The adamant attitude of the crowd was pierced. Dan could see a ray of hope flash on what had been the cheerless prospect of strangling to death at the end of a rope. The men broke into little groups and started to argue among themselves as whether or not to lynch him. All at once the tide of opinion changed to Dan's favor and Frank Greenwood, general foreman of the shop, made his way to Dan and said quietly, "Go home, Dan, and give the men a chance to settle down. But remember this; I want you back at work in the morning and I'll assure you there will be no trouble."

From then on Dan Cunningham resumed his place as one of the shop workers and many of the men who had been anxious to hang him became his fast friends.

So it was that a crowd of impetuous railroad shop workers almost ended the career of a man who was to devote his life to railroading, become one of the real characters in the operation of such lines as the Norfolk and Western, the Atcheson, Topeka and Santa Fe, the Denver and Salt Lake (the Moffat railroad), and the Denver and Rio Grande. From the Rutland railroad or the Boston and Maine to the Central of Georgia; from the New York, New Haven and Hartford to the Western Pacific and the Southern Pacific; from the Wabash or the Monon to the Southern or the Louisville and Nashville; from little short lines with two engines and half a dozen cars to the mightiest railroad dynasties, one will find someone who has known or worked with "Big Dan" Cunningham. The renown of the six feet four, 250 pound railroader, has almost reached the legendary stage of Casey Jones. He is as much a part of the great Rocky Mountain region of the United States as Pike's Peak, the Great Salt Lake or the Continental Divide.

But there was nothing legendary about a baby born on

April 19, 1873, at The Big House, on a plantation in Bedford county, Virginia.

That day George and Susan Cunningham welcomed a third son. They named him Daniel Goode Cunningham as Daniel had been a family name on both sides for some years. Otho Thomas Cunningham had arrived November 13, 1867 and George William Cunningham was born August 17, 1871.

Dan's mother, Susan Sabra Saunders, was born in Bedford county, Virginia, at The Big House, an old southern mansion, February 12, 1848. Her father, who was of Pennsylvania-Dutch ancestry, owned four plantations and over four hundred slaves. Her father's tobacco sold readily in Lynchburg and Susan was reared in the country luxury of plantation life. She had ample playmates as she was the youngest of twelve children.

On the plantation was a private distillery and every year the cellar at The Big House, sometimes known as Five Oaks or Big Oaks, was restocked with thirty barrels of peach and apple brandy. This, explained the master of the house, was in case "somebody takes sick." There was never any unusual amount of sickness at the Saunders' place but always thirty barrels needed replenishing at the end of the year.

The Saunders' holdings were run as a business and, consequently, the master was never cruel to his slaves as their being in good physical condition was necessary to the successful production of crops. He never sold his slaves and unless there was reasonable justification, would not allow his overseer to punish the negro workers. The Saunders family enjoyed a pleasant, prosperous life.

But when the War Between the States moved conflicting forces into the Bedford section of Virginia, the easy calm of life at The Big House was shattered. As the defending Confederate forces grew weaker, Yankee soldiers invaded Bedford county. The Union troops strode up the steps of The Big House, forced the occupants to open the dining room and cook meals while the negro kitchen help looked on. After the Yankees had eaten, they would call in enough slaves to fill the dining room; then force the Saunders girls to wait on the negroes. This action embarrassed the slaves who, after the Union troops had marched or ridden away, would endeavor to erase the memory of the rude actions of the Federal soldiers, who could not realize the deep affection many slaves held for "their white folks."

As more and more Northern soldiers came up the driveway to the mansion, the Saunders girls, warned of the enemy's approach, fled to the negro cabins and hid. Never once did the slaves betray their mistress' sanctuary to the blue-uniformed soldiers of Abe Lincoln, who arrived with shouts of freedom for the blacks.

Dan's father, George Lodiwick Cunningham, was born in Bedford county, February 1, 1845. His father was descended from the Scotch-Irish, who first settled in Mecklenburg county, North Carolina. One of his ancestors was a signer of the Mecklenburg Declaration. This was a group of rebellious resolutions adopted at Charlotte, North Carolina, at a midnight convention, May 20, 1775. The convention was comprised of representatives from the militia companies in the county and proclaimed the good folk of Mecklenburg county independent of the British rule. The Mecklenburg Declaration, of course, antedated the Declaration of Independence and since 1831 many North Carolina people have celebrated May 20 as a legal holiday.

On the Bedford Cunningham place, a profitable tobacco plantation, life was much the same as on the Saunders plantation.

When Virginia seceded from the Union, George selected his favorite mount, left his father's home and enlisted as a private in the Second Virginia Cavalry, Company G, and fought throughout almost the entire war. At Chancellorville he helped pick up a wounded Confederate officer, shot by his own men who had mistaken his party for Federal scouts, and who said in his dying words, "Let us cross the river and rest under the shade of the trees." Lee, on hearing of Stonewall Jackson's death, sadly commented it was as if he had lost his right arm. George Cunningham participated in many battles; the Valley Campaign, Yellow Tavern, the Wilderness and both battles of Bull Run. Not always did he escape the hail of Yankee bullets which riddled the Confederate ranks. He was wounded at Gettysburg and, when General Lee surrendered, Captain George Cunningham was at home on furlough recovering from a Yankee slug he had taken in the shoulder.

The twenty-one-year-old former Confederate captain and Susan Sabra Saunders were married December 19, 1866. Captain Cunningham, as he was always called, and his bride came back to The Big House after their honeymoon and the new master took charge of what was left of the plantation.

War had left its mark on the Saunders estate. Practically all the money had been invested in Confederate bonds and currency and these were worthless. Most of the horses, mules and livestock had been stolen by the Union soldiers. Until the war, George Cunningham had led the easy-going life of a planter's son. He had never worked with his hands. To rebuild, Captain Cunningham knew he must labor with everything he had. Although many of the slaves stayed on as free workers, they had to be fed and cared for. George Cunningham turned, as had his father, to tobacco and hoped that the golden weed would build again fortunes for his people.

Although the Captain bravely tried to carry on the traditions of ante bellum plantation life, the first few years after the war were difficult ones. As George and Dan went from babies to little boys, actual surplus cash in the family was scarce. The plantation was made as self sustaining as possible. Food came from the fields and the slowly growing herd of livestock and the table was well filled. Mam, as Dan's mother was called, after the negroes sheared the sheep, weaved the wool into cloth, dyed the material brown with coloring made from oak bark. The brown homespun was used to make clothes for the boys. Their hats were made of wheat straws plaited into long rows and then ironed. The buttonless outfits would slip over the boys' heads and hang to their knees. This single garment protected them against the summer sun. The breeze was refreshing on the young bodies and the boys felt unhampered in their play. Sometimes a bee or a wasp did take advantage of the accessibility of bare skin and the boys had anxious moments as they chased the insects from under their smocks.

In the summertime the boys would go barefooted as they loved the feel of the red earth under their toes and, too, the plantation had no facilities for shoe making. Each fall Mam and the Captain gave them a new pair of boots with brass caps over the toes and these were worn until spring came again to Bedford county.

When Dan was very young, one year Christmas found the Captain as short of gift money as he was long on Yuletide spirit and spirits. Not aware of this, the boys hung up their stockings in Grandmother Sabra's room confident Santa Claus would fill them.

Christmas morning the boys tumbled from their beds to find their confidence was not misplaced. In each stocking was an apple, a stick of peppermint candy and, topping everything a clown toy doll. At the Captain's suggestion, the boys eagerly pressed the stomachs of the dolls and music came forth to their childish delight. It was a real merry Christmas for the youngsters. The holiday table was loaded with ham and turkey and the buffet held decanters of brandy to cheer the visitors, who came to The Big House to drink toasts to the Yuletide. Neighbors dropped in from adjoining plantations; the Packing House Place, the Stone House, the Nichols Acres, and the Cunningham Place. These plantation families were equally pressed for ready cash as the Captain as they, too, had lost their resources in the war. Yet they strove to breathe life into the gentlemanly country mode of existence. The damnyankees had licked their government, not their breeding.

If the boys had caught their mother unawares Christmas day, they would have seen tears she couldn't hold back. Tears inspired by the way the Captain carried on his heritage. Mam knew the story back of the gifts of the dolls. She had given the Captain money to buy himself a new hat for Christmas. Instead of getting the needed hat, he had used the money to purchase the dolls for his boys.

Until the crops were sold, Captain Cunningham wore his tattered hat as if it were the finest one he could locate in the stores of Lynchburg, Richmond or Baltimore. Later Mam told her sons of their father's sacrifice. In years to come, Dan was given fine watches, diamond rings and other expensive presents by his friends on the railroad. None touched him as did the little clown doll.

The Big House was set a hundred yards back from the main road to Liberty, now called Bedford. Five large oak trees were in the yard. When Dan was old enough to run about he would look at the three story red brick house with dormer windows in the roof as if it were the biggest house in the world. Mam would laugh and tell him the old mansion houses on the eastern shores were bigger, yet she was certain there was no prettier home in all Virginia.

Dan would climb up to the second story porch and hang on the white columns reaching to the roof. In the distance he could see the high Peaks of Otter with Flat Top rising 4,000 feet and its companion Sharp Top a few hundred feet shorter. He often saw his father ride off in the direction of the peaks as the Captain went to Liberty, or, as the county seat was commonly known, Bedford Court House. From his high perch on the porch, Dan would wave to the colored workers in the fields. Mam liked for him to play on the porch as then she knew he was away from the well filled with free-stone cold water. The well was back of the dining room.

The bottom floor at The Big House had a large kitchen and storeroom at one end and the dining room occupied the entire other end. Both the kitchen and the dining room had large fireplaces in which were cranes used for holding pots and sometimes Dan watched the cook roast meat over the flames.

Grandma Sabra's room was the most popular spot on the second floor for the children. She had a trundle bed and the boys vied for the honor of sleeping in it. They also sought the honor of holding fire to grandma's clay pipe. The Captain did not often smoke tobacco, but grandma had to have her pipe every night.

Across a large hall from grandma's room was the parlour, seldom used except when the Cunninghams had company. Then the room would come alive with flames from the huge fireplace and the guests would sit around the fire as they swapped stories of the war, the tobacco markets and county gossip. The boys ate winesap apples, drank persimmon beer and hoped the guests would know some thrilling ghost stories.

When the fire grew too warm for them—it had ample room for a back log which would last for days—the boys retired to the corners and sat on horsehair sofas and listened to a guest play on the square spinet, usually out of tune, but Dan thought it was like music from the Heavenly Angels. By the time the guests decided to play cards on the marble top center table, it was to bed for the youngsters.

So the boys would climb up to the third floor which was made up entirely of bedrooms. Each room had a four poster bed with rope cords instead of springs and the rope cords made an excellent springboard for the boys. The beds were so high, as each had a trundle bed in it used for overflow guests and children, that the Cunningham boys had to use a chair to reach the bed covers.

Guests were always welcome as they brought news and tales of the outside world. Except for them, the only news sources were the weekly paper at Liberty and the Lynchburg and Richmond papers which the Captain would buy when he made his infrequent trips to the big tobacco market at Lynchburg.

Grandma Sabra once told of a time—long before the late unpleasantness—when a stranger rode up to The Big House. The negro stable boy unsaddled the horse, watered it and put the animal in the stable. Meanwhile the stranger went to the house and introduced himself to Thomas Saunders. The two men took a liking to each other and the stranger was filled with interesting stories. When the stranger decided to leave The Big House, Saunders asked, "Why hurry off, suh, it's been a great pleasure to have you." But the guest insisted he must be on his way. From the time the stranger walked into the house until he took his leave was twenty years!

Back of the main house stood a half circle of negro cabins. Most of these were still occupied by the former

CAPTAIN GEORGE CUNNINGHAM, C. S. A. Virginia cavalry fighter under "Jeb"
Stuart. His vision was a South reborn through railroad development.

Three Little Confederates. GEORGE, OTHO and DAN at The Big House plantation.

Franklin Pierce was president of the United States when this Virginia and Tennessee train crossed the pastoral lands of the Old Dominion in Big Dan's county of the Peaks of Otter. *Picture credit: Beyer's* Album of Virginia

Today *The Pocahontas,* fast Norfolk and Western passenger train, passes the Peaks of Otter in Virginia. *Photo credit:* Norfolk and Western.

Saunders' slaves who worked as share-croppers, and who were actually no better off financially than before the war. A negro boy named Punk was supposed to live in one of the cabins with his parents, but Punk often spent the night in The Big House. The negro was about the same age as Dan and he played with the Cunningham boys. With Dan, Otho and George, Punk would dam up the creek and make water-wheels, construct rabbit traps out of hollow gum logs and go swimming in the creek.

When night would fall, Punk was allowed to stay inside if Mam were asked permission. Mam told the boys they must never sleep with Punk. The colored boy had a pallet on the floor beside Dan's bed and Punk shared his pallet with Turk, the boys' favorite hound dog. Sometimes Dan, frightened by a noise in the night, slipped out of his bed and laid down beside Punk and Turk. Guarded by the negro boy and the hound dog, Dan knew he was safe from all ghosts and haunts. If Mam knew of this, she never mentioned it.

Dan and Punk had a parallel in the Captain and Uncle Nace. For many years Uncle Nace had been the Captain's personal servant. George Cunningham had taken him to war and Uncle Nace was as loyal a supporter of the Confederacy as the most ardent South Carolina secessionist. Many of the Southern cavalrymen brought their own personal servants with them and these were shared with the less fortunate company members.

When the Confederate cavalry was campaigning around Petersburg, Uncle Nace was granted permission to spend the afternoon fishing if he would return by five o'clock. As long after that hour Uncle Nace had not shown up in camp, Captain Cunningham started looking for him. There was always the danger the negro might be captured by a roving Yankee patrol. Such was not the case. Uncle Nace was located sitting happily on the side of a stream with his line in the water. The Captain started to give his servant a verbal lashing when the negro interrupted him with "Afore God, Marse George 'taint my fault, suh. I jest ketched half a fish and 'twas staying round to get the tuther half afore I quits." To prove his contention, Uncle Nace held up an

almost paper-thin flounder. The negro had never seen any
fish except the mountain variety in the Piedmont district
such as perch and suckers. The Tidewater flounder was only
half a fish to Uncle Nace.

Naturally Uncle Nace stayed on with the family after
the war as he felt he was a member of the household rather
than a servant. One of his favorite pastimes was accompanying his master on turkey shoots and he beamed in delight
as he brought home three or four turkeys bagged by the sharp-
shooting captain.

Before the family moved to Roanoke in 1883, Uncle
Nace's big expansive heart stopped beating. Mam and the
boys cried and the Captain said it was almost as sad a day as
Appomattox. He rode over to Liberty to get a white parson
and Uncle Nace was put away in one corner of the family
burial place. The Confederate flag flew during the services
as the Captain insisted Uncle Nace had been as much a Rebel
as any of them. In death as in life, Uncle Nace remained a
part of the family.

Aunt Violet, another former slave, wept for Uncle
Nace at the funeral. She, too, felt a part of the family and
it was not long until she took her place in the corner of the
burying ground.

After Uncle Nace's death, the Captain gradually lost
interest in squirrel hunting as the negro had been his constant
companion on these forays against the bushy-tailed rodents.
Uncle Nace's task had been to go around a tree and make a
noise which would scare the squirrel into the high branches
usually a hundred or so feet above the ground. Then the
Captain would draw a bead on the rodent's head with his
Kentucky squirrel rifle. To shoot a squirrel anywhere but
in the head was considered poor sportsmanship as was the
act of picking off a squirrel when it was anywhere but the
topmost branches of a tall tree. Uncle Nace would bring
back the kill and smack his thick lips over the prospects of a
squirrel pie or stew.

If the squirrels had known the rules of hunting, they
wouldn't have ended up in a pie. In their efforts to get away
from the noise, they fell prey to the keen-eyed riflemen.

Uncle Nace said some mighty intelligent squirrel someday would just walk up to the hunter and be as safe as a baby in his mother's arms. But the mighty intelligent squirrel never made his appearance.

Sometimes Dan and his brothers watched the Captain as he rode off for a fox hunt. The boys' chests filled with pride at the sight of their father sitting on his horse like a true Southern cavalryman with no fear of a wide ditch nor a high fence. Such obstacles hadn't stopped the Captain when he had hunted Yankees with Jeb Stuart and certainly they wouldn't stop him as he sought elusive Reynard.

One day while the Captain was on a fox hunt, Dan and George put their heads together and planned a trick on Otho. As Otho was six years older than Dan and four years older than George, sometimes he would give his younger brothers a licking. The younger boys dug a hole about twenty inches deep and dared Otho to put his leg in. Taking the dare, Otho soon found his leg covered with dirt which the two brothers tramped on. Next the younger lads dared Otho to pull his leg out and, although he tugged and tugged, Otho could not free his leg. Confident their brother was trapped, Dan and George began to pelt him with rocks. Otho was screaming when the Captain unexpectedly returned home. Dan and George fled to the fields while their father dug Otho's leg loose. The Captain was furious, but Otho explained his brothers had outsmarted him and, too, he deserved what he got for picking on them. This saved Dan and George from a whipping and never again did they play any tricks on their older brother.

The Captain had returned home early that day as he had bought a horse and was expecting its delivery. Immediately the family offered suggestions for a name. None met with the Captain's approval and the family learned that none would. A name had already been selected by him. Could anyone guess the name, suggested the Captain, and as a hint he told them it started with a P and had meant a big noise in Lee's army.

Mam laughed and said, "Now you've given it away, Captain. Pendleton. That's it. Brigadier General W. N.

Pendleton was Lee's Chief of Artillery. Imagine a horse named Pendleton."

"I cannot imagine such a thing and you are wrong, my dear."

"I'm just as happy as if I were right because now I know the answer. If it's not Pendleton, it must be Pelham!"

"And Pelham it is, my dear. I've named the new horse for Major John Pelham, the late commander of Stuart's Horse Artillery. That blonde lad who fell at Kellysville with the battle cry of 'Forward' on his lips. He will always be 'The Great Cannoneer.' "

The Captain ran his hand through his curly black hair and said softly:

"Just as spring came laughing through the strife,
    With all its gorgeous cheer,
In the bright April of historic life
    Fell the great cannoneer.
O mother of a blessed soul on high!
    Thy tears may soon be shed—
Think of thy boy with princes of the sky,
    Among the Southern dead."

Captain Cunningham was quoting from the poem *Pelham* written by James Ryder Randall, noted poet, who had been a professor at Poydras College in Louisiana when the war broke out.

The Cunningham boys loved stories and they had three sources, Mam, the Captain and the negroes. Mam would tell fairy tales, the Captain would become reminiscential about the war, and the negroes would spout folk tales and ghost stories.

Mam would sit by the fire before bedtime and tell such stories as the one about The Iron Man and the Golden Knight which was Dan's favorite. Once upon a time The Iron Man, who lived in a home under a lake of pure gold, captured a lad hunting on the lake shore. The Iron Man grew fond of his young captive, whose hair had turned to gold as he was whisked through the lake, and finally set him free near a King's palace. The boy became the King's gardener but, as his golden hair was different from any other hair, he always kept his head covered. That is, until one very hot day and then he removed the covering as he thought no one was looking; however, he was seen by the King's daughter and soon the two fell in love. As he was only a poor gardener, the lad felt he could not marry the Princess and so went back into the lake of gold to seek his friend The Iron Man.

Welcomed by The Iron Man, the lad explained soon the King was having a tournament and the winner would receive the hand of the beautiful Princess. Immediately The Iron Man dressed the boy in a suit of golden armor, put him on a snow white horse fitted with a mantle of silver and diamonds, and gave him a troop of knights mounted on black horses.

As a foreign nobleman, the lad returned to the King's palace and with his knights won all the matches up to the final test; this was to shoot an arrow through a golden apple thrown into the air. Every contestant for the Princess' hand failed and only the golden knight remained. When the lad in his golden armor skillfully pierced the apple, the Princess grew sad as she loved only the gardener. As the winning knight rode up to the Princess, his helmet fell back revealing his golden locks and the Princess recognized her lover. So the two were married, were happy ever after, and The Iron Man saw they were well supplied with money from his lake of gold.

Perhaps stories of this nature were "escapist philosophy" to offset the hard times which had come to the South. They relived the days of knights and cavaliers and gay balls and told of gold so plentiful it would fill a lake. And the only gold in the postwar South was the gold of the sunshine warming the graves of the soldiers.

Uncle Nace often told the boys of the planter who owned a pack of faithful hound dogs. He was hated by a cruel witch and she locked his dogs in the smokehouse, sent out a wolf pack to eat the man. Treed by the savage wolves, the man called his dogs to save him, "Here, Ranger! Here, Roller! Here, Music! Here, Sounder!" As the trapped man called vainly for aid, the wolves gnawed at the trunk of the tree until it began to sway and the mean witch shrieked in pleasure at the thought of the wolves eating the man. Precisely as the tree was starting to fall, the loyal dogs, who had broken out of the smokehouse, raced to the rescue, killed the wolves and then gobbled up the witch.

As many times as the boys heard this tale, they always wondered if the brave dogs would arrive in time. Although the hounds proved themselves as faithful as the marines in getting the situation under control, sometimes, after this yarn, Dan had a hard time going to sleep as he pictured what would have happened to the trapped man had his dogs been another minute late.

Fat, black Aunt Violet told in a rollicking voice of the adventures of Brer Fox, Brer Wolf, Brer Rabbit and others in the animal world. Actuated, perhaps, by the love of colored people for rabbits—both alive and fried—Brer Rabbit was made the hero of the folk lore stories. Brer Rabbit's enemies were Brer Fox, Brer Wolf and Brer Bear, and he always out-witted these foes. Brer Rabbit and Brer Turtle were friends and Brer Turtle chuckled with pleasure when Brer Rabbit triumphed against all odds. Joel Chandler Harris became famous with his *Uncle Remus* stories, the best known of which is probably the one about Brer Rabbit and the Tar-Baby. But long before Dan heard of *Uncle Remus*, Brer Rabbit was a real character in his childhood days. It is in-teresting to note that animal folk stories, such as those told by the Southern negroes, have also been found in the tales of India, Siam, the Amazonian Indians, and the American Indians.

As the boys grew sleepy, Aunt Violet would finish out her story and then take them to bed. She sang them to sleep with such songs as "Snake bake de hoe cake, set de frog to mind it, frog got to noddin' and de lizard came and stole it."

Dan would dream about the Jack O'Lantern which led pursuing negroes through the woods and briar patches until the blacks fell exhausted. Many tales of this elusive light in the darkness were told him by the field workers.

Sometimes Dan looked apprehensively at Turk asleep on the pallet for the negroes told of dogs—fortunately not hounds such as Turk—which ran in front of your feet and would not get out of your way. When you kicked at them, your foot went right through their bodies and the dogs vanished in the air. Once in a while Dan slipped his foot from under the covers and wondered if maybe he should suddenly push Turk the dog would vanish.

Occasionally at night Dan was awakened by the trotting of a horse on the hard road. He heard the front gate click and a visitor call "Hello, there, hello." Then the visitor's footsteps could be heard as he walked up the steps to the second story porch. As the footsteps stopped, Dan would run to the window. Ever he saw the porch empty of all but the moonlight.

The Captain's stories concerned the War Between the States. Merriment entered the Captain's voice as he related how the infantry and the cavalry continually joshed each other. The infantrymen claimed when they deployed, the cavalry riding through their ranks splashed mud on them and, too, they said the cavalry would charge the enemy, pick a fuss, and then fall back. The mud covered infantry would have to cover the horsemen's retreat to keep them from being captured by the Yankee riders.

Captain George Cunningham had a passionate devotion to the cavalry and he told his sons how the fighting horsemen of the South had a tradition fostered by such leaders in the American Revolution as Francis Marion, "the Swamp Fox," and "Light Horse Harry" Lee; how the cavalry played a decisive part in enabling General Harrison to win the famous battle of Tippecanoe in 1811; and how at Thames, two years later, Kentucky horsemen successfully charged the British and their Indian allies and Tecumseh, the Shawnee Indian chief, was killed.

Dan and his brothers learned of the activities of the cavalry in the many Indian wars and in the Mexican conflict. It was for the Indian wars that the famous Dragoons were formed. Many of the cavalry leaders, both North and South, were long experienced in the Indian fighting on "The Plains."

Exploits of famous Southern leaders with whom the Captain served were told and retold. Men such as handsome, black-whiskered Colonel Thomas T. Mumford, commander of the Second Virginia cavalry in which George Cunningham rode and who later as a brigadier general headed a brigade when Fitzhugh Lee, Robert E. Lee's nephew, became supreme commander of the cavalry of the Army of Northern Virginia. The Captain told how only forty-eight hours before Appomattox and Lee's surrender, Mumford's cavalry had downed Union horsemen commanded by Crook.

Then there were General Joe Wheeler, cavalry commander in over a hundred battles with sixteen horses shot from under him, and whose valor inspired General Sherman, U.S.A., to say, "In the event of a war with a foreign country, Joe Wheeler is the man to command the United States cavalry;" and curly-haired University of South Carolina educated Lieutenant General Wade Hampton, commander of Lee's cavalry after Jeb Stuart's death and who, at the start of the war, financed with his own money "Hampton's Legion" which fought the length of the conflict.

The deeds of Brigadier General Turner Ashby reminded Dan of the elusive Jack O'Lantern of the negroes. Mounted on his white horse, Ashby was the "will-o-the-wisp of the Confederacy." His raids were so daring many Yankee officers refused to admit such an audacious warrior existed and he was said to be a creation of Confederate propagandists. Yet there was an early end to the supposed myth when, in the summer of 1862, a Southern general was killed at Harrisonburg, Virginia, and with his final breath cried, "Charge men! For God's sake charge!" So died the valiant Turner Ashby.

The boys thrilled to the story of their father with Jeb Stuart when the picturesque lancers of the Sixth Pennsylvania vainly sought to whip Jeb. Wily Stuart had a faculty of seeing to it the Northern cavalry often would arrive too early or too late to stop his military operations. Dan shuddered at the idea of a Pennsylvania horseman with a twelve foot lance outstretched riding down on his father.

After a few years the tobacco crops showed a good profit and the financial strain was lessened at The Big House. As the boys grew older they helped out in the fields. When hot and tired they, along with the share-croppers, picked out watermelons and cantaloupes to refresh themselves. The boys would top the tobacco plants to make them spread out and pull off suckers and tobacco worms. When the tobacco was cut and hung in the barns to cure, Dan watched the charcoal fires for any stray sparks which might fly out and ignite the tobacco. The tobacco lands of the South were scarred with barns lost in this manner.

When the tobacco was cured to a bright golden brown, the hands would wait for a rainy day ideal for stripping as then the tobacco would be moist and not crumble. Dan and his brothers helped strip the leaves alongside the negroes and the hands of the white boys would turn black with the heavy tobacco gum. Never in his life has Dan smoked or chewed tobacco as he feels he had enough contact with it when he was a boy.

Finally the tobacco was packed for the market and loaded on wagons. Soon would come the payoff for months of toil.

CHAPTER II

*W*ITH the tobacco packed into hogsheads, the Cunningham family prepared for the exciting trip to the markets. Mam, the Captain and the boys, would ride in the first wagon and the colored drivers would pilot additional wagons. At Liberty a small amount of tobacco would be sold to the warehousemen there, and the empty wagon would start back to The Big House, the negro driver bemoaning his fate at not being able to make the trip to Lynchburg which was the mecca of tobacco men in that part of the state.

Aristocratic Lynchburg had its beginning in 1756 when seventeen-year-old John Lynch built a ferry to replace the difficult ford on the James river. Lynch had been reared by a practical father, Charles Lynch, who had commenced his life in Virginia as an indentured worker, but had seen to his future by marrying Sarah Clark, pretty daughter of his master. The ferry prospered and soon John Lynch was building tobacco warehouses to which farmers rolled hogsheads over the dirt roads. From the warehouse these would be lowered by ropes to the bateaux on the river for their journey eastward. More and more tobacco came into the Lynch warehouses and by the turn of the century Lynchburg was the world's best known dark tobacco trading center. Blacks—proud of their bulging muscles and eager for any adventure that might come along the river—poled flatboats piled high with tobacco down the stream to Richmond; returned with cargoes of whiskey and molasses, and bearing tales of flirting negro girls, who worked for the "white folks" in the mansions of Richmond. Tobacco dealers were prosperous and of their number none was more picturesque than Colonel Augustine Leftwich, who in the summertime always dressed in immaculate white linen and, as he felt the tobacco leaves for their texture, sniffed a sample for its odor, was ever shielded from the heat by a big emerald green umbrella held by a negro slave.

The advent of the James River and Kanawha Canal in 1840 and the Virginia and Tennessee railroad in 1852 increased the tobacco trade and Lynchburg flourished until the depression that followed the Rebellion. But in a few years the tobacco trade had been restored and Lynchburg smoking and chewing tobacco was known around the world. By the time Captain Cunningham was bringing in his crops, more than 25,000,000 pounds of tobacco were being marketed there each year.

When the Cunningham tobacco wagons came into the city, Dan would be left with his mother and brothers to explore the town while the tobacco was being auctioned. Mam would go into the stores to look at new yardage, though she could do very little buying until the money from the sale of the crop was actually in her hands. Later in the day, if his transactions had been profitable, the Captain would give his family a treat with a meal at an eating house and the boys would look with awe at the other diners. If the sale hadn't been profitable, Mam would forget all the gaily-colored yardage and her dreams of trips to the dressmaker, smile a little and tell the boys that next time they would celebrate. But whether the tobacco was sold at a profit or not, Lynchburg meant the ultimate in excitement for the boys.

To Dan not even Coleridge's words, "In Xanadu did Kubla Khan, a stately pleasure dome decree," were sufficient to describe the fascination of the city. To him the town was more romantic than Camelot with its palaces, high hills, and tournament plains; more breathtaking than Bagdad with its turbaned sorcerers and its perfumed venders of frankincense and myrrh. Perhaps the most splendorous people, in the lad's eyes, who came into Lynchburg, were the medicine men, who set up miniature theatres on street corners and vacant lots. The air vibrated with the twang of the banjo as the colored helpers to the loquacious "professors" sang the song that, introduced in Dan Bryant's minstrel show on Broadway in New York shortly before the outbreak of the war, had become the rallying cry of the South:

> "I wish I was in de land ob cotton,
> Old times dar am not forgotten;
> Look away, look away, look away,
>   Dixie Land!"

At these words youngsters would wave their hats and former soldiers in the crowd would pick up the tune and shout out the Southern version as the negroes played:

"For Dixie's land we take our stand,
And live and die for Dixie!
To arms! To arms!
And conquer peace for Dixie!"

Often the more erudite medicine men would highlight their shows with recitations of favorite Southern poems such as Sidney Lanier's *Death of Stonewall Jackson,* Henry Timrod's *Charleston,* Father Abram Joseph Ryan's *The Conquered Banner,* John Maurice Thompson's *To the South* and the oft requested *Stonewall Jackson's Way* by John William Palmer and *Little Griffin of Tennessee* by Francis Orray Ticknor. Dan and his brother would thrill to the thundered words:

"The sun's bright lances rout the mists
Of morning, and by George!
Here's Longstreet struggling in the lists,
Hemmed in an ugly gorge.
Pope and his Dutchmen, whipped before:
'Bay'nets and grape!' Hear Stonewall roar;
'Charge Stuart! Pay off Ashby's score!'
In Stonewall Jackson's way.' "

Men with an empty sleeve tucked in their jackets, men with an empty trouser leg pinned up, women with an empty heart covered with gingham listened to the eloquence and realized that war isn't poetry, that it isn't and never will be as magnificent as these lines of William Henry Thompson in *The High Tide at Gettysburg*:

"Then, at the brief command of Lee
Moved out the matchless infantry
With Pickett leading grandly down
To rush against the roaring crown
Of those dread heights of destiny."

The spectacle made a grand show for Dan. There was no time for a youngster to think that the illness caused by the War of Secession, the lives ruined, the homes broken, could not be erased from bodies and nerves by bottles of medicine, tin boxes of pills, oils and herbs, potions and liniments, all held aloft by the jocular medicine men while grinning negroes did a soft shoe shuffle—and children laughed once more.

Sometimes Dan would take long walks with his father. Hand in hand they would puff up the steep inclines, walk up Wise street by the Victorian Gothic house which, in 1856, was the first Methodist Protestant College in the South, or go by the Claytor-Miller House where Thomas Jefferson once ate a tomato to prove to the children of the occupants that the "love apple" was not a poisonous fruit. But Captain Cunningham would chuckle most when they walked by the Spring Hill cemetery and he would relate how John Crouse had sold the land to Bishop John Early in 1855 for a "seminary," only to find that the Bishop had said he wanted it for a "cemetery." And, when adjoining homeowners protested in vain against the new burial grounds, the initial funeral party found the mourners protected by a liberal supply of firearms!

Dan always wanted to go by the railroad station. He watched the trains come in and the black smoke rising up over the Hill City. His father took a long stogie from his dusty linen coat, bit off the end, and turned the thin roll of tobacco in his lips; then looked through the railway cars as if they were made up of some phantom train from the netherworld.

"Daniel," he said slowly, "that's what beat us. Trains and engines and supplies. . . . and a fellow named General Herman Haupt. When you go to school, maybe college, you'll read about General Grant. But Grant couldn't have whipped us if it hadn't been for Haupt. The Stars and Bars would be over Washington now, I tell you, if the Feds hadn't had one unbeatable man whose work offset the raids that Morgan and Mosby and Forrest made on the trains that always seemed to bring more Yankees and guns and food against us. Remember Herman Haupt, lad, and how he and the railroads kept Abe Lincoln sitting in Washington."

The train's whistle broke the thread of thought; George

Cunningham took his son's hand and turned back to his wagon. As the horses pulled against their halters, the wheels jogged and the shreds of tobacco leaves were golden brown dancers on the stage made by the bumping wooden floor.

Doubtless the memories of days when shattered transportation had held up needed supplies for the Southern armies battling against the invasion forces riding down against the South on the apparently exhaustless rail communications held by the Federals, had colored Captain Cunningham's conception of the loss of the war. But certainly Herman Haupt—seldom mentioned in present histories of the great conflict—had played a decisive part. Haupt was, during a critical part of the war, general superintendent of the United States Military railroads.

Born in Philadelphia in 1817, Herman Haupt was graduated from West Point at the age of 18, and shortly after graduation, helped survey the Norristown and Valley railroad as well as a line from Gettysburg to the Potomac (now a part of the Western Maryland railroad) and the York and Wrightsville railroad. In 1846 committees made a house to house canvas of Philadelphia seeking stock subscriptions for a new railroad which had been chartered by the name of the Pennsylvania railroad. News of the proposed line reached Gettysburg where Haupt was a professor at Pennsylvania College. Immediately young Haupt sent in his application for a position to the railroad's president, Samuel V. Merrick. The application was considered unfavorably.

So Haupt kept teaching, little knowing that Gettysburg would play so important a part in the conflict that was to come and that he would be an integral part of it. The Pennsylvania tracks began to lengthen; however, the construction had been in charge of prominent canal men and they found that building a railroad offered complications far beyond their waterminded capacities. Soon Haupt had an offer made to him by the railroad and, accepting it, he was quickly general superintendent. Well he handled his task and no detail was too small for his inspection. In 1853, Haupt took the position of chief engineer for the Southern railroad of Mississippi; returned, within a year, to the Pennsylvania as chief engineer.

By this time Haupt was an international authority on bridge building. Tunnels and bridges go hand in hand. The first railroad tunnel in the United States had been outside Johnston, Pennsylvania, built in 1833 for the Alleghany Portage railroad (now a part of the Pennsylvania). A gigantic proposal was the Hoosac Tunnel on the Troy and Greenfield railroad in Massachusetts and Haupt was asked to take charge of the construction.

Tackling this job brought Haupt into conflict with Chester W. Chapin, president of the Western Railroad Company (now the Boston and Maine), as the proposed tunnel would open a rival line. No punches were pulled by those opposed to the great tunnel and Haupt got his basic training for a role he was to play in uniform ten years later.

Putting aside his work on the tunnel, Haupt's entry in the War Between the States, came in April, 1862, when Secretary of War Edwin M. Stanton called him to Washington, put him in charge of restoring transportation on the military railroads which had been cut to pieces by Southern raiders as well as rendered of reduced value, even before that, by conflicting authorities who gave and countermanded orders without any knowledge of railroad problems.

With fearless energy Colonel Haupt took charge of the reconstruction of the railroad from Aquia Creek to Fredericksburg and this was the first truly military road operated by the government in the war. After bridging Accakeek creek—a span of over one hundred and fifty feet—in a little over a dozen hours, Haupt's construction men found themselves facing a deep crossing of the Potomac creek which would require a bridge four hundred feet long and eighty feet high to replace one destroyed earlier in the war. Haupt recalled the book he had written on bridge building, but didn't remember any chapter which covered such a bridge to be thrown up with the inexpert help, inadequate tools, improper food for the bridge gang, and a Virginia rain that fell more caressingly on the White House of the Confederacy than it did on the harassed workers, who looked wonderingly across the creek's waters.

Yet Haupt planned a deck bridge—crib and trestle work

—and so inspired his men that in two weeks the railroad engines crossed it. Word of the bridge reached Washington and President Lincoln came to see it, commented, "I have seen the most remarkable structure that human eyes ever rested upon. That man Haupt has built a bridge over which trains are running every hour and, upon my word, there is nothing in it but bean-poles and corn-stalks!"

Other eyes were upon the bridge. Eyes that sparked to Confederate gray and the scarlet-lined cloaks of men like Mosby who rode the wild wind. Abe Lincoln could wait his time, they vowed, but someday he would watch that bridge burn.

Lincoln had his worries as the campaign went against the North. Burnside's troops evacuated Fredericksburg as the whole Federal line fell back before the Second Bull Run campaign. Orders went out to burn the bridge at Potomac Creek before the Confederates seized it. Despite Haupt's protests, the bridge went up in flames. As the tide of war changed, another bridge was built and, before the war's end, a more substantial bridge carried the trains of the Richmond, Fredericksburg and Potomac railroad.

But in war bridges are built for a life span that is as long as they serve those who build them. One bridge used by the Orange and Alexandria railroad was destroyed seven times by contending forces. The large bridge over the Tennessee river at Bridgeport, Alabama, was valuable to Union troops, who were sending supplies to Chattanooga via the Nashville and Chattanooga railroad. Three times the Confederates destroyed the bridge, but the fourth time the bridge was rebuilt, in 1864, the United States troops held it firmly.

Haupt's engineers supervised the reconstruction of the Manassas Gap railroad when Stonewall Jackson invaded the Shenandoah and McDowell planned to trap him. But the elusive foot cavalry of Jackson slipped out of the trap laid by the Federal trains.

When on June 26, 1863, General Pope assumed Union command, he promptly shoved aside Haupt and his men and would give him no co-operation despite McDowell's plea that Haupt should run the military railroads. Pope dismissed the subject by saying such matters were the problems of the Quartermaster.

Haupt felt he was needed on the Hoosac Tunnel project and, after all, he was serving in the army as a volunteer without any compensation. He retired to his Massachusetts home in July, 1863. Hardly had he unpacked before a telegram came from Assistant Secretary of War P. A. Watson (later president of the Erie railroad). Immediately Haupt repacked and was soon with Pope's army. The telegram had read "Come back at once; cannot get along without you; not a wheel moving on any of the railroads."

Soon Haupt found that although he was with Pope he was headed in the direction of Massachusetts, for Pope, badly defeated, retreated toward Washington. By now a brigadier general, Haupt threw all the resources of his railroad group to the aid of Pope's retirement. Yet the conflict between railroad officers and the regular army officers resulted in almost chaos, especially when officers schooled in combat would not follow the railroad men's instructions.

Even as priorities became a household word in World War II, so they had their place in the War of the Rebellion. Haupt felt that a priority system must be followed if the railroads were to be efficient. The list was headed by food for combat troops, and in order followed forage, ammunition, medical supplies, veteran infantry troops, and finally, new infantry troops. No priority was established—except when necessity demanded it—for artillery, cavalry, wagons and ambulances.

The fortunes of the Confederacy ran high and Lee invaded Pennsylvania for the second time; his soldiers marched up to a quiet little town named Gettysburg. Herman Haupt had helped General George Meade arrange his troops for battle as Meade had been a student of his at Pennsylvania College. But Meade—as victory tended to swing toward the Union defenders—was too cautious for his former professor, who, on a Sunday midnight, leaped abroad one of his own locomotives, rode back to Washington. There Haupt urged authorities to order Meade to throw his whole strength against a weary Lee so that the power of the Southern cause would be

broken quickly. Climbing back on the locomotive, Haupt
returned to the battlefield confident his advice would be followed.

It wasn't. Meade failed to strike. The crippled Gray
army slowly recrossed the Potomac, entrenched itself for
many more battles.

But Haupt's reorganization of the railroads and his building up of the Construction Corps had been of greater value
than his unheeded words at Gettysburg. In September, 1863,
with the transportation crisis for the Union apparently
passed, General Haupt was relieved and returned home. His
successor was Colonel D. C. McCallum, who was appointed
superintendent of military railroads. The efficient operation
of the roads continued under McCallum, who was long an
official on the Erie railroad.

One of McCallum's first tasks was one which would
have delighted Haupt. Joe Hooker and an army of 25,000
men was transferred from the East to the aid of General
Rosecrans before Chickamauga. The movement, some 1,200
miles, was made in less than two weeks. Soon Colonel Mc-
Callum was Major General McCallum.

The Construction Corps and the United States Military railroads at the end of the war had some 25,000 men
(approximately the same size as the army Lee surrendered);
419 engines; 6,330 cars; had built 137,418 lineal feet of
bridges; had laid or relaid 650 miles of track; and controlled
some 2,000 miles of track. The gross expenditures during the
war had been around $42,500,000.

As to Haupt, the Hoosac workers reached the end of
their four mile and a half task of digging through the mountain in 1872. The first cars went through the tunnel in February, 1875, and it was used by Boston-Troy passenger trains
in October, 1875. Today it is the oldest great railroad tunnel
in the United States.

Ever lured by actual railroad operation, Haupt became
general manager of the Richmond and Danville railroad
around 1875 and followed this with the position of general
manager of the Northern Pacific. In 1884 he became president of the Dakota and Great Southern railroad.

When the Northern Pacific was opened, Haupt first met the man who had won the West for the Union while Haupt was handling the railroads in the East so capably that ultimate victory for the Union was to become a reality.

Yes, almost twenty years after Appomattox, Herman Haupt was introduced to Ulysses S. Grant!

Sometimes Dan and his parents would drive by beautiful Sandusky, near Lynchburg, built in 1797 and surrounded by magnolias and boxwood and which, in 1864, was used as quarters by three soldiers named James A. Garfield, Rutherford B. Hayes and William McKinley; all rose to the same public office, president of the United States.

Then again they would drive out to tiny New London which at one time, in 1754, had been the county seat for sprawling Bedford county and where Patrick Henry pled his famous beef case. He defended a client being sued by John Hook for seizing two steers for the Colonial army, by reciting the glorious victory of American and French troops at Yorktown and his audience gave him tumultuous applause as he ended his plea with, "But hark! What notes of discord are these which disturb the general joy and silence the acclamations of victory? They are the notes of John Hook hoarsely bawling through the American camp, 'Beef! Beef! Beef!' "

And as the Cunningham wagons rolled along the roads winding up to The Big House, Dan and his brothers would get sleepy. Otho, George and Dan would huddle together in the rear of the wagon. The Captain and Mam occasionally glanced back at their "Three Little Confederates" until the time came when the boys were asleep.

All would be quiet except for the beat of the horses feet on the road and the song of the night birds.

CHAPTER III

*D*AN took many steps to get his early education. He had to as the county school was over two miles from The Big House. No school bus picked up the children. Dan walked.

At school the boys cut wood for the stove in the corner and brought in water from the well. The girls swept the floor and dusted the benches. These hard benches, made of slabs with the cut side up, were softened none by the contents of McGuffey's arithmetic-spelling-reading text book.

Noon day recess was welcomed as then the children could take down their lunches, which had been hanging in boxes on pegs along the wall, and go outside to eat. During lunch the boys played a game called "Anthony Over" in which they threw a ball over the top of the one story school. The girls, more domestically inclined, sat under the trees and dreamed of their future homes as they built houses of rock and used broken china for dishes and moss for tiny beds.

Some of the prettiest girls were from the unfortunate "poor white" class, known to the negroes, who saved their admiration for the "quality white folks," as "poor white trash." Boys such as Dan could not associate with these girls outside of the school unless they wished to bring on themselves the scorn of the girls from the landed families. In his heart, Dan felt sorry for the "poor white" children.

The "poor whites" lived in crude log cabins often without even a cook stove. Dan would occasionally drop in to see a classmate in such a home. As a visitor from The Big House, he would be welcomed and invited to dinner. This meant Dan could eat ashcake and he loved the corn meal and cracklins food. Ashcake was baked on the hearth after the wood burned down to coals. Then ashes and coals were put over and around the cake and when it was done it was eaten piping hot. The "poor whites" did not seem to resent the landed gentry and many a man from such a family had died fighting for the Confederacy.

Sunday was the big day of the week at The Big House. In the early morning, the Captain would hitch up Pelham and Button and have a wagon filled with hay. He and Mam would sit up front and drive to the country church. The boys would stay in the back of the wagon and on the way the Captain would stop to pick up boys and girls who were friends of his children. After church, the youngsters would snuggle down in the hay and the boys would hold hands with their little sweethearts.

Later the country preachers rode to The Big House for dinner. Uncle Nace and Aunt Violet brought in platters of chicken, turkey, young shoat, sweet potatoes, corn, brandied peaches and hot biscuits. Nothing was more popular with the preachers than the brandied peaches and Dan recalls one old divine who, when Mam would insist on a second or third helping of brandied peaches, always said, "No, sister Cunningham, no. But I will take another cup of the juice."

As the evening progressed, neighboring tobacco planters dropped in and the men folk retired to the parlour for smoking and drinking. Captain George fixed mint juleps and Uncle Nace saw no glass ever remained half-filled. By this time, the Captain ordered his sons to bed and they would tell the guests good night. Instead of going to bed, they gathered outside the cat hole—all the doors had holes cut for the family cat—and listened to what went on inside the parlour. The parsons and the planters joked with one another. One evening the laughter was extremely uproarious after the Captain read a passage from one of the books in his library. Later Dan looked up the passage and read this:

"Some of the parsons in Colonial Virginia—yes, perhaps many of them—were men who loved fox hunting and liquor and gaming. It would seem they thought more of the flavor of their congregation's brandy than the condition of their preparation for a Heavenly abode. This lamentable situation among the clergymen grew so widely the Virginia Assembly, in 1776, voted a law punishing every preacher who was 'notoriously scandalous for drunkingness, swearing, ffornication, or other heinous and crying sins.'" Perhaps some of the censured parsons were ancestors of Sinclair Lewis' *Elmer Gantry*.

As Dan's reading advanced in school, his father, remembering his remarks to his son on General Herman Haupt, bought him a book on railroads.

Some time after Dan had received the book, he walked cautiously into one of the barns, made his way through the feed for the horses until he reached a table on which were paint streaked cans as colorful as the autumn leaves in the Virginia hills. Carefully lifting one of the cans, Dan carried it over to the Studebaker wagon. Soon he had a brush and was slowly lettering on the wagon's side. When he had finished, he stepped back to admire his work and spell out slowly the red letters "O—r—u—k—t—e—r A—m—p—h—i—b—o—l—o—s." Quaker Philadelphia had come to the tobacco lands of Virginia!

The *Orukter Amphibolos* was the first steam propelled vehicle in the United States. Invented by Oliver Evans, this 1804 vehicle ran both on the streets of Philadelphia and in the waters of the Delaware river. Philadelphians looked on with as much awe as they had in January, 1793, when Jean Pierre Blanchard, the great French balloonist, made the first air voyage in the United States. Above the watchful eyes of George Washington, Blanchard flew from Philadelphia to Woodbury, New Jersey.

Although this curious mechanical wagon built by Evans was a big step in arousing public interest in new means of transportation, the advancing years saw more important developments. Colonel John Stevens in 1815 received a charter from the state of New Jersey to build a railroad from Trenton to New Brunswick, the first railroad charter ever granted in the United States. After four years of unsuccessful attempts to finance the proposed railroad, Stevens turned to Pennsylvania and proposed a line from Philadelphia to Pittsburgh. Again he found no adequate backing although he had the support of such a man as Stephen Girard, the great banker and founder of Girard College. Even the memory of the *Orukter Amphibolos* did not sway enough of the stolid Pennsylvania bankers to make the road possible.

To prove the practicability of a railroad, Stevens constructed a track around his Hoboken estate and built a locomotive. This was the first engine to run on wheels in the United States. It was not until five years later that Colonel Stevens actually put across his idea of rail transportation. Then he and his sons, Robert and Edwin, received a charter for the Camden and Amboy railroad and construction was, in time, carried to a successful completion. Robert Stevens designed the first rail now commonly known as the "T" type as well as spikes to fasten it. In England, Robert Stevens ordered the *John Bull,* the engine which was to be the first to run on the Pennsylvania railroad, the outfit which took over the Camden and Amboy.

Strictly speaking the initial railroad company to build and operate a railroad was the Granite Railway Company which had a line, opened in 1826, two miles long and built by Gridley Bryant. The embattled farmers at Bunker Hill were the inspiration for this line as it was laid from Quincy to Milton to carry granite used in the construction of the Bunker Hill Monument and the loaded cars were pulled by horses. In 1846 the company began to use steam power and carried freight and passengers. The Granite right-of-way became a part of the Old Colony railroad which, in turn, was taken over by the New York, New Haven and Hartford.

Sharing pioneer railroad honors with Colonel Stevens was Horatio Allen, who became interested in locomotives while an engineer for the Delaware and Hudson Canal Company. Young Allen went to England and purchased four locomotives which were the first European engines to arrive in the United States. The subsequent history of three of the locomotives is unrevealed, but the fourth, *The Stourbridge Lion,* was tested by Allen at Honesdale, Pennsylvania, in August, 1829, but the seven ton monster proved too heavy for the tracks and was converted to stationary use. Onlookers marvelled at Allen's bravery when he ran the engine across a trestle at ten miles per hour but refused to accompany him.

Nevertheless, the test won Allen the position as chief engineer on the Charleston and Hamburg railroad, the pioneer railroad of the South—later the South Carolina railroad and now part of the Southern—where he recommended steam be used as the only motive power on the road. The line had been experimenting with sail power among other methods.

This railroad was a tribute to the civic-mindedness of the citizens of Charleston who financed almost the entire nearly one million dollar cost and the 136 mile railroad was said to be the longest in the world. Because of light motive power, for a time the railroad handled only cotton on its run out and light weight merchandise on the return trip. Passengers rates were set so low a poor man found it cheaper to ride than wear out precious shoe leather. Unfortunately this pioneer railroad was so badly damaged during the War for Southern Independence it went into receivership in 1878 as a result of the expense of rebuilding it.

But when Allen joined the railroad it was in the midst of expansion. On Christmas Day, 1830, the people of Charleston received a present which really made the holiday a momentous one; the first engine to pull a train in the United States was placed in service and named, appropriately enough, the *Best Friend of Charleston*. Designed by E. I. Miller and built by the West Point factory in New York, the locomotive pulled a three car train at a speed of slightly over 21 miles an hour. Charleston residents were advised the train would not be allowed to run at night and female passengers courageous enough to ride it were presented with flowers by the railroad.

The *Best Friend of Charleston* was not the first locomotive to run on a common-carrier railroad; this honor had gone to the *Tom Thumb*, built by Peter Cooper and tested on the Baltimore and Ohio railroad in September, 1830. This one ton experimental locomotive performed successfully as the first engine to pull passengers, but lost a race to a horsecar!

A few months after the Charleston locomotive was placed in service, a negro fireman, annoyed by the noise of escaping steam, held down the safety valve lever. So came about the first boiler explosion and the resultant death of the fireman. After the accident, a buffer car filled with cotton, was placed in back of the locomotive. Soon the South Carolina line had its second locomotive, the *West Point*, and was the original railroad to carry the United States mail. Horatio

Allen came to realize trains must travel at night as well as day even as the aviation transportation industry, a century later, found it was imperative to carry on for the entire twenty-four hours. Allen had a flat car put in front of the loco-motive, covered the bottom of the car with sand and built a bonfire of pine knots.

The Iron Horse was lighting its way to fame!

Yet with all its progress and pioneering the Charleston and Hamburg was not the inaugural common carrier railroad in the United States. This was the Baltimore and Ohio, which opened a regular run between Baltimore and Ellicott's Mill—a distance of 14 miles—May 24, 1830, with cars being pulled by horses. Two years earlier, the first ground for the con-struction of the B. & O. had been turned and Charles Carroll, of Carrollton, last living signer of the Declaration of Inde-pendence, had been one of the principal speakers. The dis-tinguished 92-year-old Carroll had said, "I consider this among the most important acts of my life; second only to the signing of the Declaration of Independence, if even second to that." By the time of Carroll's death in 1832 the Baltimore and Ohio stretched out all of some 75 miles.

In reading about the early development of the railroads, Dan learned that what is now the great New York Central had its start as the Mohawk and Hudson railroad which, in 1831, was opened between Albany and Schenectady and whose first engine was the *DeWitt Clinton*. And in 1832 an ex-jeweler and watch repairer built the four wheeled *Old Ironsides* for the Philadelphia, Germantown and Norristown railroad—now a part of the Philadelphia and Reading—and sold it for $3,000. The builder's name was Matthais W. Baldwin. At this time the standard rate of pay for engineers was $2 a day and the fireman made all of $1.25.

The end of 1830 had found only 23 miles of railroad track in the United States, but ten years later this had in-creased to 3,000 miles and by 1850 to some 30,000 miles. The railroad boom was interrupted by another boom; the South Carolina guns firing on Fort Sumter!

While Dan was on the plantation at The Big House, red-haired, freckle-faced William J. Jenks was a youngster on a

North Carolina farm in Wake county, who, later, in his early teens became a railroad telegrapher at $10 a month and board. At the time Dan went into the Roanoke shop, Jenks had, a few years previously, gone to Bramwell, West Virginia, working for the Norfolk and Western for $45 a month. At nearby Bluefield, Nicholas D. Maher was trainmaster; Arthur C. Needles, yardmaster; and James T. Carey, an engineer. These men were destined to play leading roles on the N. & W. Maher was president from 1918 to 1924 and Needles from 1924 to 1936. Carey became general superintendent. And what of the fate of the $10 a month telegrapher? William J. Jenks was named Norfolk and Western chairman of the board in 1946 after having been president from 1936. New president of the N. & W. is Robert H. Smith, who has spent his entire years of railroading—begun in 1910 while he was on vacation from Princeton University—on the same line.

Captain Cunningham watched his son poring over the railroad book and he walked out to the stable. There he patted Pelham on the flanks and stood quietly with his thoughts. He could hear the negroes singing in the field:

> "Swing low sweet chariot,
> Coming for to carry me home."

The higher, rich voices of the negro women joined in to repeat the words and together the men and women sang lustily:

> "I looked over Jordan
> And what did I see,
> Coming for to carry me home. . ."

Yet back of the melodious song of the negroes, Captain Cunningham imagined he could hear the shrill whistle of a locomotive and the heavy clang of a bell and the rumble of freight cars riding the iron roads across Virginia.

CHAPTER IV

CAPTAIN CUNNINGHAM spoke, "You remember, Daniel, one day at Lynchburg, we watched the trains come in and I told you how the South lost the war because of the railroad situation?" Young Dan nodded his head in assent.

"Well, Daniel, I'm going to tell you how it happened and I want you to remember it. In years to come when you study the war and the railroads you will recall some of the things your Dad has said."

It all started with McClellan (said Captain Cunningham). He won the first important engagement of the war in July, 1861, in what is now West Virginia. One of the reasons the South was experiencing difficulty in planning a defense of the western part of Virginia was because the Union forces could enter it both by rivers and by the Baltimore and Ohio railroad. McClellan moved in with 20,000 men and found himself opposed by the Confederates under General Garnett and among the Southern force was the student body of William and Mary College. Brave Garnett walked back and forth in front of his lines to inspire his men. A Federal sharpshooter drew a bead on Garnett and that was the end of General Garnett's role in the war. In the ensuing battle, McClellan's men won not only victory, but control of the turnpikes and with it the mastery of the Baltimore and Ohio in that section; part of this railroad had been the old Winchester and Potomac which had reached Harper's Ferry in 1836.

"Little Mac"—General McClellan was so named because of his short stature and his somewhat Napoleonic complex—probably was the most beloved of all the Northern generals; certainly he knew the value of communications from his railroad experience.

George McClellan was president of the Ohio and Mississippi Railroad Company when the war broke out. Formerly he had explored in Washington territory "to ascertain the most practical route from the Mississippi Valley to the Pacific ocean." While at Fort Vancouver, Washington, McClellan was a guest of the regimental quartermaster—Captain

Ulysses S. Grant. It was to be Grant's destiny to succeed where McClellan, Pope, Burnside, Meade and all the rest failed —the conquering of Lee's army.

Well, (continued the speaker) McClellan didn't have any success in his search for a railroad passage in the Cascade Range, although later passes were discovered which were to be used by the Northern Pacific and the Great Northern. So George McClellan returned to the midwest and by the time he was thirty years of age he was chief engineer of the Illinois Central and shortly thereafter he became vice president of the road. One of the men he hired was Ambrose Burnside, who later became an official of the road and, in the war, the Union commander in the East.

But "Little Mac" wasn't always sure of his decisions in the war—it was said that he so realized the faith his men had in him that he was afraid an important decision might result in defeat—and in the railroad business McClellan made a decision in judgment of men which later events proved erroneous. One day McClellan received a letter from his friend Simon Bolivar Buckner—he was later a famous Confederate general—recommending a certain man for employment on the Illinois Central. The man was living in Lancaster, Pennsylvania, the town that was the national capital—for one day —and the site of Wheatland, President Buchanan's home. This man was unemployed and was staying at the home of his father-in-law, the former Secretary of the Interior, Judge Thomas Ewing.

This person for whom Buckner unsuccessfully sought a job was an ex-railroader named William Tecumseh Sherman!

Young Dan looked up quickly to his father's face, "Sherman—who burned Atlanta—and said 'war is hell.' Golly, Dad, I'm glad McClellan didn't give him a job."

A faint smile flecked the tan cheeks of the captain as he spoke, "Now, son, Sherman was fighting a war when he swept through Georgia. Seems hard that he had to destroy so much. Maybe his victories saved lots of lives on both sides as they brought the struggle to a quicker conclusion. People who know Sherman say he wasn't really a hard man at heart. No, son, McClellan was turning down a real man in Sherman. The Illinois Central railroad could have used him."

Captain Cunningham didn't know what a varied life Sherman had led up to the time Buckner recommended him; how he had helped pioneer the first railroad on the Pacific coast.

As an army officer in the Mexican war, Sherman had been stationed at Monterey, California; had fretted that he was so far away from the scenes of action which were training schools for future military leaders of the North and South. After the war, Sherman had gone into business and risen to the position of the head of the San Francisco branch of Lucas, Turner and Company, a St. Louis banking house. He also accepted the position of vice president of the proposed Sacramento Valley railroad, which against extreme difficulties, was trying to construct a rail line to Folsom, a distance of some twenty miles from Sacramento.

The day after Sherman became an official of the railroad, the backers put a handcar on the tracks in Sacramento and poled it down the streets. This was as much excitement as Sacramento had seen since the days of Sutter's empire and the discovery of gold outside the city.

Actually this moving handcar was the initial rail movement west of the Rockies and Sherman felt that his midwest banking associates would see the future of the brave little railroad that hoped to conquer the high Sierras and open the treasures earth-locked in the mountains. A year or so later, in 1856, the rails of the Sacramento Valley reached Folsom and Pacific coast railroad history was written through Chapter I, even if the S. V. R. had only four little engines and a debt, to repay which, would require a train of flatcars loaded with greenbacks.

The opening of the railroad was celebrated with an excursion to Folsom, where Sherman, awaiting his turn to speak, listened while Senator Flint shouted to the happy—and high-spirited in more ways than one—crowd, "The Iron Horse, that mightiest triumph of human art, pants along the metallic way, tireless, and uncurbed in strength, and impatient to dare the far off."

And across the continent in far off Atlanta, Georgia, people talked of King Cotton and paid little heed to the printed words of Senator Flint nor to the speech of William Sherman. Little did they know that the Iron Horses "tireless and uncurbed in strength" that were lancing through Georgia, were doomed to destruction in the flames set by the victorious Federal army under the general marching through Georgia, Sherman.

The following year, Sherman displeased with the lack of support given him as General of the Militia, when he was trying to suppress the violent outbursts of the Vigilantes, who were in popular favor, instructed his St. Louis bankers the California branch could make no profits under the turbulent coast conditions, returned East.

Sherman had a brief career as a lawyer in which he had one client. He "won" the case which was a judgment on a house his client owned, by moving—with the eager arms of his client aiding him—the house away under the cover of darkness.

When McClellan found no place on the Illinois Central for Sherman, the former railroader and banker took the position of president at the Louisiana State Military Academy (now Louisiana State University). It was from there that he went into the Union army at the commencement of the war.

With Sherman teaching many young men who were to die under the blood-soaked Stars and Bars, the Sacramento Valley railroad was progressing despite the absence of its former vice president. This railroad, which had awakened the west to the future of rail transportation, carried the Comstock gold and was to become, in 1865, a part of the Central Pacific, later the Southern Pacific. And it was gold—riding over the newly laid rails spiraling down from the rich young mountains of the West that met many a payroll of the Federal armies.

Around the time McClellan took no favorable action on Sherman being added to the Illinois Central staff, he had a counsel for both the Illinois Central and the Rock Island who amused McClellan considerably. McClellan said this of him:

"More than once I have been with him in out-of-the-way county seats where some important case was being tried, and, in the lack of sleeping accomodations, have spent the night in front of a stove listening to the unceasing flow of anecdotes from his lips. He was never at loss, and I could never quite make up my mind how many of them he had really heard before, and how many he invented on the spur of the moment. His stories were seldom refined but always to the point."

McClellan was speaking of a railroad counsel named Abraham Lincoln.

Now back to McClellan and the start of the War Between the States. When the nation split, the United States had some 30,000 miles of railroads of which about 10,000 miles were in the South, and some 1,400 in Virginia; however, not all the southern mileage was in states which actively aided in the secession. The development of railroads in states which are in what is now the midwest proved of great value in sending troops against the outposts of the Confederacy and it was the success of the Federal armies in the West that offset the victories of the Southern armies in the East.

Too, with the war underway, the Union forces were able to operate not only on railroads, but on the waterways, whereas the Secessionists were, in the main, confined to their own railroad lines which were far more vulnerable than the Northern lines as the war progressed. Sometimes the South did not take the fullest advantage of its limited transportation system. For example, the Confederates had an excellent rail line from Lynchburg, Virginia, to Chattanooga, Tennessee, but, for some unknown reason, the Confederates were dilatory about using this rapid means of troop transportation until the North had the teeter-totter of war rising toward a Federal victory.

The northern country west of the Alleghanies had only some thousand or so miles of railroad in 1850, but by the time Lincoln assumed office in Washington and Jefferson Davis took over the presidency of the Confederate States at Montgomery, Alabama, the mileage of the western railroads had increased to approximately that of the Confederacy. Authorities state that had the South seceded ten years earlier, victory could have been theirs because the midwestern states would have been unable to furnish the support by railroads necessary to the invasion of the South. And, too, in 1850, Jefferson Davis was among the leaders in the United States Senate and President Millard Fillmore might have sought means of handling the sectional feud less drastic than actual conflict.

Such was the railroad background when McClellan stormed into extreme western Virginia and won control of the Baltimore and Ohio in that district. Troop trains steamed out of the midwest—though the Confederate cause had a sizeable following in that territory—for the Eastern front. Several months after McClellan's victory, the Nineteenth Illinois, under Colonel Turchin, entrained in five cars, suffered one hundred men killed and injured when a bridge collapsed one full moon night as the train was crossing a river along the route of the Ohio and Mississippi railroad.

Captain Cunningham related how further east the railroads from Washington and Baltimore west were being attacked by Rebel partisan raiders—independent commands—acting under the authority of the Confederate government, but attached to none of the regular Confederate armies. These groups were, in a sense, similar to the adventurers sailing under the "Letters of Marque" used by Southern privateers on the sea.

Workmen on the Philadelphia, Wilmington and Baltimore, and the Baltimore and Ohio railroads would suddenly be surprised by charging cavalry groups which would burn bridges and tear up the tracks. To combat this, the North hurriedly built railroad batteries. One of the most remarkable was constructed of heavy boiler iron, had a 24 pounder cannon mounted on a pivot, and had rifle holes for fifty guards. Impervious to rifle fire, such batteries would be attached to construction trains. "Never cared much about charging one of them," Captain Cunningham admitted.

Northern engineers were sometimes protected by iron plated cabs as every gully was a potential source of enemy fire. The Southerners often would loosen the rails, attach telegraph

Top—Victorious Southerners with a locomotive thrown over a bank by Pope's retreating army after the Second Battle of Bull Run. Photo credit: *National Archives*

Bottom—The mighty *Dictator,* famous Federal railroad mortar, 1864, at the siege of Petersburg. Photo credit: *Confederate Museum*

Inset: Brilliant Northern railroad genius—GENERAL HERMAN HAUPT. Photo credit: *National Archives*

Railroad fighting in Virginia. The First Ohio Regiment, guarding the railroad between Alexandria and Leesburg, rallies after a surprise attack by masked Confederate batteries.

Sketch by Henry Laurie
Picture credit: *National Archives*

Five locomotives built at Vicksburg for the United States Military railroads after Pemberton's surrender to Grant.

Sketch by F. B. Schell
Picture credit: *National Archives*

wires to them, and, as the Federal train would roar down the tracks, the Confederates would jerk the rails out of place. With no time to halt the train, the engineer, if he were lucky enough to find himself alive, would pull himself from his wrecked engine and look wearily back at his derailed train. Often culverts would be broken by the raiders and the trains would be hurled into deep cuts in the countryside or into rivers.

Of course, the Northern troops were not adverse to wrecking Southern trains when they could get to them. Virginia had many short railroads when the Federal troops invaded her territory; lines such as the Potomac, Manassas Gap, South Side, Alexandria and Loudon, Orange and Alexandria, Richmond and York River, Weldon and Petersburg, and the Virginia and Tennessee. The V. & T. was called by plain-spoken Lincoln, "the gut of the Confederacy."

After his success in western Virginia, by June, 1862, McClellan found himself in trouble as his Peninsular Campaign was being brought to a conclusion that bore no mark of success. The Southern troops under their new commander, Robert E. Lee, held Richmond inviolate and Lee and Jackson joined forces with such strength that "Little Mac" hastily prepared to withdraw. General McClellan ordered train after train loaded with food and war material. His railroad engineers were amazed when orders came to destroy all the railroad bridges over the Pamunkey river. Such an order meant that the trains could not be moved back into Federal-held territory. It was soon apparent that McClellan had no intention of trying to save the trains as he feared that the Confederates would capture them.

"Dan," spoke Captain Cunningham, "after the war I talked with one of McClellan's men who stood on the banks of the Pamunkey and looked out for maybe somebody like your pappy in a gray uniform as the engineers steamed up the Yank locomotives. He told me how the trains would start moving, then the engineers would jump, and every fully loaded train would run right off the tracks into the river where, on the riverbed of the Pamunkey, it rested safely out of the hands of Johnny Reb!"

In August, 1862, General Pope found the power of the
famed Virginia cavalry pitted against his transportation.
Stonewall Jackson learned that Pope had left his baggage and
personal papers at Catlett's Station on the Orange and Alexandria railroad and also at Manassas Junction the Federals
had stored over one million dollars worth of supplies. As
Manassas Junction was only some thirty miles from Washington, Pope felt the supplies were safe.

Pope didn't know what type of men were against him.
At Jackson's command Jeb Stuart took fifteen hundred men,
rode day and night, fell upon Catlett's Station, bagging
among other prizes, Pope's dress uniform and favorite hat.
Previously a well planned attack by Federals on Stuart had
resulted in the loss of Stuart's plumed hat. Gay cavalier that
Stuart was, he wrote Pope a note, sent back the uniform and
hat by a special messenger. Pope, not to be outdone in polite-
ness, returned the captured plumed hat to Stuart.

But the South was to receive more than Stuart's hat. As
Pope sought to reinforce Manassas Junction, Stuart and Jackson joined as the "foot cavalry" of Jackson covered fifty miles
in thirty-six hours. Back of Pope's army struck the Confederates and at Manassas Junction captured seven trains and
ten locomotives. The half-starved, half-uniformed Confederates feasted on German lobster, Rhine wine and clothed
themselves in the seized uniforms of the North. "An onlooker
would think he had come across Pope's army, the way we were
all done up in blue," commented Captain Cunningham. But
the soldiers soon were running engines off the track, destroying much of the railroad, and raising such a din it resounded
almost to Pope's headquarters.

With the railroad lines cut, Pope was forced into the
second battle of Bull Run, badly mauled by the victory-
minded Confederate army until his retreat stopped only in
the shadow of Washington. It was after this battle that
Herman Haupt's prompt action to supply transportation for
the retreating Federals helped save Pope's forces from utter
disaster.

Soon Robert E. Lee was crossing the Potomac and
marching into Maryland as his men sang:

> "The despot's heel is on thy shore
>   Maryland!
> His torch it at thy temple door,
>   Maryland!
> Avenge the patriotic gore
> That flecked the streets of Baltimore,
> And be the battle-queen of yore,
>   Maryland, my Maryland!"

As the words of James Ryder Randall's famed Confederate song rang out in the air of the Old Line State, Baltimore, Washington and even Philadelphia were in panic as the citizens could imagine the Stars and Bars waving in their streets. The high tide of the Confederacy, swept forward by the unlocking of the enemy control of northern Virginia railroads, reached Antietam.

Neither army could score a decisive victory, but McClellan, again in command, stopped Lee's advance, and the Confederates retired back across the Potomac. Again United States military locomotives were fired up for their runs into Virginia territory and back in the Alleghanies and the Blue Ridge Southern chieftains summoned their raiders and planned to destroy the new spears of steam clouded rails that were thrown against them.

Jeb Stuart took particular delight in raiding the railroads and Captain Cunningham told of the time he was with Stuart on a jaunt against the Orange and Alexandria when Jeb seized the telegraph station, put his own operator on the key, and sent through a message to the Federal commander opposing him. Capricious Stuart wired his opponent that he hoped Washington would furnish better grade mules to the Northern army as those which Stuart had been capturing were of decidely inferior quality.

Whereas victorious Confederate leaders in the East could taunt their harassed foe, the war in the West was of a different nature. Although every mile of their advance was contested bitterly, the United States western forces were pushing the Confederate States defenders both up and down the Mississippi.

The smiles on Captain Cunningham's face vanished as

he told the story of the war in the West, but he brightened up when he left the subject of Shiloh and went on to a tale of the railroads at Cornith. After the victory at Shiloh, when Confederate General Albert Sidney Johnston was killed, Halleck, with Grant as his second in command, advanced on to Cornith, Mississippi, where he threw more than 100,000 troops against an effective force of 53,000 Rebels under General Beauregard, who, with some clever use of the railways, saved his army with a surprise evacuation.

As the overwhelming Northern forces prepared for an assault, they could hear the noise of trains arriving in Cornith and the enthusiastic cheers of the defenders. Obviously the under-manned Confederate garrison was being reinforced. The invaders were thrown off balance as there was a possibility the Southern troops would charge out from their trenches against the beseigers. So fast did the trains arrive in Cornith that the Federals felt all the Confederate soldiers in that territory were being rushed to Cornith's aid.

But as the hours passed, no gray-coated men plunged forward the battle flag of Dixie and the movement of the trains grew less and less. Finally Federal railroad men put their ears to the rails, reported that trains coming into Cornith sounded as if they were empty, but those going out sounded as if they were heavily loaded.

As soon as the order could be given, Halleck's army advanced; Union pickets crossed over into Confederate lines; Colonel Washington L. Elliot's brigade, one regiment of which was commanded by Colonel Phil Sheridan, dashed into Cornith, rode in the shadow of the Cherokee saloon and by the long, rambling two story railroad station with its sloping overhanging roof.

Cornith was captured!

But not in enemy hands fell the elusive Beauregard. He had never received the supposed reinforcements; instead, had ordered his men to cheer as they were being evacuated so as to fool the Yankees. By this ruse he had saved his army.

Railroad evacuation could not save the territory that Beauregard had been forced to yield and only Vicksburg stood as a barrier between the northward bound fleet of "Oak

Heart" Farragut and the southbound flotillas of Union gunboats.

After the fall of Cornith, Buell was ordered to advance toward Chattanooga by Halleck and to rebuild the Memphis and Charleston railroad which was the dividing line held by the contending armies. Southern raiders broke up efforts to rebuild the line and Buell switched his operations to the Nashville and Chattanooga railroad which was within Union lines. The Construction Corps had the railway repaired in short order and the initial military train moved from Nashville to Buell's men. By the next afternoon General Nathan Bedford Forrest—the wealthy businessman who had enlisted in the Confederate army as a private at the age of 40 and who had twenty-nine horses shot from under him—had charged into Murfreesboro, a score or so miles below Nashville, captured the garrison and torn up the new railroad line.

Undaunted although unhappy, Buell repaired his railroad communications below Nashville and hoped for a change. He got it. Instead of Forrest cutting his N. & C. tracks, that meteoric lash of the Confederacy, General John H. Morgan, led his men across the Cumberland river, blew up the tunnels on the Louisville and Nashville railroad.

"You see, Daniel," talked on Captain Cunningham, "we were wrecking our own railroads rather than Northern railroads." This was the damning weakness of the method used by the Southern defenders, who, it is wholly true, had little choice. Yet, not always, did they take the opportunity of breaking rail lines in their occasional forays deep into the North. When Morgan made his famous ride into Kentucky, Indiana and Ohio and came within fifty miles of Indianapolis, the raider paid small heed to destroying the railroads and the Northerners, wisely enough, did not tear up their own tracks, but merely felled trees across them. On this daring raid—said to have been timed so that the Southern sympathizers, the so-called Copperheads, could arise—Morgan, unfortunately for Lee battling at Gettysburg and Pemberton struggling to hold Vicksburg, let his command get out of hand and friend and foe alike were pillaged. Thus was alienated the powerful "underground" support for the South in the midwest and

Morgan in the future had only the opportunity to wreck
the railroads of his own beloved South. This he did until that
early morning in 1864 when, surprised by a Federal raid on
his headquarters at Greeneville, Tennessee, he shouted, "They
have sworn never to take me a prisoner," fell from a cavalryman's bullet and lay silent amidst a bed of rain-drenched
flowers such as had been picked by the students of nearby
Tusculum College since the days before the American
Revolution.

Before Morgan's death, Vicksburg had long been in
Federal hands. Pemberton had burned the railroad shops in the
starving river port, but Federal engineers were so ingenious
they had the shops soon rebuilt and from the machinery
wreckage constructed five new locomotives for the United
States Military railroads.

With Grant in the West was William Tecumseh Sherman,
who, from his railroad experience on the Pacific coast, knew
that the South's railroads must be crippled. After the Vicksburg triumph, Sherman with 20,000 men struck against
Meridian, Mississippi, the most important railroad center of
the Southwest. To aid him Union horsemen were ordered
down from Memphis under General W. S. Smith. This force
was stopped by the Confederates at Okolona. But no one
could stop Sherman, who successfully accomplished "the most
complete destruction of railroads ever beheld." With Secessionist rail communications disrupted the small Union
garrisons along the Mississippi were safe from co-ordinated
attack.

In March, 1864, black-bearded, cigar-chewing Lieutenant General Ulysses S. Grant, fresh from important victories in the West, arrived in Washington to take over
command of the Union forces which time after time failed to
capture Richmond.

Captain Cunningham often took any occasion to tell
how Grant got his introduction to the war in the East. Young
Dan listened attentively each time. It seems that when
Grant's unguarded special train pulled into Warrenton
Junction, the beat of horses hoofs was raising the Virginia
dust in the not too far distance. Momentarily stepping from

his train, Grant peered at a group of onlookers, took a bite on his soggy cigar, asked what was causing the commotion.

One of the civilians at the station recognized Grant, spoke, up, "This isn't Vicksburg, General Grant. You're in Virginia now, suh. That dust is from horsemen who crossed the tracks. Mosby and his men are chasing the Feds. General, if you'd been here a few minutes earlier, you'd had the pleasure of meeting Mosby yourself!"

Grant bit down on his cigar hard. Soon the train was pulling out of the station. The new Federal commander looked at the ashes of the station which Mosby had burned months previously. There must have been a bit of wonderment in Grant's agile mind as he realized that Confederate train raiders rode successfully in back of the Union armies.

If Grant hadn't been a drinking man, perhaps Mosby would have converted him to hard liquor. Colonel Mosby was soon burning the Baltimore and Ohio stations and his successes so infuriated Grant that he supported an order put out by Brigade Commander George Custer to hang without trial captured "irregular" troops. And Mosby's derring-do comrades were not always successful in escaping after their destructive actions. At Front Royal, while golden-haired Custer, dapper in his velvet uniform, ate fruit picked from Virginia trees, half a dozen of Mosby's captured men were executed as the blue-clad band played *Love not, the One You Love may Die*.

About this time General Jubal Early was riding so close to Washington that at night the planks were taken up on bridges approaching the capital. Captain Cunningham recalled that Lee often affectionately referred to Early as his "bad old man." On this raid, "the bad old man" with 17,000 men had swept up with Lynchburg in forced marches, torn up many miles of the Baltimore and Ohio in Maryland and driven to within five miles of Washington. The United States capital was in a panic; rushed to man the defenses went convalescent troops from hospitals and government employees. Lincoln, himself, hastened to the front lines at Fort Stevens. Not until a Confederate sharpshooter brought down an officer standing three feet from Lincoln, did the president seek a sheltered spot. But although Early had destroyed the B. & O. lines, the North so controlled enough important railroads in territory conquered in the South that the Federals received reinforcements from around Petersburg and New Orleans and "Old Jube" retired.

"We almost captured Washington, didn't we, Father?" Dan asked as he nibbled on an ashcake which one of the negroes on the plantation had brought in to him. Ashcakes were "poor white" food and never were they made in The Big House. But the negroes would bring in the ashcakes as they knew the Cunningham children liked them.

"Don't know what would have happened if 'Old Jube' had succeeded," the master of the house said as he nipped off a bite of the bread for himself. "Guess maybe Jefferson Davis and Abe Lincoln might have changed places in that prison cell after the armistice."

Perhaps. But in the Deep South, the North's military might was steadily lopping off hunks of territory formerly in Confederate hands. Sherman reached Atlanta wrecking the railroads as he progressed. The Federal transportation was in charge of Colonel W. W. Wright, who had been a student of Haupt's at Gettysburg, and who had received valuable experience in the Virginia campaigns. Yankee forces controlled nearly 500 miles of rail line from Louisville to Atlanta, although half the route—from Nashville on to Atlanta—was subject to numerous assaults by the roving Confederate bands.

But the assaults were overcome and the railroads supplied the 100,000 Union soldiers so well that Sherman said, "the Atlanta campaign would have been impossible without the railroads." As fast as the Confederates would break up the enemy's rail advance and fall back, the United States Military railroad workers would repair the damage and by the time the Rebels would make camp, the Federal Iron Horses would come up puffing and ready to renew the conflict.

General Hood's troops in Atlanta were powerless to stop Sherman, yet the Union general realized that taking the city by storm would mean a terrific loss of men. Instead of a bloody seige, Sherman turned his garrote on the city by cutting off its communications. Sherman fooled Hood at Atlanta even as Beauregard did Halleck at Cornith and had the defenders thinking his army was in retreat. Actually Sherman was moving his entire forces against the West Point railroad which he destroyed. This was followed by the destruction of the Macon and Western railroad, the only remaining line of supplies to the Confederates as the Georgia Central had been badly crippled.

Four months after the Atlanta campaign started, Sherman could not sleep the night of August 31 because of the noise of Atlanta's death-rattle. Valiant Hood found himself with ammunition and supplies but no means of getting them away safely. His only alternative was to destroy them and he ordered hundreds of railroad cars blown up. By September 2, Hood's men had left Atlanta and the campaign was won by Sherman at a cost of over 30,000 Federal troops killed, captured or wounded.

But Atlanta's fall justified the cost as the North was electrified by the news and this victory was one of the decisive factors in the presidential election in which former Illinois Central attorney Abraham Lincoln won his re-election over former Illinois Central vice president George McClellan.

Northward, the peripatetic Mosby was astir as the execution of his men had aroused him to even greater activity. Phil Sheridan's cavalry protected the Manassas Gap railroad, but Mosby's men cut its rails and sent Union trains smashing themselves to wreckage. Finally Union forces destroyed all homes within five miles of the railroad and forced important Southern civilians to ride exposed on the trains as hostages. Out of the blue-star night Mosby rode boldly and Sheridan recommended that efforts to reinforce the main Federal army be confined to the B. & O.

Of all the Southern railroad exploits in the war, none brought more of a twinkle to Captain Cunningham's eye than the "Greenback" raid made by Mosby October 13, 1864. A Baltimore and Ohio train that night passed Harper's Ferry and was nearing Kearneysville when bullets, plunging into the coaches, brought the train to a sudden stop. Rebel raiders leaped on the cars, ordered out the passengers, set fire to the

train with captured copies of the New York *Herald Tribune*.
Prize loot was a Federal army payroll of some $200,000.

The raiders commander stood on top of a cut, received
some of the passengers, spoke quietly, "I regret having to
interrupt your journey, but it seems that since General Stevenson will not guard the Baltimore and Ohio, it becomes imperative that I make Stevenson attend to his duties. As my
men have probably told you—I'm Colonel John S. Mosby."

As a result of the "Greenback" triumph—so called be-
cause of the large amount of seized currency—traffic on the
B. & O. was almost paralyzed and Mosby returned to his
Virginia haunts.

The flames in the fireplace were burning low as the wood
around the back log was consumed. Captain Cunningham
rose from his chair, picked up some small logs, threw them on
the back log. Soon the fire flared up again and Dan looked
with pleasure at the mounting flames. His father resumed
speaking, "It's like Atlanta flared up, Daniel. When Sherman
decided to abandon Atlanta and set out across the country,
much of the business section of Atlanta was put to the torch.
One of the biggest fires was when the railroad roundhouse
was burned. Must have been quite a sight for the Yanks. One
of their newspaper reporters wrote, 'In more ways than one
it was a parallel to the burning of Rome for the Union bands
accompanied the roar and crackle of flames, the boom of
monster explosions and the crash of falling debris with martial
airs that soldiers love so well.' "

As Sherman started for the sea, on his flank Federal
officers ordered complete annihilation of all means of enemy
communication and the red and yellow light that played
across the blue uniforms of the marching troops was born
in the burning bridges of the Georgia Central.

With many of the Deep South railroads in Northern
control, the South battled to keep Petersburg, the railroad
center of Virginia. The terrific contests were taking a deadly
toll even if some Confederate pickets, who held a long chat
with Northern soldiers opposite them in outposts, made an
interesting report to their officers.

"I was at headquarters when our lads came in," Captain

Cunningham remarked, "and we were amused at their tales of how they had exchanged copies of our newspapers for those out of Washington and Baltimore which had been read by the Yankee pickets. Then the boys told us they had exchanged some of their tobacco for Northern coffee and even brought us a poke full of coffee. One of the soldiers, aged far beyond his years by the conflict and with creases in his face almost as deep as our trenches, came up to me and said, 'Captain, while we were making the exchanges, we and the Yanks talked this whole mess over and if it had been left to us in 1861 we would have settled this damned war in half an hour!' "

But the settling of the war before Petersburg was anything else but conversational even considering the "loud talking" of the 17,000 pound railroad mortar, *Dictator*, which was manned by the First Connecticut Artillery. The huge mortar, which broke the first railway car on which it was mounted, sometimes was difficult to adjust to range and its shells fell into the city proper rather than on the Confederate lines. The North had other seige guns—gunboats on wheels—mounted on railroad cars and protected with massive timbers and iron plate.

Even as the South had used submarines against the Northern sea blockade on the Atlantic coast and built the *Davids*—steam torpedo boats which were forerunners of the famed "expendable" torpedo boats of World War II—and even as one Southern inventor had built a model airplane which he had hoped would herald air attacks against Washington, so the South had been the first to use a gun mounted on railway trucks. When Richmond was successfully defended during the Seven Days battle, the defenders had put a field cannon on a flat car and an engine had run it from point to point to fire against the Federals.

As had taken place at Atlanta, the North severed the railroads until the Petersburg Confederates were so short of supplies that their food was cut to one-sixth normal daily rations which meant the troops instead of getting three meals a day were actually receiving only one-half a meal. Yet General William Mahone was to save Petersburg as "The Hero of the Crater," and for nearly a year the railroad center held out.

Finally at Five Oaks, Sheridan cut the line of the South Side railroad, the only railroad in possession of the Confederates, and Lee was compelled to evacuate both Petersburg and Richmond. Lee's starving army fought a running retreat until it reached Appomattox Courthouse. The morning of April 8, 1865, a Confederate provision train arrived at Appomattox Station and, as supplies were being unloaded into wagons and ambulances, Federal cavalry charged and captured the railroad line. So ended the last effort to provision Lee's men and the following day General Lee surrendered his 28,000 warriors to Lieutenant General Ulysses S. Grant.

Other Confederate generals, including General Johnston in North Carolina, with whom Lee had hoped to make a junction, fought on briefly until the final commander, General Kirby S. Smith, surrendered his Army of the Trans-Mississippi on May 26 to Major General E. R. S. Canby.

The conflict between brave men who wore the blue of Washington and the gray of Richmond had closed. Railroads —what was left of them in the South—could again move along the rails in peace and no rebel yells came out of the misty hills from which careening horsemen had galloped for a cause that had long been lost.

CHAPTER V

THE big red bound book lay against a rocker on the porch at The Big House and Captain Cunningham looked out to the trees laced with shadows as the sun moved down toward the Virginia hills. Under the trees his three sons were building a fort out of broken sticks and red soil. At their father's call, they stopped playing, ran up to the porch.

"Sit down," he said gently, as he leaned back in his chair and the green rocker moved back and forth slowly. The big red book slipped to the floor and the boys could see that it was a history of the War for Southern Independence.

The lads listened as their father spoke: "I bought this book while I was down in Lynchburg, boys, and I'm going to tell you something I've learned from it. The war's long over and General Lee was right when he told students at Washington College something about their first duty was to be good citizens of the United States. We have to build for the future. That's what our Southern generals have been doing; building so that a new South will grow strong and prosper and the nation will not be made up of loosely bound sections, but will be a country held together by bonds of iron. That, sons, is what the railroads can do."

"I know the railroads are doing a good job of carrying our tobacco, sir," spoke up twelve-year-old Otho.

"Yes, Otho, but we must have more railroads," answered his father. "I'm going to read to you what some of Lee's former generals are doing." Captain Cunningham picked up the big book, began reading thoughtfully and his words rolled out toward the closest rows of tobacco as if they, too, were in the audience. And the boys listened to their father's voice punctuated by the creak of the rocker on the uneven platform of the porch.

Captain Cunningham was right. The South was rebuilding and many of its former military leaders were seeking and had sought to bring the roar of the Iron Horse along the levees, through the cotton fields, across meandering rivers shaded by trees dripping with Spanish moss. Brilliant General Nathan Bedford Forrest, after the South had capitulated, had organized and become president of the Selma, Marion and Memphis railroad. Perhaps Forrest had been inspired by the memory of Isaac Ridgeway Trimble, who, at almost sixty years of age, had left his railroad pioneering in Maryland to be a general in the Confederate army. Or, perhaps, tall Viking appearing Robert Emmett Rodes, whose drooping moustache aged in appearance the 32-year-old Confederate brigadier general. Rodes had been a former railroad civil engineer in Alabama before he taught at V. M. I.

The South still loved dapper General Peirre Gustave Toutant Beauregard, who resigned as Superintendent of West Point to take command of the defenses at Charleston, South Carolina, and who opened fire on Major Robert Anderson at Fort Sumter the morning of April 16, 1861. It was the courageous Beauregard who led the South to its great victory at Bull Run; who later defended Charleston against seige operations and held Petersburg against Grant; who, along with Joseph E. Johnston, had surrendered to General Sherman in April, 1865. His Confederate military career concluded, Beauregard had become president of the New Orleans, Jackson and Mississippi railroad.

Joseph E. Johnston, himself, was interested in railroads and was a railroad commissioner after the war. He could look back on the bloody days when he had commanded the Southern forces in Virginia at the war's start; when he was the supreme commander of the Confederate armies in the southwest after Braxton Bragg had been defeated at Chattanooga. Johnston could recall it was partially because of the lack of proper rail communications that Lee's retreating forces, after the evacuation of Richmond, were unable to consolidate with Johnston's army in North Carolina. After the war, Johnston had been nominated for the presidency of the Richmond and Danville railroad, but the Union supported "Restored Government of Virginia" had blocked Johnston's election. Brigadier General E. P. Alexander, who at Gettysburg had commanded Longstreet's guns, which almost to the last shot had blasted the way for Pickett, was a railroad president.

And there was the heroic figure of General William "Billy" Mahone, "The Hero of the Crater," hailed as the South's greatest railroad figure when he created the consolidation which resulted in the Atlantic, Mississippi and Ohio railroad.

Northern military leaders, as well as those who wore the gray of the Confederate States, were active in railroad development after the war. General Ambrose Everett Burnside, who had succeeded McClellan as commander of the Army of the Potomac; later was superseded himself by Major General "Fighting Joe" Hooker; and who was later prominent in the seige of Knoxville, and the battles of the Wilderness, Cold Harbor and Petersburg, went back to railroading after the war. During the conflict, while on the Virginia front, Union soldiers would watch Burnside ride a handcar on inspection trips, his tall bucket-shaped hat polished so brightly it would reflect the faces of the perspiring negroes who propelled the handcar.

Irish born General James Shields was a railroad commissioner; General Henry Halleck was managing a western railroad; and General Granville M. Dodge was chief engineer of the Union Pacific from 1866-70 and of the Texas Pacific from 1871-81. At Gettysburg, the Federal cavalry had been commanded by General Alfred Pleasanton, who later, in 1864, forced Virginia-born Hampden-Sydney College graduate General Sterling Price out of Missouri to Arkansas, where he was in command of the Confederate troops at the war's close. It was a different kind of movement which Pleasanton directed in the days of peace as he became president of the Terra Haute and Cincinnati railroad.

One of the most interesting postwar experiences had been that of General Daniel Tyler, first colonel in the Connecticut Volunteers, later a leader in the Army of the Mississippi, and commander at Harper's Ferry and Maryland Heights. Even as some of the defeated Southerners sought haven in Brazil, where they thought they would grow cotton and continue the plantation life they enjoyed prior to the war, so General Tyler decided he would like the Southern way of living himself. He didn't go as far south as Brazil. Tyler left

Connecticut for Alabama where he became a cotton planter, built the now well-known town of Anniston, and was president of the Mobile and Montgomery railroad from 1873-1879.

The railroad fever had hit the Captain, but he had no chance to do anything about it until 1882. When the new Shenandoah Valley railroad announced it was coming through Stony Battery, near Bedford, the Captain took Otho, who was then 15 years old, and set out to Stony Battery. So for six months the Captain helped "boss" the construction of the railway line running deep into Virginia from Hagerstown, Maryland.

His work finished around Stony Battery, the Captain returned to The Big House and he and Otho were brimming over with exciting stories of the railroad. As the family was reunited around the dinner table, the Captain spun his yarns.

It seems (he said) some of the farmers had never seen a train when the first Shenandoah Valley trains came through rural western Virginia. Such a farmer, who lived about five miles from a new S. V. R. station, decided to take his family down to see the trains arrive. He hitched his mule to a wagon, loaded up his wife and six children, and the family started out on its great adventure. All was well for four miles. Then, as he had heard tales of the terrible sight presented by a running locomotive, the farmer became perturbed and, feeling his mule might be frightened by the iron monster and wreck the wagon, he stopped half a mile from the station, unhitched the mule and tied it to a tree. The farmer, himself, got between the shafts and, as there was a slight downward grade, the wagon proceeded on its way. Just as the farmer and his family came in sight of the station, the incoming train rounded a curve. The locomotive let out a loud blast of the whistle and the wide open cylinder cocks threw out clouds of steam on both sides of the engine. As the farmer saw this come-to-life nightmare rushing toward him, he let out a cry of terror and, plunging ahead with his hold on the wagon shafts, ran wild and turned the wagon over an embankment, killed his entire family as well as wrecking the wagon.

This story, as Dan recalls it today, reminds him of another story he heard later on when he was working for the

Norfolk and Western. The N. & W. was building the short cut out from Pepper to Bluefield and track had been laid up to the water's edge at the New river; however, the bridge had not been built and, to an outsider, there was no indication of preparations for bridge building. Across the river the railroad tunnel had been started and it ran nearly through the mountain leaving visible a large hole.

A farmer chanced to come up to the track's end, spoke to a railroad workman, "What in tarnation is that hole for, mister?"

The workman grunted, "Hole's for the train to go through."

First the farmer looked at the track ending up at the river bank; then he looked at the expanse of water; finally at the hole in the mountain. After his thorough examination of the situation, he turned to the railroad workman and said crisply, "It may be all right, brother. But when the train jumps the river, if she misses that hole, it will be the damndest smashup you ever saw!"

Railroads won over tobacco at the plantation and, in 1882, the Captain went to Roanoke where he supervised the unloading of all material and machinery used in the building of the Roanoke Machine Works. This was being erected for the handling of all repair work and the construction of new equipment for both the Norfolk and Western and the Shenandoah Valley.

Some months later the Captain returned to The Big House and told his family he had bought a home in Roanoke and they were to move immediately. The Big House was put up for sale and so another planter turned from the rural life to urban pursuits. Uncle Nace, Aunt Violet and Grandma Sabra had passed away by then. Perhaps what Captain George hated most to leave was his beloved Pelham, who stood in the fields and watched the family move out.

The Captain looked at Pelham, reached in his billfold and took out a wad of greenbacks. "Take this, son," he said to Otho, "and go over to Liberty and buy a buggy. Ride over on Pelham and bring him back with the buggy. Then you and George and Mam—and Pelham—drive on to Roanoke."

Steve Mustgrove, a neighboring planter, had offered to carry the personal belongings in his canvas topped Conestoga wagon. So the Captain and Dan rode along with Steve. The thirty-five mile trip took two days and the men spent the night at a friendly farmer's house. After a breakfast of salt pork, eggs and coffee, they continued on to Roanoke.

Near nightfall the wagon reached the new Cunningham home. It was quite different from the mansion house in Bedford. White frame and small it stood near the railroad tracks for the Captain had said he wanted a place where his boys could watch the trains go by.

Pelham neighed a welcome from the place he was tethered in a field.

After old Lynchburg, the Cunninghams found Roanoke a baby town the life blood of which was the railroads. Although some early pioneers had gone through what is now Roanoke Valley in efforts to "discover the South Seas," settlers did not come until 1740 to this land, a hunting ground for Indians as animals were attracted to the territory by salt deposits. By 1800 Old Lick was a cross roads on the turnpike from Lynchburg and the Grand Road down the valley. Turnpike travel brought about the little town of Gainsborough, soon known as Big Lick where, in 1852, the Virginia and Tennessee railroad built a depot. Around 1874 Big Lick was incorporated and, in 1881, the half a thousand or so inhabitants of Big Lick raised $10,000 so that the Shenandoah Valley railroad would make it the southern terminus. Big Lick became Roanoke—the Indian name for wampum or "shining money"—and, when the first S. V. R. train pulled into the town, industry which was to make Roanoke "The Magic City" began. One year after the Cunninghams arrived, Roanoke had 5,000 inhabitants.

A few days after getting settled in the new home, Captain George took his boys out to see the railway shop he had helped to build. Dan saw a one story brick building about 70 by 340 feet with metal trusses and skylights. As they walked through the building, the Captain explained how power was supplied from a straight line engine and distributed through the railroad shop by means of shafting. Dan watched the crane travelling along the center of the shop and operated by an endless cable powered by a steam engine. Some of the workmen were busy building railroad cars. The Roanoke Machine Works had opened September 1 and in three weeks the first car had been completed. The Norfolk and Western used the south end of the building and the Shenandoah Valley the northern portion.

Dan thought of the waterwheels he and Punk had built in the little Bedford streams and all the machinery fascinated him. Maybe, he suggested to his father, someday Dan Cunningham would work in a railroad shop. Already Otho had signed up as a machinist apprentice.

Further interest in railroading was evinced by Dan when he started jumping on the steps of the caboose as freight trains lumbered by the house. A quick end to this particular interest was brought about by the Captain applying the bottom of a large hairbrush to Dan's posterior.

Because of this, Dan's railroad riding was confined to his imagination which was stimulated by the fact every time the trains passed the house, the building would shake. At night Dan would listen to the roar of the Norfolk and Western trains and peer out of the window at the advance of the azygous-eyed locomotives.

For many years other Virginia boys had looked at locomotives and dreamed of railroading. Virginia had been interested in railroads from the time of South Carolina's Charleston and Hamburg. In 1833 the first steam railroad to operate in the state, the Petersburg Railway Company, received its charter, ran from Petersburg to Weldon, North Carolina. Weldon, in 1837, became the terminus for the Portsmouth and Roanoke railroad, now the oldest part of the big Seaboard railway. Other early developments were the Richmond, Fredericksburg and Potomac, chartered in 1834; the Richmond and Petersburg and the Louisa railroad, both chartered in 1836. The latter railroad was to become the oldest section of the great Chesapeake and Ohio railway.

The mighty Norfolk and Western railway system of today is a result of many consolidations and the original Norfolk and Western railroad came about through the foreclosure sale of the Atlantic, Mississippi and Ohio in 1881. The A. M. & O. was the outcome of a consolidation fight made by William Mahone in which he successfully welded the old City Point railroad, the Virginia and Tennessee railroad, the Southside railroad, and the Norfolk and Petersburg railroad into one line which was to be so powerful it could combat the encroachments of the Yankee Baltimore and Ohio said to be threatening to dominate the Virginia rails by buying up the Orange and Alexandria.

The oldest and smallest unit of the N. & W., the City Point, opened September 7, 1838 and ran nine miles from Petersburg to City Point, with a passenger fare of 75 cents for grownups and 37½ cents for children and servants. This short railroad was established, according to its backers, because "a longer period is consumed in transporting goods from City Point to Petersburg than from New York City to City Point."

The Virginia and Tennessee had been proposed as early as 1830 by citizens of Lynchburg and, after numerous attempts to finance a railroad, the line was opened to Liberty (Bedford) in April, 1852, and to Big Lick (Roanoke) in November, 1852.

That year, 1852, the South Side was opened from Petersburg to Burkeville and two years later to Lynchburg, a distance of 123 miles, and the new line purchased the tiny City Point (which had been bought by the Corporation of Petersburg and renamed the Appomattox railroad) about the same time so as to obtain a tidewater terminus. The report of the first annual stockholders' meeting of the South Side included this neat juggling of words in a description of the railroad bridge built near Farmville:

"The bridge is 3,400 feet long, varying in height from 60 feet at the abutments to 100 feet near the river; the clear spans are 105 feet each. There have been higher bridges not so long, and longer bridges not so high, but taking the height and the width together, this is perhaps, the biggest bridge in the world."

Chief Engineer for the Norfolk and Petersburg had been William Mahone, who constructed the railroad over the

1838—City Point Railroad. Little wood burning engines puffed over nine
miles of track between City Point, Virginia, and Petersburg at a speed of
18-20 miles per hour.   Picture credit: *Norfolk and Western*

Father of the Norfolk and Western. GENERAL WILLIAM MAHONE, "hero of the
Crater," pioneer railroad builder and leader in the movement which resulted
in the A. M. & O.   Photo credit: *Norfolk and Western*

Top—The old *Dick Thomson* operated on the Cincinnati and Eastern, one of the units which later made up the Norfolk and Western Railway.

Center—An A. M. & O. passenger locomotive built by William Mason, at Taunton, Mass., in 1871.

Bottom—One of the early locomotives used by the Shenandoah Valley, one of the predecessor lines of the N. & W. Photo credit: *Norfolk and Western* difficulties of finances, disease—in the fall of 1855 Norfolk had a yellow fever epidemic which killed one-third of its population—and the Great Dismal Swamp. The line was commenced in 1853 and operation over its entire length came about in 1858. President of the railroad at the time of the War Between the States, Mahone was to become Virginia's first railroad magnate.

Born in 1826 at the now non-existent town of Monroe on the banks of the Nottoway river, the sandy-haired boy of Irish descent entered V. M. I., was graduated in 1847, and taught at Rappahannock Academy and V. M. I. He then turned to engineering as "internal improvements seem to be the order of the day far and wide," and became a surveyor for the Orange and Alexandria, the president of which, George H. Smoot, received the munificent salary of $1,000 a year. By 1852 Mahone was chief engineer for the Fredericksburg and Valley Plank Road. The fad for plank roads was sweeping the country and one advocate, William Gregg of South Carolina wrote in Debow's *Southern and Western Review*: "The plank road is capable of meeting all the needs of our country and superior to the rail-road in every particular, but that of indulging our fancy in rapidly passing from one point to another; it is so simple and cheap in its construction and management, that there is scarcely a village or an agricultural section of our country that cannot afford to build and maintain one."

But although Mahone built plank roads, he must have realized the fallacy of Gregg's contention for he next accepted the position of chief engineer for the proposed Norfolk and Petersburg railroad in 1853. The 27-year-old Mahone was voted a salary of $2,500 a year by the Board of Directors and won engineering fame by conquering the Dismal Swamp with a roadbed which is still standard railroad construction for handling swamp lands. In 1860 he became the railroad's president.

The outbreak of the war interrupted railroad construction plans in Virginia. The popularity of railroads in the decade before the conflict is illustrated by this quotation from newspaper verse appearing in the Richmond *Dispatch* in 1852:

> "For the Steam-King rules the travelled world
> And the old Pike's left to die. . .
> We have circled the earth with an iron rail
> And the Steam-King rules us now."

Immediately after the War Between the States, General Mahone regained the presidency of the war-torn Norfolk and Petersburg and a few months later was made president of the South Side railroad. The latter line, too, played an important role in the Southern war effort as is shown by the annual report for 1865 which said, "During the period from October, 1864, to April 1, 1865, the Confederate Government monopolized nearly all the motive power of the company, at rates about one-fourth those charged individuals." With the war's cession, the South Side had a profit of $674,000 in its Treasury, but $671,500 was in valueless Confederate money.

Mahone called on Southern workmen to rebuild the railroads with a wage of "bread and meat and a promise to pay." The workmen responded. Contending the Virginia railroads needed to consolidate, Mahone carried on a bitter fight with his opposition which was spear-headed by the Virginia and Tennessee president, Robert L. Owen. In 1867 Owen was replaced by Mahone as president of the V. & T. A New Yorker wrote, "Mahone is now the biggest railroad man in America, having control of more miles than Vanderbilt." Mahone became known as "our railroad Bismark." His employees were determined his lines would not be second to the Baltimore and Ohio. The consolidation plan had brewed up "the most terrible legislative railroad fight ever known in Virginia;" however, in 1870 the "consolidation bill" was passed and so was born the Atlantic, Mississippi and Ohio railroad, some 408 miles long. Mahone's foes soon dubbed the A. M. & O. the "All mine and Otelia's"—Otelia was Mrs. Mahone—and claimed that "Billy" Mahone had won his fight with the liberal use at the most advantageous time of elaborate dinner parties featuring terrapin soup and champagne.

But the $25,000 a year—less than five feet five and one hundred pounds—president of the A. M. & O., wearing his silk-lined shoes, laughed at the jibes, travelled over his transportation lines on inspection trips; often his party was carried on two handcars, one of which carried Mahone and the other his baggage and personal servant. The A. M. & O., backed by $15,000,000 of English money, prospered until the financial panic of 1873, brought on by the failure of Jay Cooke and Company, hit the railroad so hard that a bondholder came to Mahone and threatened to take "his" locomotive off the railroad if the bond wasn't made good. Mahone hadn't forgotten his warring days under Lee, replied, "So you think it is your locomotive, sir. Then, I beg you, take your locomotive off my tracks or I'll rip the rails from under it and then you can get the engine off my right of way!"

Battling "Billy" Mahone could not stave off the inevitable and, in 1881, the A. M. & O., at a foreclosure sale, was bought by a little man in a long gray overcoat, Clarence H. Clarke, and the railroad was renamed the Norfolk and Western, but so well had Mahone done his pioneering that Poor in his *Manual of the Railroads in the United States* wrote: "The Norfolk and Western railway is to this day a magnificent monument to Mahone. It has realized his dreams. It follows his right of way. The stations he located and named are prosperous little towns and villages. Many of the buildings he planned and constructed are still in use."

Today William Mahone's vision has materialized into the great Norfolk and Western railway system; the tracks of which are in six states, Virginia, West Virginia, Maryland, North Carolina, Ohio and Kentucky, and stretch over 5,000 miles!

Dan and George attended the grade school on Commerce street. Friday was Visitors' Day and the exercises included spelling matches and poetry recitals. The children repeated such poems as *The Blue and the Gray* and *Curfew Shall Not Ring Tonight*. Dan's turn to recite came up and, although Mam had coached him faithfully, when he stood up his tongue stuck in the roof of his mouth. The boy from Bedford had attracted a school sweetheart and she slyly whispered the words to him so that he was able to falter through his assignment.

Later Dan repaid the girl for her help. She had plastered the schoolroom walls with stickers and, when the irate teacher demanded to know who had disfigured the walls, the girl started to stand up. But Dan was on his feet before she could speak and shouldered the girl's guilt.

The principal of the school was well exercised in the afternoon. He had given Dan a tanning.

A month or so later Dan was given a chance to redeem himself on Visitors' Day. This time he didn't miss a word as he started off:

> "I'm sorry that I spelt the word,
> I hate to go above you;
> Because you see, because you see,
> Because you see—I love you!"

The little girl in her starched dress looked up at her hero in admiration and tears welled in her big, blue eyes. Dan and Monte Cristo shared the feeling that the world was theirs.

As the years went by the pretty blue-eyed little girl, as little girls do, grew up; and, as most big girls do, she married; and, as not all married girls do, she led a happy life. Her husband was Dan's best schoolboy friend.

After the Captain had finished several contracting jobs for the Norfolk and Western including laying the foundation for the new West Roanoke shop, the city asked him to handle the work grading streets over new additions to the booming city. Dan was promptly put on the payroll as water-boy for the road gang.

Five cents an hour was Dan's remuneration. Sometimes he had to bring water from springs a mile away to the gang of thirty negroes. Some of the negroes were good and some were bad. That is, to Dan's way of thinking. The good negroes took only the amount of water they wished to drink; the bad negroes dipped their cups into the water bucket, took a few sips, and threw the rest on the ground. As Dan watched the water sink into the ground, he wondered what Uncle Nace would have said to the bad negroes. Dan did not regret it when his father finished the road work and he went off the pay roll.

With the nickles he had earned, Dan bought books: *Calamity Jane, Old King Brady, Deadwood Dick, Buffalo Bill, Sun Flower Sam of Shasta*, and many others in the dime novel school. Mam and the Captain objected to Dan reading paper-backed books and Dan had to hide out when he perused the melodramas. He traded dime novels with his friends even as the children of today trade the adventure cartoon books. Big Dan is quite sure these tales in the "ten-twenty-thirty" tradition did him not one whit of harm and in those days substituted for the coming period of *Hawkshaw the Detective, Hairbreadth Harry* and later *Dan Dunn* and *Dick Tracy.*

As with all growing children, Dan became a part of a gang in his neighborhood. This gang was known as "Mustang Jack's Gang" and it was made up of six white boys and one negro lad. The colored boy acted as a personal servant to all the boys and his name was the result of his parents having worked for a family the head of which had been a professor of history at Davidson College. The negro's name was Ulysses Columbus Boneparte Patrick Henry Madison Peery Dige Jones. Dan could figure out everything but the Dige part of the name.

The gang called the colored boy—Joe.

Chapter VI

A TALL, clean-shaven man, middle-aged and wearing a Texas sombrero, a Prince Albert coat, and a string tie and cattleman's boots, eagerly watched dusty travellers get off the train at San Marcos, Texas. Spotting a group, he strode forward, took hold of a woman and kissed her. He said lightly, "First time I've had a chance to kiss such a pretty woman in years. 'Course she is my sister. Welcome to Texas, kinfolks, and a right powerful mess o' them there is, by gad!"

Mam smiled and hugged her brother, said, "John Henry Saunders, no one in Bedford county would recognize you in that getup. Folks down Texas way certainly do dress as if they were going to a Fancy Dress ball. You look mighty imposing, though, brother."

The Captain laughed, "Maybe I should have worn my uniform, suh, as there was no state which was devoted to our noble Confederacy more than Texas. From New Mexico to Gettysburg, Texas soldiers fought and died for the Stars and Bars and we in Virginia remember the Texas contribution and always will. But come, we will have plenty of time for such discussion. The important thing is now that you know my boys. Otho's the oldest, and George is next. The tall fellow, he's holding the baby, is Dan. And the baby, well that's the new addition. He's Frank Henry Cunningham and he was born May 23, 1886, just a year ago. Dan's really taken to the young one.

"Pears I got a little tired of the city after The Big House, so I thought I'd do some planting down in Texas. Mam made the trip fine, but I reckon she's a mite tired as we couldn't get anything but coaches all the way through and it is a mite wearisome sleeping in those hot seats."

John Henry Saunders called to a negro to get the collection of baggage and told him to pile it in one of the two buggies waiting for them. He turned back to the Captain and Mam, "I've got exactly the place for all of you folks. My ranch is about ten miles out at Wimberly and you all are going to stay there until the Captain finds a place. I'd like to know what you think of my planting after the tobacco lands of Virginia."

Dan was all eyes as they drove through San Marcos in Uncle Saunder's big buggy. They went down the main street and Dan could see the houses clinging to the oak-covered hillsides. The buggy passed the courthouse and Uncle Saunders spoke up, "That building Hays county got as a gift, sister Susan. San Marcos was settled in 1846 and a few years before the war a criminal trial was shifted from Travis here. There was a $2,000 bond put up by the defendant and when the trial came up he decided not to put in his appearance in San Marcos. So the bond money was used to build the first Hays county courthouse. I thought we might have at least named the building after its donor."

Mam and the Captain were amused at this historical incident and they talked about what had happened since John had left the Virginia plantation. Mam's brother was superintendent of schools for Hays county as well as a prosperous rancher.

When the party reached the ranch, the Captain found out about his host's planting. The "crop" consisted of angora goats and mustang ponies. John Henry Saunders had been one of the first men in Texas to import pure bred angora goats and from his extensive herd goat raising was to spread through much of Texas. The Texas rancher had done some other raising too; he had a family of six girls and seven boys.

After several weeks of rest, the Captain moved to his own place about two miles from San Marcos. He stuck to planting and specialized in cotton and sugar cane. The sugar cane was the more profitable crop; sown by hand like clover, the sugar cane would produce two or three crops a year and was mowed and used for cattle feed.

Dan, hungry for Virginia apples, had a substitute in the sugar cane. He cut the ribbon sugar cane—so called because its stalks were colored like ribbons—into ten inch sections and sucked the ends. The juice was sweet and plentiful.

School in Texas was different from school in Bedford or Roanoke as the young cowboys attended. Not that the cowboys had any abnormal desire for schooling, but the teacher

was an attractive twenty-year-old girl named Annie Mc-
Laughlin. The cowboys, lured by the sight of the pretty girl,
came to classes in their chaps and spurs and lined up with the
children in the spelling matches. As Dan stood in line with
the tall cowboys, he felt as if his *Deadwood Dick* characters
were coming to life.

Uncle Saunders often dropped by the Cunningham ranch
and he told many interesting stories of Texas. George and
Otho rode in their spare time as they thought they wanted
to be cowboys, but Dan was always present to hear Uncle
Saunders' yarns. These tales concerned David Crockett,
Stephen E. Austin, Sam Houston and other Texas heroes. And
there were tales of characters not as noble such as Sam Bass,
who had terrorized the section around San Marcos in his
career as a bandit, but who had been killed in a gun fight.

Learning that Dan was interested in railroads, Uncle
Saunders told of the Buffalo Bayou, Brazon and Colorado
railroad, the first line started in Texas in 1851 and how railroads had sprung up until by the time of the War Between
the States Texas had eleven different railroads operating a
total of 500 miles of track. But with the end of the conflict
only one line, the Houston and Texas Central, had escaped
bankruptcy. Too, Texas had shared in the transcontinental
railroad race as the Central Pacific tracks, laid by Chinese
workers, came East in an effort to beat Jay Gould's Texas
Pacific to El Paso. The Central Pacific won.

Two of Uncle Saunders' stories were Dan's favorites.
One was the story of Jefferson Davis' camel trains in Texas
and the other was the story of Prince Carl Zu Solms-Braunfels.
When Jefferson Davis had been Secretary of War in Washington, he was quite active in promoting transcontinental transportation. Along with aiding railroad development, he had
camels imported for baggage trains in the southwest. The
camel stations were known as "khans" and, for a time, the
camels, often ridden by natives from Egypt, carried freight
from Texas west.

Prince Carl Zu Solms-Braunfels was a character right
out of one of G. A. Henty's books. He came to Texas as
Commissioner-General for a German immigration society

headed by European noblemen. Establishing a colony at what is now New Braunfels, Texas, the adventurous Prince, in full Austrian army uniform, raised the Austrian and Texas flags over his headquarters. There he ruled for a short time around 1844 with a guard of fancy uniformed soldiers and velvet dressed aides. This old world show had a tendency to awe the Indians and Texans. When the republic of Texas was annexed later in 1845, the Prince returned to Europe, but the colony continued under the management of the German society until 1853 when Texas creditors were given the control of the town and the society's influence ended.

One reason Dan was always home, even when Uncle Saunders unexpectedly dropped by, was that he acted as the nurse for baby Frank. He rocked Frank's cradle, read a book and sang to him simultaneously. There were no dime novels available and Dan read Charles Dickens, Sir Walter Scott and Dr. Pierce's *Golden Medical Discovery*.

Now and then the Captain would bring in the weekly paper from San Marcos. Dan found a thrilling story in it which started off with the adventures of a girl captured by bandits. One night the heroine escaped from the outlaws' den and the desperadoes leaped on their horses and started in pursuit. At this exciting point Dan found the words "continued next week." By the time the Captain brought in another edition of the weekly, the thriller had concluded. Dan says the girl's ultimate fate has rested on his mind for going on sixty years and he still wonders how she eluded the bandits.

Although Texas planting was profitable and the people almost to a man former Confederate supporters, the Captain did not become attached to the strange country. He had no love for cotton nor sugar cane and the attachment he had for the tobacco fields of Virginia never was duplicated. If he turned to the railroads, it would have meant being on constant move and Mam didn't approve of such a migratory life.

But the Captain made up his mind to leave Texas and get closer to Virginia. He located a railroad contracting job at Bessemer, Alabama, and decided this would be the place for him. Too, Dan had developed serious rheumatism and could hardly walk. The Texas climate, the Captain contended, had caused it.

So the Cunninghams packed up and Uncle Saunders drove them to the station and wished his kinfolks well on their trip to Alabama.

Afterwards, Uncle Saunders bought a home in San Marcos as well as his ranch. After his death, for many years citizens of the town would uncover as they passed his old home out of respect for a man who had done so much for Hays county and its people.

The first thing the Cunninghams noticed about Bessemer was the water which was so full of sulphur one almost had to hold his nose to drink it. But the sulphur water proved a quick cure for Dan's rheumatism and the Captain said it was the will of the Lord they had left Texas.

The Lord's will, nevertheless, didn't keep the Captain from desiring to return to Virginia. As soon as he had finished the contracting work, he made no attempts to find further jobs in Alabama, but announced he was going back to Roanoke and the Norfolk and Western. Mam was beginning to get enough of the shifting about and said, "We move so much that when the moving van stops in front of the house, the chickens lie down and cross their legs to be tied."

The trek back to Roanoke was the final one for the Captain. At Roanoke he bought a larger home, a two story white frame house with green shutters and a large yard with cherry trees. This was his home until his death in 1911 at the age of 66 and Mam's home until she died in 1928 at the age of 82.

The Captain went to work for the Norfolk and Western as a foreman in the car department. Otho did not like the confinement of railroad shop work, especially after the open spaces of Texas, and took a place with the Railway Express Agency, a company he stayed with until his retirement several years ago to a pretty brick home atop a hill in Roanoke.

Dan found life at Commerce Street High School not as colorful as schooling in Texas. He liked history and Latin, but he disliked mathematics. His speaking ability, developed from the days he had to recite poetry on Visitors' Day, led to his participation in high school dramatics and he played the role of James Fitz James in Scott's *Lady of the Lake*.

After school hours, Dan worked as a part time apprentice machinist at the Norfolk and Western shop. The railroad had bought the Roanoke Machine Works and renamed it. In 1892, following graduation from high school, Dan began his real railroad career as a full time machinist apprentice in the shop his father had helped build.

At the shop, Dan had watched the men build Engine 227, a Class G locomotive which was to become famous along the N. & W. because of the loving care with which Engineer Thomas W. Goodman piloted it. Engineman Goodman drove the 227 until 1916 when it was scrapped and two years later he retired from service after thirty-three years of railroading. On his death in 1929, his widow, knowing the devotion he held for the 227, commissioned H. E. Nichols, Roanoke stone-cutter to mark his grave with a granite replica. Blueprints of the engine were followed so as to make the grave marker perhaps the most faithful reproduction of a locomotive ever cut in stone.

While Dan had worked as a part time apprentice, he was the victim of all the pranks played on neophytes in the shop. He was sent for "the Johnson bar," "Red Light Oil," "a left handed monkey wrench" and "a bucket of electricity to fill the light globes." Dan would be sent on a quest to Dick Woods, say, who would tell Dan that Bill Smith had taken away the desired tool and Dan would have to find him. Bill Smith, finally located, would say that Jack Jones just took the tool to the far end of the shop, and around Dan would go like a squirrel in a cage. Finally he would return empty handed and receive a mock bawling out for all his trouble.

On one occasion Dan entered the oil house and said, "I've been sent over for some strap oil."

Several workers had walked up to him and one of them said, "Young fellow, how much strap oil do you want?"

"I was told to get all I can take," Dan replied.

"You will, son," answered one of the workers. With that Dan was seized and put over a barrel and one of the shopmen with a piece of belting gave the apprentice "all the strap oil he could take."

Dan took the rough house tactics in good spirits as he felt they made him more alert and taught him the right time to speak. This "right time to speak" subject was brought to Dan's attention many years later by a story E. G. Fuller, of the Hunt-Spiller Manufacturing Corporation, told him. This is Fuller's story:

"I was leaving Pocatello, Idaho, one evening, shortly after the end of the World War, with our former president Mr. Ellet, whom you know very well. We were twenty miles west of Pocatello when I felt a sharp application of the air brakes and the train came to a stop. I looked out of the window and could see lights, but felt certain this was not a regular stop for the train and I mentioned it to Mr. Ellet. When we had boarded the train we had taken seats in the smoking compartment of the pullman, but after the train resumed moving, we decided to go back to the observation car. There we learned from fellow passengers the reason for the stop. A young bandit had held them up at the point of a gun and, when well stocked with money and valuables, he pulled the train cord and, as the train slowed to a stop, jumped off into the night.

"Of course, train robbery being a serious offense, a heavy reward was offered by the Union Pacific and I understood the offer was $5,000 for the capture of the bandit. All the Union Pacific special agents went to work and I learned about three weeks afterwards the young bandit was shot and killed trying to escape from custody.

"It seems that a night or two after he held up our train, he attended a dance at Twin Falls, Idaho, where he was attracted by the beauty of an Idaho girl. While dancing with her he boasted about being flush with money and he was asked where he got all the money and he boldly told the girl, 'I've been robbing trains.' Union Pacific authorities quickly seized the young man and were prepared to deliver him to the proper authorities when, in trying to escape, he was shot and killed. His pretty dancing partner to whom he had boasted of his crimes was the daughter of a Union Pacific section foreman."

At the Roanoke shop Dan learned the language of the railroad men. The engineer is called a "Hoghead" and the fireman a "Tallow Pot." The master mechanic is always "The Old Man;" the superintendent "The Brass Collar;" and the conductor "The Skipper." Apprentices are known as "cubs;" the trainmen are "Brakies" and the chief dispatcher is "The Chief Train Detainer."

Railroad cafes have their own lingo too. The waitress is a "hasher" and the dishwasher a "flunkey." Food is ordered by such terms as "lye" for coffee, "a string of flats" for hot cakes, "Sampson" for butter, "sand" for sugar and "baby" for mustard. So when a "brakie" calls for plenty of "hot baby" he doesn't mean the full bosomed "hasher." Well, not always!

The railroaders and the waitresses carry on a good natured feud. A "tallow pot" will open up the slices of his ham sandwich and call out, "Hey, hashie, take this back. The ham is cut so thin a dog could not smell it on the knife!"

When Dan started his apprenticeship on the N. & W., boilermakers were much in demand and all top boilermakers were capable of using a hammer equally as well in either hand. The boilermakers and the machinists fussed with each other until some other group picked a fight with either of them and then they united against their enemies. The boilermakers called the machinists "nut splitters" and the machinists termed the boilermakers "lost motion machinists." All a machinist had to do to make a boilermaker mad was to say to him, "Listen, pal, you don't have a trade. All you have is a habit!"

Freight trains in those days did not have any air brakes, but were equipped with a vacuum brake which operated from atmospheric pressure. Freight cars had only hand brakes and link and pin couplers; this meant the cars had to be coupled by hand.

Dan watched a gang of boomer (transient) brakemen and switchmen come in the yards and ask for work. The yardmaster asked them to hold up their hands in lieu of references. If the applicants had several fingers missing, the yardmaster knew they were "old timers" and would be able to go on the job as experienced workers and not students.

The machinists were careful of their own safety considering the fact there were no supervisors of safety. Eyes, especially, had to be guarded and Dan was adept at getting foreign substances out of the eyes of fellow workers. Very few of the N. & W. machinists had an eye missing.

There were no air tools and all drilling and reaming was done by hand. The machinists became expert chippers with a hammer and chisel and were taught to use a file without rocking it. Dan looked enviously at the experienced machinists, who could file the head off an Indian penny without touching the rim.

Boilermakers drove rivets by hand. If a boilermaker, in coneing up a rivet, touched or scarred the sheet with the edge of his hammer, he was a failure. John Doarnberger, who afterwards was master boilermaker for the N. & W., and Steve Wigmore made up a team and could drive thousands of rivets without touching the sheet. Dan watched the two men grind the face of their riveting hammers flat and finish off the edge with an oil stone with as much care as a barber would whet his best razor.

Working in the shops was no quick way to riches. The highest rate paid a mechanic was 25 cents an hour and the laborers received ten cents. Dan worked ten hours a day, and later on, when he got time and a half overtime after 10 o'clock at night, he thought he had the world by the tail.

The Roanoke shop then built one 60 ton engine a month and turned out twenty small engines a month, the largest of which weighed 120,000 pounds and the tanks held 3,000 gallons of water and six tons of coal. The Roanoke shops now turn out over sixty engines a month which weigh over a million pounds and the tenders hold 25,000 gallons of water and 28 tons of coal. Whereas the engines built around 1893 carried 140 pounds of steam and had a tractive effort of 30,000 pounds, the locomotives built now carry 350 pounds of steam that is superheated before it goes into the cylinders and have a tractive effort of 125,000 pounds.

The modern locomotives are stokered, superheated, airbraked. They have electric hand and cab lights, power reverse gears, steam grate shakers, water pump and steam exhaust injectors, air sanders, air bell ringers, windshields, automatic protection valves which permit the engine to run downhill and not build up pressure.

Several years ago Big Dan was giving talks to the engineering classes at the University of Utah and Brigham Young University and he said in his conclusion:

"The modern locomotive can be fired by a girl perhaps as well as by a man as everything is automatic. Since women are invading many fields formerly held by men, we may expect someday to see women climbing into the cabs of locomotives. This reminds me of Samuel Johnson's observation on women preachers when he wrote, 'Sir, a woman preaching is like a dog walking on its hind legs. It is not done well; but you are surprised to find it done at all.' "

At Roanoke the Cunninghams did not have to worry about an alarm clock nor, for that matter, did any of the railroad people. Their lives were regulated by *Old Gabriel*, the powerful whistle atop the shops, which could be heard for seven miles. Six times a day the whistle sounded off; 6:50 a.m., 7 a.m., 12 noon, 12:50 p.m., 1 p.m., and 4 p.m. The whistle of *Old Gabriel* was accepted as final authority by the Roanokers and once, when the noon whistle was blown by mistake at 11 a.m., all of Roanoke rushed down to the watchmaker to have their time pieces adjusted. From 1883 on up to the present time the strident wail of the whistle has been as much a part of Roanoke as the Norfolk and Western itself.

When, in 1938, the Denver and Rio Grande Western railroad built its new powerhouse at Salt Lake City, Big Dan, who was the D. & R. G. W.'s master mechanic at Salt Lake, wrote the N. & W. and obtained specifications on *Old Gabriel* so that he could have a replica built for Salt Lake. This whistle Dan named *Old Gabriel's Colt*. In writing about this incident for the *Norfolk and Western* magazine and the Rio Grande's *Green Light* publication, Dan said:

"When memory keeps me company and moves to smiles or tears, my mind goes back to the early days when I first heard the vibrating tones of *Old Gabriel*. Since then, whether travelling far or near, when I mention the Norfolk and Western and Roanoke, invariably someone refers to the Roanoke shop's whistle.

"In Roanoke I lived just west of the Park street bridge and when I worked in the shops the 'ten minute' whistle would allow me just enough time to get to work before the seven o'clock blast. Sometimes I wonder why I didn't become a long distance runner because *Old Gabriel* certainly added wings to my feet!

"Well do I remember happenings associated with the whistle's voice. When I visit Roanoke and hear the whistle calling men to their work and releasing others from their toil, it seems a thrilling greeting from an old friend welcoming one of the N. & W. boys back home. Since *Old Gabriel* began to rule over our destinies how times and working conditions have changed. Locomotives have evolved from the old 'balloon' stacks to the present monarchs of the rails; passenger cars from wooden, non-vestibule coaches to our modern, all-steel palaces. And still *Old Gabriel* sounds his message, telling us we are only beginning to see the changes yet to come. Many railroad men, who have been called to their duties by this whistle, have passed on to their reward. Perhaps they still hear *Old Gabriel* carrying on.

"When the Rio Grande built its new powerhouse at Salt Lake, it had been my dream to install at this plant just such a whistle. My good friend, R. G. Henley, N. & W. superintendent of motive power, graciously sent me a blueprint of *Old Gabriel* and from this a replica of the Roanoke shop's whistle was manufactured. Since there is only one *Old Gabriel* and since we did not have the temerity to christen our whistle with the same name, we decided upon *Old Gabriel's Colt.*

"The D. & R. G. W. whistle was blown for the first time at 2 p.m. on January 29, 1938, when the new powerhouse opened for inspection. And far away from Salt Lake City, sheep herders deserted their flocks, cowboys ceased their cattle roundups and, with hundreds of others, came galloping into town to see what all the noise was about. Even the dogs curled their tails between their legs and took off for the Salt Flats, near the great Salt Lake, fearful of the awesome noise they had heard.

"I wonder, as time goes on, whether *Old Gabriel's Colt*

will become a tradition with the same tender memories that hover over the spirit of his father, *Old Gabriel*? I do know that at ten o'clock at night, when *Old Gabriel's Colt* blows curfew for all the little boys and girls of Salt Lake City, I sigh in contentment at the ' beautiful sound.' "

Back in 1893 when Dan wasn't listening to a whistle, he was awaiting the clang of a bell—the fire alarm. He was a member of the Roanoke Fire Department and this proved equally exciting as the railroad work. Dan was captain of the Aerial Truck and his friend and apprentice machinist, John Van Lew, ran the steamer. Mam said every time she heard the fire department go out, she was certain Dan would be sent home in an ambulance. Several times her dire prophecy almost came true. Dan's worst experience as a fire fighter was when he was combating a blaze in the tower of a grain mill. Without warning, the tower floor caved in and Dan fell five stories through smoke and flames. Fortunately the basement of the mill was filled with water and this broke Dan's fall. Led by John Van Lew, fellow firemen rescued Dan before he was badly injured.

In the Roanoke railroad yards, Dan watched the train loads of coal roll in. Coal was the "black gold" which boomed the railroad and brought alive many industries in what had been theretofore little hamlets.

In 1893 the president's office on the Norfolk and Western was occupied by handsome mutton-whiskered Frederick J. Kimball who, in 1881, played a most important role in the future development of the railroad's commercial business by taking an eight day stage ride from Hagerstown, Maryland, to Abb's Valley in Tazewell county, southwest Virginia.

Kimball, then vice president of the new N. & W., was fulfilling a desire to see the Scott coal mine; an opening in a hill used by a local blacksmith for his forge. The generous blacksmith allowed friends to dig in the mine to get fuel for their homes. This was done over the protests of his not so generous wife, who feared the deposit would not be sufficient to supply her husband's forge.

Coal had been discovered in Virginia in 1701 at Manakin Town, a French Huguenot settlement on the south side of the

James, twenty miles from what is now Richmond. Coal was first mined in the United States in 1750 at the Midlothian mines in Virginia and the "black diamonds," measured in bushels and not tons, were shipped from the Old Dominion to Philadelphia, New York and Boston. As early as 1750, coal bearing lands had been described by explorers in the Appalachians. It may be recalled that Marco Polo amazed Europeans with his tales of black stones which burned like firewood found in Cathay.

The first "railroad" in Virginia was a result of coal operations. The horse drawn Chesterfield railroad, carrying coal in cars holding 56 bushels, was opened in 1831 and went from the mines at Midlothian to Richmond. Virginia had its share of the dangers of early day coal mining. An explosion in 1839 killed 51 out of 54 miners working in the Black Heath Coal mine near Richmond and another disaster, in 1844, closed the mine until 1938.

But the real strike came when Kimball dug his pen-knife into the coal vein at Abb's Valley, set fire to the cuttings, and exclaimed, "This may prove a very important day in our lives!"

The statement was correct as Kimball had located the first of all the vast southern coal fields—the Pocahontas coal seams!

Soon the railroad was opening up the potentially rich mines. The Norfolk and Western carried in 1882 4,735 tons of coal and coke; 1883, 70,000 tons; 1887, almost 1,000,000 tons; 1893 almost 4,000,000 tons; 1917 nearly 40,000,000 tons; and in 1929 45,000,000 tons. Today the "black empire" served by the N. & W. is deep in the forest-clad, narrow-valleyed Appalachians, stretches some 200 miles from Blue-field, West Virginia on the east, almost to the Ohio river, at Kenova, West Virginia, on the west. In 1944, from this mighty domain of " fuel satisfaction," the big rolling cars of the Norfolk and Western hauled 53,000,000 tons of bituminous coal. Much of this went into the war effort and Kimball had proved that the pen-knife is as mighty as the sword.

The summer of 1894 Dan was walking down Jefferson

street in Roanoke when the Boy meets Girl situation first
came seriously into his life. Romance had entered the lives
of his older brothers. Otho had married Maybelle Cunningham in 1890 and George, who was a commercial artist, was
engaged to Mattie Dooling Oliver. They were married in the
fall of 1894. Dan, who had come out second best in an encounter with a crane at the shop, was taking a few days off
while his injuries healed. On Jefferson street he met by chance
a girl aquaintance accompanied by a visitor to Roanoke, Miss
Inez Eley from Smithfield, Virginia. Inez was a sixteen-year-
old Virginia beauty with brown hair which framed her
peaches and cream complexion, her gray-green eyes and her
pearly teeth. She weighed 120 pounds and had a figure which
Dan says "would have made the *Ziegfeld Follies* look like the
Scrubwomen's Union." Dan had always remarked he wanted
a sweetheart who could walk under his arm. Inez was five feet
one as contrasted to Dan's six feet four.

All of Inez's attraction overwhelmed Dan. He invited
the girls into an ice cream parlour for a claret ice.

But the ice did nothing towards cooling his feelings.

With John Van Lew and other friends Dan had a house
party at a relative's home in the country and he invited Inez.
As he and Inez wandered through the country lanes, he knew
this was the girl for him.

The house party was followed by hay rides and watermelon feasts and "dressed up" rides on Sunday after church.
From the livery stable Dan rented a yellow buckboard pulled
by two bay ponies and with Inez drove out to rural taverns
where they feasted on fried chicken and corn muffins. The
two drove back to Roanoke in the twilight and sang such
tunes as *Daisy Bell* and *After the Ball*.

Sometimes bold cyclists rode alongside the buckboard
and tried to flirt with Inez and Dan would let the ponies out
in an attempt to outspeed the wheel-mounted dandies. But
the cyclists would peddle faster than the ponies could run and
Dan found the best way to throw off the intruders was to slow
down the ponies and then Dan would start to unlimber his
tall frame.

The sight of the big fellow preparing for action quickly sent the cyclists peddling in another direction.

But this summer romance was to wait for its zenith as Dan had no money for marriage and, more important than the financial angle, was the fact Dan was entering Virginia Agricultural and Mechanical College to study engineering. Wisely, Mam and the Captain urged him to get a college background for his railroad career.

On a day in early September Dan took Inez down to the station and put her on a train for the eastern shore. A few minutes later, with Mam, the Captain, and his brothers all advising him, Dan climbed up the coach steps, the conductor gave the engineer the highball, and the train started out southward.

CHAPTER VII

*W*HEN Dan arrived at Christiansburg, he climbed into a hack bound for Blacksburg—nine miles away—as the location of Virginia Agricultural and Mechanical College was reached by no railroad. Conversation bounced off the sides of the covered hack as its occupants excitedly discussed their college future.

Blacksburg, Dan discovered was a typical small Virginia town, two thousand feet atop the Alleghanies, with its only distinguishing characteristic the college campus. Blacksburg had its place in history, though, as it was built on the site of the Draper's Meadows Massacre. Homesteaders had pioneered on lands, once owned by Colonel James Patton, around 1745. Ten years later, Draper's Meadows rang with the war cry of raiding savages. Shawnee Indians, who had held the lands before the arrival of the homesteaders, slaughtered the whites, shot Colonel Patton, who, as chance would have it, was visiting at Draper's Meadows when the attack occured. Blacksburg was not founded until some forty-four years later.

V. A. M. C. owed its beginning to the Land Grant college bill, passed by Congress in 1862, and which authorized a liberal appropriation of the Public Lands for the endowment and maintenance of at least one college in a state where the leading instruction would be in agriculture and mechanical arts. In 1872, when the state of Virginia was readmitted into the Union—it had been Military District Number One— V. A. M. C. was founded at Blacksburg around the nucleus of old Preston and Olin Institute. The college's early history was marked by the short term of office as president held by Colonel Scott Shipp, later superintendent of V. M. I. Colonel Shipp arrived in Blacksburg one morning and by that evening he had resigned. His term at Blacksburg had been all of one day. When Dan Cunningham came to V. A. M. C. its destiny was guided by capable Dr. J. M. McBryde, formerly president of the University of South Carolina.

Soon Dan had filled out his enrollment papers and was assigned to room 57 in Old Barracks. Another Roanoke boy,

J. I. Palmer, was his roommate and the two started straightening up their room after the evening mess had already instilled in them a nostalgic memory of home-cooked food.

Throughout the day, the freshmen had heard the cry "Rat, rat, take to your hole!" The new cadets, puzzled by this, found all first year men were known as "rats" and the upperclassmen had a program in mind that was definitely "rough on rats."

Dan and his roommate could hear the Old Boys going from room to room and the agonized cries of the rats mixed with the blatant laughter of the Old Boys. Dan and Palmer apprehensively awaited their turn from the "welcoming delegation" of the cadet corps.

Suddenly the room door swung open and ten huskies poured in. One of the Old Boys shouted "Rats Cunningham and Palmer, attention!"

The two rats snapped to attention, but their eyes were not straight ahead. Instead they were on the ropes and barrel staves the Old Boys carried. The older cadets were gripping the staves as if they were experienced in using them and they would slap the improvised wooden paddles against their legs as if anxious to put the staves into action.

Following orders, Dan and Palmer stood face to face, commenced singing different songs suggested by the upperclassmen. As the boys would get off key, the hazers would take a wide swing and bring the barrel staves sharply against the unpadded bottoms of the rats. With the jolting smacks lifting them off their feet, the rats tried to keep up their spirits and their harmony. Neither was achieved.

After the singing was concluded, Dan was told to drop a penny in his wash bowl which had been filled with water. Immediately the cry was "root, rat, root!" and Dan dropped to his knees, started to root the penny out with his nose. As Dan, choking with water in his mouth and nose, pushed the penny up to the edge of the bowl, a hard wallop from a stave landed on him; the penny fell back in the bottom of the basin.

Vociferous laughter filled the room as the command was, "Keep it up, Cunningham!" Several times Dan pushed the copper almost out of the water only to receive a paddling for his efforts. But Dan kept probing for the penny and finally moved it successfully to the edge of the basin and rat Cunningham felt his torment was almost at an end.

But one of the Older Boys was not satisfied. He picked up a stave, examined it, and struck Dan with all his might. As the striker drew back, Dan sprang to his feet, swung a haymaker with his right arm, and landed a terrific blow on the cadet's jaw. Without a sound, the upperclassman fell to the floor. Palmer's mouth flew open as he watched the cadets try to revive their fallen comrade. Dan looked for an escape route while the hazers muttered what dire consequences he had brought on himself as the result of his retaliatory action unheard of on the part of humble rats.

There was no escape as the door was blocked. Dan readied himself to fight the whole bunch, though he knew it would result in his taking a bad licking. Several cadets moved in on him threatening to beat him until he had wished he had never heard of Blacksburg.

At that moment, the fallen cadet regained consciousness, pulled himself up, started for Dan. This was it, Dan thought. Now he would get an undeserved beating for a brutal hazing. Dan raised his fists. Certainly this couldn't be as bad a situation for him as when the angry workers had threatened to lynch him in the Roanoke shop. Nor was it as bad as when the rioters had sent bullets cutting through his militia cap as he fought the mob.

The oncoming cadet pulled his friends away from Dan. At least, Dan thought, we'll fight it out man to man and a bit of admiration for the upperclassman partially replaced the hatred in Dan's mind.

Unexpectedly the upperclassman stuck out his hand toward Dan. The rat dropped his guard and looked at his opponent.

"I want to shake hands with a real man," the Older Boy said. The speaker turned to his perplexed friends and said contritely, "All of you get the hell out of this room and lay off this fellow. From now on Dan Cunningham is my rat and he's going to be treated right."

The hazers walked slowly out of the room and looked at

Dan as if he were some Merlin in a military uniform. Only the one upperclassman remained. Dan still hadn't said anything. The repentant hazer spoke, "Fellow, you gave me exactly what I had coming to me. Anybody who would hit another college student with a stave in which is a big nail deserves to get his head knocked off and, brother, you practically did just that to me. But, Cunningham, you've got too much strength to waste it on hitting me. I'm on the football squad here and I want you to turn out for the team tomorrow!"

Dan was pleased that he had been asked to join the football squad, but realized that he knew little about the game. Palmer, who had stood by while all the action took place, agreed to finish up the room while Dan made a quick trip to the college library so that by the next afternoon he could "talk football" even if he couldn't handle the pigskin in Walter Camp fashion.

William Webb Ellis, Dan learned, on a chilly November afternoon, 1823, heard the school bell at Rugby, England, commence its signal which would end the ball game of Bigside in a scoreless tie. As a punt came into his hands, he, disregarding the rules which said the ball should be kicked and not carried, brushed aside his opponents and ran across the goal line. So it was that Bigside became Rugby and from the latter game developed football.

Spectators sat around a rail fence at New Brunswick, New Jersey, on November 6, 1869, to watch the first intercollegiate game of football. Princeton, led by William S. Gummere, later Chief Justice of New Jersey, bowed to Rutgers six goals to four. So it was that Rutgers has the honor of being the first victorious football team in college history.

A year later Columbia played its initial contest, lost to Rutgers 6-3. In 1874 McGill and Harvard played both in Cambridge and Montreal and Yale's initial squad tripped Columbia 3-0. By 1876, the Intercollegiate Football Association was formed with a membership comprised of Harvard, Columbia, Princeton and Yale and thus came about the first organized conference football with a set of intercollegiate rules.

After a few years football had caught public favor and the game spread from its narrow confines of the Ivy League colleges. Washington and Lee and Virginia engaged in what is said to be the first college game in the South. Michigan came into the sports pages downing Racine 7-2. Georgetown and Transylvania had started their Kentucky state feuding in 1880 and plans were being made for a football team at Hanover College in Indiana which was to win all of forty-six games in the next forty-five years. Williams and Amherst were practicing for the commencement of their famous rivalry. The year 1882 saw the Navy first sail down the gridiron and in 1887 Notre Dame's mighty Irish made their debut with a spring game lost to Michigan. The Army team came forth in 1890 and lost to Navy 24-0. By now football was so popular that the Lafayette team played a twelve game schedule in twenty-seven days!

When the 1894 Virginia Agricultural and Mechanical College football team took the field, way up in Chicago a young Yale graduate named Amos Alonzo Stagg, who had had to play on his initial University of Chicago team so as to make up a squad, was entering his third year as coach. Stagg had previously coached at International Y. M. C. A. College (now Springfield College), where his Massachusetts gridders had played the original indoor football game. Also in 1894 Lehigh and Lafayette were introducing their conflict which was to become the longest unbroken series in the gridiron world. Pennsylvania and Princeton were readying themselves for the bloody competition which was to cause cancellation of football relations between the Tigers and the Quakers until 1935. Until 1892 the Pennsylvania team had lost twenty-four straight games to their Trenton opponents. Georgia Tech, with Lieutenant (later General) Leonard Wood as player-coach, was entering its second year of football, having beaten Georgia 25-0 in its first year and fled Athens in a box car to escape the wrath of the University's followers. Out Texas way the first games were being played by Texas and Texas A. & M.

At Ithaca, New York, the 1894 Cornell team was being captained by Glenn Scobey Warner, later to become the famous "Pop" Warner, coach at Georgia, Iowa State, Cornell,

Carlisle, Pittsburgh, Stanford and Temple. Ike J. Armstrong, Drake graduate, who was to coach Utah to many Rocky Mountain Conference championships, hadn't been born and wouldn't be for two years, but Bernard William Bierman, famed coach of Montana, Mississippi A. and M., Tulane and Minnesota, was a baby of six or seven months and Dana Xenophon Bible, later to become dean of the grid mentors down in Texas, was a three-year-old playing on the campus of his future alma mater, Carson-Newman College at Jefferson City, Tennessee.

And keeping his eye on the national picture of football as it was to be unfolded in 1894 was the immortal Walter Camp, who was scouting possibilities for his sixth All-American football team.

Football at V. A. M. C. was of recent vintage as the maiden team had played in 1892, practiced on a plowed field. At the beginning the students did not take kindly to the idea of a two-team squad as all the players wanted to be on the varsity. Only four regular games had been played by 1894, the Cadets having won and lost to St. Albans, defeated Emory and won from Randolph Macon Academy.

President McByrde felt that the college needed a more comprehensive sports program, allowed the Athletic Association to use part of the college farm. The ground was plowed, harrowed and rolled until it had some resemblance to a playing field.

When Dan Cunningham reported for practice he met the new football coach, J. A. Massie, a former V. A. M. C. student, who had starred with the University of Virginia squad. A walrus-type moustache gave a certain touch of dignity to the new coach and Massie instilled a fighting spirit in his squad; so fighting, in fact, that Dan found his competition for a place on the team so strong all he could do was act as a substitute as V. A. M. C. rolled to victories over Emory and Henry, Roanoke and St. Albans without even being scored on. Then came the final game with V. M. I., which held the "Blacksburg Farmers" in little regard. At Staunton the first of the famous Military Classic of the South games was played and V. M. I. spoiled V. A. M. C.'s record with a 10-0 victory. Dan packed up his uniform and hoped for a more exciting time the next season. He was to get it!

Shortly after Dan had entered college, he was assigned to the Artillery Battery as he was more proficient in military than most of the new cadets because of his experience with the Roanoke Light Infantry. This was a good break for Dan so far as sleep was concerned, as the Battery fell in at reveille right in front of Old Barracks and this meant a few minutes more to stay in bed. As he had learned to be speedy when he was with the Roanoke Fire Department, Dan was a quick dresser. When the fire alarm would sound he would literally jump into his boots and slide down the brass pole almost all in one motion. At college Dan decided he could get some additional winks of sleep if he would leave his shoes unlaced. This would enable him to jump into them and his long overcoat would cover up the fact he hadn't laced his shoes. By this method, Dan could stay in bed until he heard the call "Fall in!"

One morning Dan leaped from bed at "Fall in!," started to jump into his shoes only to find that someone, during the night, greased his laces and tied the strings in a double knot. It was impossible to get into shoes so laced. Dan had no choice but to get into his overcoat and cap, race barefooted to take his place in ranks. Outside he found ten inches of snow on the ground. The hour hadn't reached six and it was still dark; his bare feet went unnoticed to all but himself. That particular morning the adjutant had a long list of orders to read and for twenty minutes Dan stood in the snow and his feet got so cold he felt he was with George Washington at Valley Forge. From then on Dan behaved properly so far as dressing for reveille was concerned.

Dan made no effort to uncover the culprit who had tied his laces as he realized that actually the fellow had done him a good turn. In time, the battery officers would have discovered the unlaced shoes and Dan would have been punished with heavy "penalty tours"—extra guard duty—for his infraction of the cadet rules.

When Freshman Class elections took place, Dan found that room 57 had both vice presidents of the class; Palmer was first vice president and Dan was second vice president. Class Sergeant at Arms was a cadet from Richmond named Julian Ashby Burrus. Cadet Burrus was to make a career for himself in education and, in 1919, was to become the first alumnus to be president of Virginia Polytechnic Institute. Burrus was president of V. P. I. until 1945.

One afternoon President McBryde stood on the campus peering at a tree. One thousand new maple trees had been planted recently at the college, but this tree was different from all the rest; it was growing right out of the mouth of one of the four War Between the States muzzle-loading cannon used by the cadet artillery.

The college president looked from the young tree to the gun crew completely lacking in *sang-froid*. The first detachment, Battery E, had no idea that the school's head would pop in on them. Dr. McByrde also observed the spot on the campus near the gun from which obviously the tree had been uprooted.

Dan Cunningham was thinking fast. Why had he done it? He was number one man and his work was to shove the powder and shot home when it was put in by the number two man, as well as use the ramer to swab out the gun barrel. One of the cadets had sneaked a bag of powder and as it was rammed in sod had been added to give the gun a resounding "crack." The cadets wondered how far they could shoot one of the young trees. Forthwith went the uprooted tree into the cannon's mouth. It was then that Dr. McBryde walked up. None of the artillery men could say the infantry cadets had played a joke on the batterymen as the infantry was drilling a distance away from the gun.

Dan and his batterymates decided they were as stuck with their maple tree as George Washington had been with his cherry tree. So they confessed their error in respect to the tree.

According to Parson Weems, the nation's first "star reporter" in the highly colored feature story category, George Washington said, "I cannot tell a lie, Pa; you know I cannot tell a lie. I did it with my little hatchet." And to these upright words, George Washington's father replied, "Run to my arms,

you dearest boy. Glad I am George that you killed this tree;
for you have paid me for it a thousand fold. Such an act of
heroism in my son is worth more than a thousand trees, though
blossomed with silver, and their fruits of purest gold."

The college president's reaction was not similar to that
of Augustine Washington, George's father. Dr. McBryde said,
"So you young men confess you pulled up the tree and put
it in the cannon. Why? You said it was merely because you
weren't thinking. Perhaps I should do something to make
you think. Each of you will donate one dollar to the college
library fund. At retreat I shall order the entire corps assembled in front of where you uprooted the tree. Then, as the
band plays a suitable number, perhaps *The Rogue's March,*
you shall have the pleasure of replanting the tree!"

And so Dan and his batterymates paid the fine and later
replanted the tree to the music of the college band and the ill
concealed snickers of the cadet corps.

Such a spectacular punishment doubtless made Dr. Mc-
Bryde certain that the artillerymen of the first detachment,
Battery E, would be exemplary in their demeanor in the
future.

They weren't.

One evening the detachment was assigned to fire the
evening gun at retreat. While one cadet was on his way down
to the basement of the mess hall where the cannon were kept,
he picked up a round river rock about the size of a croquet
ball. The gun was brought out to the drill ground; the battery team put in the powder, then the sod, and then the round
rock was slipped in and the gunner put in the friction primer.
With the signal for firing, the artillery cadets "broke away"
as all artillery men do with a muzzle-loading gun as they
have to stand near the mouth. To "break away" meant they
leaned to one side, opened their mouths and stood on tip toe
so as to break the sound and shock as the old cannon would
bounce six inches off the ground when fired.

Crack!

The gun's crew wasn't the only open-mouthed group on
the drill field. The entire student body had its mouth open in
astonishment. When the cannon had been fired, the rock had

gone out as if it had been solid shot and, almost simultaneously, part of the roof of Commandant David C. Shanks' house disappeared and shingles rained down on the campus like the stars that fell on Alabama!

Lieutenant Shanks, a Virginian of the 18th United States Infantry, came to Blacksburg that year as Commandant and Professor of Military Science and Tactics. He had little idea that his cadets would raise his roof.

Came the court martial in a few days. The gun crew reasoned that maybe even George Washington would have hedged a bit in a matter like this and told the examining officers that the accident must have been caused by something in the sod put in the cannon. Lieutenant Shanks, a very pleasant officer who had the admiration of the entire cadet corps, dropped the entire matter.

Many years later when Dan was living in Salt Lake City as an official on the Denver and Rio Grande railroad, Brigadier General David C. Shanks arrived for an inspection of Fort Douglas. He and Dan had luncheon together and, despite the fact that they had not seen each other since Dan's college days, General Shanks said, " Certainly I remember you from the days at V. P. I. At the time I was called Old Buck and you, well, you were on the gun crew which blew off the roof of my house with the hardest bit of sod that was ever dug out of Virginia ground!"

As with boys at practically all colleges, the cadets complained that the meals served were not to their liking. The cadets insisted all the months of the year at Blacksburg had the same name, Ramadan. This is the ninth month of the Mohammedan year and the time of the annual thirty day fast. This "beefing over the beef" was one of the traditional duties of the first year class and often before evening mess Dan would be asked to offer up this college prayer:

"Oh! God of Love look from above
Upon my discontent,
And give me meat that's fit to eat
For this ain't worth a cent.
The bull was found upon the ground
(Left there by Uncle Noah)

> Stuck in the mud just before the flood
> And filled with salty water.
> Our college bought the carcass,
> Fraught with incense rare and sweet
> And then it was boiled until 'twas spoiled
> And given poor cadets to eat!"

During his freshman year, Dan was elected one of the "feelers" of the Plutonian Euterpean Academy, an organization formed "because it is necessary to combat pain more intense than the chilling of the winter's wind and more oppressive than the hottest summer's sun that ever drew perspiration from the brow of man. This pain heard daily is caused by the howling match of the V. A. M. C. Glee Club. We will not destroy the Club, but invent means to improve it for the angels are required to sing according to the scriptures, but these mortals would have a poor show if not taught better before knocking at the golden gate."

The Plutonians elected a Board of Instructors consisting of Captain, Catcher, Pitcher, Toater, three Bassmen, Short Stop, and three Feelers. Their duties were defined in a manner foretelling the coming comedy reign of such buffoons as Abbott and Costello and the writer would have delighted present day radio audiences.

These duties were: The Captain shall act as Leader. It shall be the duty of the Catcher to catch popular tunes and submit them to the Board of Instructors for adoption or improvement. It shall be the duty of the Pitcher to pitch the tune and it shall be the Toater's duty to toat the tune after being pitched by the Pitcher. It shall be the duties of the Bassmen to hold down 1st, 2nd, and 3rd basses respectfully. It shall be the duty of the Short Stop to collar any man having incorrect tune and submit him to the College Glee Club for membership. It shall be the duties of the Feelers to feel for the effects produced by the music and report their feelings to the Instructors immediately after each class.

V. A. M. C. had a student body of about 300 cadets and the evening bull sessions would usually turn to cycles and women with all 300 cadets speaking their minds as cadets had their preferences in both subjects. Although it wasn't until some seven years later that Glenn Curtiss was to construct his motorcycle factory and build the Hercules and Curtiss cycles as an introduction to his aviation fame which led Curtiss to become the "Pioneer of Naval Aviation," the cadets were as interested in motorcycles and bicycles as are the youth of today in automobiles and airplanes. Cadets would engage in heated arguments over the merits and demerits of the Columbia, Western Wheel Works, Eagle, Rambler, Victor, Waverly and the Stearns.

Concerning girls, many of the students held a cynical attitude, although there was always "one girl who is different from the rest." If one could take an H. G. Well's Time Machine and drop in on the bull sessions of the collegians he would have heard such comments on the fair sex as:

"The Nineteenth Century woman prefers to wear bloomers and ride bicycles than look after her family...Milton believed in the good in women and was determined to find it. He married a second and third time—but he died blind. . . Trust not a woman even when she's dead. . . . Flies and mosquitoes, like women, have their proper place in life."

Two of the favorite quotations of the cadets were:

"He is a fool who thinks by force or skill
To turn the current of a woman's will."

—

"I have seen your stormy seas and stormy women
And pity lovers rather than seamen."

Yet the cynicism was a mere veneer which, in most cases, could be wiped off with dance invitations from Randolph Macon, Hollins, Sullins, Virginia College, Stuart Hall, Blackstone Female Institute or any of the other Virginia girls schools.

One of the alluring attractions of the Christmas vacation was it meant getting back home where the cadets could see their steady girls or meet new ones. As the Blacksburg vacation period started earlier than the holidays of the girls schools around Roanoke, Dan and his Roanoke classmates lost no time in appraising the beauties of Virginia College or Hollins Institute (since 1911 Hollins College). Girls from the rose red brick buildings of Hollins, which dated back to the Valley

Union Seminary opened in 1842, tended to favor the V. M. I. keydets with their prettiest smiles, whereas many of the girls of Virginia College reserved the sparkle in their eyes for the Blacksburg boys.

Roanoke's most imposing theatre was the Academy of Music out from the business section on Salem avenue. When road shows came to the city, the girls from Hollins and Virginia College would attend in a body. The boys would get stiff necks from looking at the Hollins student body on one side of the theatre to the Virginia girls on the other. Well chaperoned, the girls would look slyly over their fans at the uniformed cadets and blush furiously if their eyes met. Yet the thrill of Boy Meets Girl was there and Dan humorously says the beginning of what the railroads call "Remote Control" must have been inspired by such a situation.

The Cunningham house would be crowded with Dan's classmates at holiday time. Among them were Julian A. Burrus; Jack Danforth, whose stepfather, Charles T. O'Farrell, was governor of Virginia; and Joseph P. Watkins, later a top reporter on the Richmond *Dispatch* and who won renown as the editor of the Charlotte, North Carolina, *Observer*.

One of the upperclassmen who was a friend of Dan's in his freshman year was William Edward Dodd, of Clayton, North Carolina, who was prominent in debating and about whom the editor of the college yearbook wrote on his graduation, "Billy proposes to edit a Southern Journal in which he will advocate a triple division of the Union." In Dan's second year at V. A. M. C., Dodd was on the faculty as assistant instructor in history. William Dodd never edited that Southern Journal, but he did become famous as an educator, author and diplomat. After receiving advanced degrees from V. P. I., Leipzig, Emory and Alabama, Dodd became professor of history at Randolph-Macon College. Staying from 1900 to 1908 at the historic Ashland, Virginia, school, which was the first college in the United States founded by the Methodist Episcopal Church, Dr. Dodd became professor of American history at the University of Chicago and later was a Trustee of Sweet Briar College. From 1933 to 1937 he was Ambassador to Germany and he died in 1940. Among his many books were *The Life of Jefferson Davis, Statesmen of the Old South, The Cotton Kingdom, Woodrow Wilson and His Work* and *Lincoln or Lee.*

The faculty of Virginia College invited Dan and five of his friends out to the school for supper. The six cadets were overcome by the several hundred girls who, in turn, were awed by the boys. What all of them ate for dinner that night would not have made an ample meal for an undersized sparrow.

When the boys were returning from the evening at the college, they passed a beautiful old home near Crystal Springs and Dan, in the lamp light, noticed a pretty girl standing on the bottom rail of the fence holding a toy Manchester dog little larger than a rat. The Manchester barked sharply at Dan, who jumped away, said facetiously, "Oh, Miss, please don't let that big dog bite me."

The girl turned her nose upward, spoke haughtily "Don't worry, tin soldier, he wouldn't even want to taste you!"

Broken was the spell of conquest cast over the cadets by the worshipping Virginia College girls. Joe Watkins was so taken with one of these girls that Dan's mother had to get out a broom and playfully shake it at him to get him to return to college on time. And Ralph Frazier, another classmate of Dan's, unbeknownest to Dan, fell for a Virginia College girl with whom Dan had been corresponding.

After the holidays, Dan received a letter starting "Dearest Ralph" and Ralph received one commencing "Dearest Dan." The girl had written the boys the same day and had mixed up the letters. Ralph and Dan promptly went back of Old Barracks and fought it out until both were so weary that their hurt pride vanished. They shook hands, resumed their friendship, and both stopped writing the coquette. The coquette? Oh, she later married an engineer on the Norfolk and Western and later Dan was entertained many times at her home in Portsmouth, Ohio.

Dan wrote regularly to Inez at Smithfield and also to a rather extensive list of other girls. He planned to visit Inez when the summer vacation came. But when the school term was concluded, Dan found himself short of money, a condition prevalent among college students of any day.

As a result, Dan spent his summer in Blacksburg instead of Roanoke and Smithfield. He worked in the college machine shop for fifteen cents an hour; built a 10 horsepower Westinghouse engine for the Mechanical Laboratory. This was valuable experience as the students had to make their own work drawings, followed by their own patterns and forgings in the foundry, and then the finished work in the machine shop. After working hours, the students would practice football.

Toward the end of the summer vacation period, the cadets yearned for a change in scenery, made up a pot and hired a wagon, a team of horses, and a colored cook. The wagon load of students set out for Mountain Lake, a fashionable vacation spot, found the hotel rates too high for their finances, set up a tent on the lake shore. The arrival of the cadets was hailed with glee by the many college girls vacationing at the hotel.

The negro cook saw to it that the boys and their dates had plenty of fried chicken, corn on the cob and cold watermelon. As the boys had given the cook a limited amount of money to spend for provisions, they marvelled at his buying ability and thought he would do well in the kitchen at V. A. M. C.

When the cadets arrived back at Blacksburg after a week of summer-romancing, they were received by Dr. McBryde. The genial president greeted them warmly, expressed his wish that they had enjoyed the beauties of Virginia—both geographic and feminine—and presented them with a bill for fifty dollars. It seems that the cook had been quite proficient with obtaining provisions, but he had carried his enthusiasm for good eating too far. He had carried it into watermelon patches, hen houses and corn fields owned by farmers around Mountain Lake. There was nothing for Dan and his friends to do except raise the money among themselves and thank their fate that the farmers hadn't called in the local sheriff!

Shortly before the scheduled opening of the fall session, a farmer came to the college and asked to have four wagon bows made for his wagons. Dan was assigned to make two and a senior cadet was told to make the other two.

Dan took hickory lumber, ripped it in the mill, planed the pieces on a jointer to exactly the right size for wagon bows, took a knife and trimmed down one end to fit the staples on the wagon. Then he bent the bow over to the other side, shaved it down to fit and in several hours he had the bows completed and the wagons were ready for delivery.

The following day the farmer returned for his wagons. Dan proudly showed him the bows he had made and the farmer was well satisfied. But, asked the farmer, where were the rest of his wagons? Dan explained that all he had been assigned were the wagons which had been finished, yet he would be glad to hunt the other two and find out what was delaying the job.

Dan looked up the senior cadet and found him deep in scrap papers.

"Say, have you finished the farmer's wagons?" asked Dan.

"Finished them? Why I haven't even begun the bows, Dan."

"Well, the farmer has come back and wants his wagons. I've got him stalled off for awhile, but I can't keep him in a peaceful mood much longer. What in the world has delayed you?"

The senior cadet waved toward the piles of scrap paper which covered the floor. "That's what did it, Dan. I don't know how you worked out the bows and got them finished so soon. I've done all this figuring to work out the curve of those damned bows by differential calculus!"

Such was the conflict between practical knowledge and applied higher education!

The senior cadet had the bows ready for the farmer that day. He closed his calculus book and he and Dan went to work on them in exactly the same way Dan had made the bows the day before. The incident recalled to Dan the words of Oliver Wendell Holmes in *The Autocrat of the Breakfast-Table*:

"Knowledge and timber shouldn't be much used until they are seasoned."

CHAPTER VIII

*W*HEN Dan turned out for the first formal football practice in the fall of 1895, he found the coaching staff had been enlarged and that an all University of Virginia trio was to guide the destiny of the V. A. M. C. team. Besides Massie were Saunders Taylor and A. C. Jones.

There was little time to get the team into real shape for a big test. The schedule makers had given V. A. M. C. a big game for the season's start—the mighty University of Virginia team—and the Cavaliers were one of the dominant squads in Southern football. The V. A. M. C. team, under Captain J. Lewis Ingles, journeyed to Charlottesville fired up for an upset victory. These gridders had no way of knowing their school's greatest upset would come in the late 1920's when Grantland Rice predicted a 60-0 win for Colgate only to find that when the scores came in the Blacksburg team, led by its All-American back Frank Peake had downed Colgate's Red Raiders at Hamilton 6-0.

A large delegation of students followed the V. A. M. C. team to Virginia and the historic campus of Thomas Jefferson and Edgar Allen Poe resounded to the Blacksburg football war cry:

> "Rip! Rah! Ree!
> Va! Va! Va!
> Virginia! Virginia!
> A. M. C.!"

War cries were not enough to down the Cavaliers and Virginia scored a 36-0 victory; the worst defeat the Black and Gray had taken. Dan and his teammates had a sad trip back to their campus.

The following week, in the St. Albans game at Blacksburg, the signal was called repeatedly by both sides for a "guards back" play as this was a favorite play of that time. It must be remembered there were no forward pass plays as the first pass thrown was by Wesleyan against Yale and this play didn't come until 1906. In "guards back" the guard would

line up behind the tackle and the ends and half back behind
him. The only way to stop the play was "to fall down and
grab as many legs as possible." In blocking such a play, Dan
found himself in a tangle of bodies; pulled himself up with
his body suddenly aching. Nevertheless, he finished the contest without saying anything about his condition to the
captain or the coach.

With the score 12-0 in favor of V. A. M. C. at the end of
the game, the teams trailed off to the showers which were in
back of "Old Barracks." Soon cold water—there was no
hot water—splashed against weary bodies and the gridders
howled in anguish. But Dan's yelling was a bit more realistic
than that of his fellow players or even the beaten St. Albans
boys. Following the shower came a rub down by teammates
as there was no professional trainer to condition the squads.
There was no rub down for tackle Cunningham. He had a
broken shoulder and ribs.

Yet with his shoulder and ribs patched up, Dan was out
the next day for practice. Football was a rough and tumble
game in those days and anything short of a near-fatal injury
was laughed off. The players bought their own uniforms,
which consisted of knit jerseys with no real padding and
canvas or moleskin pants. No helmets were worn—players
today are put out of the game unless they keep their helmets
on—and the means of head protection was the thick hair
grown by the gridmen as their mark of distinction. As it
sometimes happens in modern football, frequently instructions were to knock out the opposition's best players. The
Black and Gray used a "flying tackle" that meant hitting a
foe with sometimes 200 pounds of beef from a distance of six
feet and players, beaten to a pulp under the extreme physical
conflict, tried to keep in the contest as there were few substi-
tutes available.

Coach Jones was talented at the "between halves" pep
talks and would arouse his squad until it wouldn't hesitate to
tackle a stone wall. The attitude he conjured up reminded
Dan of the story of the farmer who sold a mule and, when the
purchaser started away with the animal, it ran into the side
of a barn. Immediately the buyer protested the mule was

blind, but the former owner scoffingly replied, "That mule ain't blind. He just don't give a damn!"

Sometimes after rawhiding it all night in day coaches, the Blacksburg team played the following day without any rest and didn't give a damn themselves—except to win the game.

With St. Albans licked, V. A. M. C. practiced for its inaugural game with Washington and Lee which was to be played at beautiful old Lexington, home of both W. & L. and V. M. I. and consequently one of the leading true "college towns" in the nation.

Because of his injury, Dan was playing on the scrub team in practice, recalls now, "The varsity knocked the living hell out of us as they knew our signals and when we would get the ball they would gang up on us. We got tired of this and at night had a meeting and got new signals the varsity didn't know. The next day we made two touchdowns on the first team. Furious, 'Monk' Jones gave the regulars such a tongue-lashing they charged us with such force that we were practically swept off the field. I had begun to think Jones made a mistake putting me on the second team to save me further injury. In the final scrimmage before we were to leave for Lexington, William Lewis James, one of the most popular students in college and star left tackle, picked up a scrub fumble and started for the goal line. He had about fifteen feet start on us. I raced after him, tackled him so hard on the five-yard-line he fell and broke his instep. That meant he was out of the W. & L. game. Well, I was about as popular about the campus that evening as a skunk at a country dance. I certainly was sorry about injuring James and it was most unintentional. I knew that football taught team work and what it meant at times when you could let a fellow player make a score by your assistance."

When the V. A. M. C. squad reached Lexington, "Monk" Jones called Dan to one side as the team came on the field. After the Virginia walloping, Jones was in no mood to drop a game to the Generals. Dan felt a heavy hand on his arm as the coach spoke firmly, balanced a football in his hand:

"Daniel, it's a mighty long way from that covered bridge

over North river up by V. M. I. to House Mountain which you see there on the horizon to the west. You're going into this game to replace the player you injured, James. If we don't whip W. & L., boy, I'm going to see that you run from North river to House Mountain and how you get back to Blacksburg is your own lookout, son. You'd better make this a worst day for Lexington than the time the Federals came in and burned V. M. I.!"

As the coach was talking, a group of W. & L. students paraded down the football field. They marched in slow cadence, carried a draped coffin marked "V. A. M. C." Dan noticed that it was an extra large casket and felt that it was measured right for him.

It would be pleasing to write in true fiction style that the game was a scoreless tie until the final second when Dan picked up a Big Blue fumble and ran for a touchdown. The truth of the matter is that the Washington and Lee team was no match for the opposition that day and—with Dan contributing his share of good playing—V. A. M. C. romped to a 30-0 victory.

With the game over, the hospitable Lexington students laughed off the coffin incident, entertained the victorious invaders. Dan walked along the white columns of Washington College, the main building on the campus, looked across the sloping lawn at Lee Chapel. A friendly W. & L. student accompanying him said:

"You all beat a time-honored school today, Cunningham. We've been going since 1749 when the Presbyterians founded Augusta Academy some twenty miles from Lexington. With the revolution we became Liberty Hall in a building not far from the present campus. Later, after George Washington made a liberal donation of James River Canal stock the school expanded and became Washington Academy. During the War Between the States, the Yanks allowed the frantic pleas of the Lexington citizens to keep the troops from burning the school. Robert E. Lee became president of Washington College, after Appomattox, put in the first school of journalism in an American university. Some of the professors recall Lee riding around Lexington on Traveller, his famous horse, on which Lee had ridden from Richmond when he came to the college. General Lee died in 1870, his last words, 'Tell (General) Hill he must come up!' The following year the name of the college was changed to Washington and Lee University."

Dan looked around the front campus, where, at the start of the Southern War had walked the educator and journalist George Junkin, the college's president, founder of Lafayette, early president of Miami in Ohio and famed scholar of his day. Although Junkin's late daughter, Eleanor, had married a V. M. I. professor named Thomas J. Jackson (the immortal Stonewall Jackson), he tore down the Secessionist flag from the college, resigned, and returned to the North. In the twilight Dan could see the passing V. M. I. cadets stopping by Lee's resting place to salute. In a few years a V. M. I. football tackle named George Marshall, later to become chief of staff of the United States army, would be pausing on the Washington and Lee campus to pay his respects to the Confederate leader. Another V. M. I. cadet, whose father and grandfather had gone to Virginia Military Institute, was to win fame along with Marshall; his name was George Patton, the late General Patton. And yet another V. M. I. cadet to rise to the top in military fame was Simon Bolivar Buckner Jr., later, as a general, killed by Jap fire on Okinawa.

V. P. I., too, contributed noted generals in World War II even as the school had done in World War I (Brigadier Generals Edward Anderson and George H. Jamerson). And it was a former Techman, Major Lloyd W. Williams, who replied to a French order at Chateau-Thierry with the famous "Retreat? Hell, No!"

Coach Jones was a happy man when the team left Lexington and he was confident of a win the coming week over Roanoke Y. M. C. A. His confidence was fulfilled and his team forged its will-to-win for contests with the University of North Carolina and Virginia Military Institute. The day before the squad was to leave for Charlotte, North Carolina, Jones showed Dan a wire which said that North Carolina was cancelling the game. The V. A. M. C. team was so disappointed that Jones replied to the Tarheels with "What's the matter? Are you afraid of us?" A prompt answer was flashed back from Chapel Hill, "Come on!" In high spirits the Blacksburg team caught the train for Charlotte confident that the North Carolina squad would be made to regret the exchange of telegrams.

The score? North Carolina 32, V.A.M.C. 5.

The beaten team arrived in Lynchburg Sunday morning only to find it had missed the Norfolk and Western connection for Roanoke and there wouldn't be another Roanoke train until evening. After a big turkey dinner at the Carroll Hotel, Dan and T. E. Dashiell, the team's fullback, decided to visit Randolph Macon Womens College as Dashiell had a cousin from Norfolk studying there. The two cadets walked up to the front door of the college and gave their names to the girl who answered. They made a strange combination as six feet four Dan was the biggest man on the team and Dashiell, who was five feet seven and weighed only 150 pounds, was the smallest.

Abruptly the girl was replaced by a man who said, "I'm Dr. Smith, the president of Randolph Macon." Dashiell repeated their names and again stated they had come to call on Miss Weymouth, his cousin.

The president eyed the tall cadet with his artillery uniform trimmed in red and the small cadet with his infantry uniform trimmed in black. Whether it was the broad red stripes on Dan's trousers which influenced Dr. Smith no one will know, but he whirled about, shouted to a large brindle bull dog asleep in the hall, "Sic 'em! Sic 'em!" The dog came out of his sleep and bounded toward the two cadets. This was no time for the boys to debate the justice or injustice in Dr. Smith's actions.

Six hundred feet of campus was between the cadets and safety from the onrushing dog. As the unwelcome visitors raced across the campus with the dog at their heels, they could hear the R. M. W. C. girls shouting from the balcony. Some of the girls cheered for the cadets; most of the young ladies cheered for the bull dog!

As the visitors reached the edge of the campus, they saw a high wire fence protected the girls from the outside world. Both men took a quick breath and leaped. Fortunately they cleared the wire and the bull dog stayed behind doubtless feeling that he had protected the morals of the feminine student body better than any other dog in Lynchburg.

By this time the cadets had made a flying tackle on a passing trolley car. Dan caught the front end and Dashiell the rear. With low spirits they rode into town. On successive days they had lost both to North Carolina and R. M. W. C.!

The North Carolina defeat made the Blacksburg team even more anxious to defeat V. M. I. The rivalry between the Gobblers of V. P. I. (Virginia Agricultural and Mechanical College became the Virginia Polytechnic Institute in 1896) and the Flying Squadron of V. M. I. has long been one of the most colorful in football as both colleges are military schools. In time the game was to become a "Thanksgiving Day fixture" at Roanoke and it still attracts the biggest crowd of the year in Virginia state football. As the Confederate gray uniformed keydets of V. M. I. and the blue and gray uniformed cadets of V. P. I. vie for the crowd's favor in pre-game parades and drills, the spectacle is comparable to that of the Army-Navy game.

But when the Blacksburg team met the Lexington squad at Lynchburg in 1895, V. M. I. looked down on the "upstarts" from the hills around Christiansburg. Long V. M. I. had been a famous school. The future "West Point of the South" had opened in 1839 with an enrollment of twenty-three cadets and with the president of the Board of Visitors, Colonel Benoit Claude Crozet, a former officer under Napoleon, who, captured by the Russians, rejoined Napoleon before the battle of Waterloo. Arriving in the United States, Crozet was first on the staff at West Point and later State engineer for Virginia and aided in the building of the state's railroads. In the War Between the States, V. M. I. furnished many officers for the Confederate army, most notable of whom was the Institute's former professor of mathematics, Thomas J. Jackson. The student body furnished one of the most brilliant chapters in the Southern cause when it answered a call for help to stop the Northern invasion at New Market. The youngsters made a courageous charge, captured Van Kleiser's Federal battery, and their deed recalled the words of Emerson:

"So nigh is grandeur to our dust
So near to God is man.
When duty whispers low, Thou must—
The Youth replies—I can."

In an honored place in the gymnasium Trophy Room at
V. P. I. hangs a picture of the V. A. M. C. team of 1895. This
team won its football immortality the afternoon of November
28 when, against a favored V. M. I. squad, it first lowered
the proud Red, White and Yellow colors with a 6-4 win.
Night bonfires flared up over Blacksburg as Dan and his teammates received the honors of a delirious cadet corps.

When the days after the V. M. I. game marked the return
of normalcy to the campus, all the excitement wasn't over for
Dan merely because the football season had ended. Unexpect-
edly he received a notice from Richmond that the Virginia
National Guard had been called out and he was to report to
Pocahontas where a serious coal strike was in progress.

In the strike-torn town Dan joined his regiment, the
Second Virginia, and was attached to the regimental staff.
He wore his artillery cadet uniform with its red trimmings
which contrasted with the white trimmings of the state infantry troops. Shortly after he arrived the regimental commander said:

"We need volunteers to guard the big powder magazine
filled with fifty tons of dynamite and powder. This is a
hazardous task as we have been informed the strikers have
wired the magazine and can blow it up at their convenience.
If they do blow it up, the guard will go along with the powder.
Remember, I'm not ordering anyone to guard it; I'm just
asking for volunteers."

In a few minutes Dan was shouldering a rifle and on guard
at the powder magazine. Years later he thought perhaps his
action in volunteering, motivated by a youthful desire for adventure, was a bit foolish. Even before the night was over, he
regretted having stepped forward for the assignment.

A small stream ran by the powder magazine and its ghostly gurgling noise masked the possible approach of any raiders
in the night. Across a ravine from the magazine was a clearing
which had been burned over leaving only the scarred tree

The "long and short" of the cadets at Virginia Agricultural and Mechanical College (now V. P. I.). Big Dan and classmate. Inset: INEZ ELEY CUNNINGHAM—"The Girl from Smithfield."

trunks. On these trunks the moon cast shadows until an on-looker could swear he saw murderous strikers crawling around intent on seizing the powder magazine. Owls hooted and from a distance in the woods a panther cried. Dan held his rifle so tight sweat ran down the barrel. Right at midnight he was re-lieved by a volunteer guard from the Richmond Blues, one of the most noted of the Southern guard units. As Dan passed on his instructions to the new guard he said, "Watch that thick grove of timber by the stream. It's full of wah-hoos, soldier."

"Wah-hoos," replied the guard, "I'll certainly keep a sharp eye on them."

What Dan didn't tell the guard was that wah-hoos were flowers which grew in trees very much as do magnolias. The next day the Richmond Blues volunteer came up to Dan and said, "Damn you, Cunningham. You scared me half to death last night. I thought wah-hoos were some foreign strikers like Poles or Hungarians."

After the Virginia guard completed its strike duty, Dan returned to Blacksburg, found he was to go to Norfolk as the V.A.M.C. delegate to the Inter-college Y.M.C.A. con-clave.

When the Y.M.C.A. session was concluded, Dan grabbed a Norfolk paper and looked up the boat schedule. Here was his chance to get to Smithfield to see Inez. Fortunately a boat, the *Accomac*, was leaving within the hour. When Dan got on board he found the skipper was Inez's uncle, Captain Delk. The college student kept his destination a secret as he did not wish to reveal any possible temper lurking in Captain Delk.

Dan had dinner on the boat; ate oysters freshly gathered from Chesapeake Bay, recalled in the early history of Virginia colonists at Jamestown had almost starved to death in famines not realizing the potential supply of food in the abundant oyster beds. The boat passed through the oyster beds and passengers watched the colored fishermen tonging oysters from the river. Oyster tongs resemble two rakes hinged in the middle and are some twenty feet long. The fisherman lets the open tongs rest on the oyster bed. Gradually the rakes are brought together; then the oysters are lifted from the river while the fisherman adroitly balances the tongs from the middle.

The *Accomac* sailed up the majestic James and into the Pagan river where it stopped at Battery Park. Arrival of the boat was the signal for the villagers to come down to the wharves, where they watched the negro deckhands unload the cargo. Underway again, the *Accomac* passed large Virginia estates and Dan could see beautiful gardens running down to the water's edge. These homes often date back to colonial days when the world-wide demand for Virginia tobacco built up an elegant mode of life for the big planters and traders. Some of the mansions of colonial Virginia stood in the midst of outbuildings, guest houses and slave quarters somewhat like the baronial manor houses of Europe. Along the James had come English ships loaded with wine, furniture and clothes; these had returned to England loaded with rich tobacco. Along the James, too, had sailed the hated ships of the Northern invaders in the war for Southern liberty and it was because the *Merrimac* (or *Virginia*) could not be taken up the James that the famous Confederate ironclad was blown up.

"All ashore!"

At these words Dan stepped off the *Accomac* at Smithfield. He stepped from the historic James into the quaint town known over the nation for its hams and its peanuts. In the world of the gourmet, there is no more famous dish than "Smithfield ham." Colonial settlers were taught the unique curing of razorback hogs by the Indians and in 1779 Mallory Todd was shipping Smithfield hams to the West Indies. The razorback hogs are allowed to grow strong and lean in the spring by roaming in the timberlands, but in the fall the hogs are rounded up, turned into the peanut fields. After the hogs have been fattened on the peanuts, they are slaughtered and the hams are packed in salt, smoked over hickory fires and stored until a thick mold accumulates on them. This mold is such that people not accustomed to seeing a Smithfield ham often think it has spoiled.

Smithfield, itself, originated in a tobacco warehouse built in 1638 and later became an important port for tobacco foreign shipments. Later it was the county seat of Isle of Wight. Dan walked past the plaster-covered courthouse— in official use from 1750-1800—at the corner of Mason and Main and up to the Smithfield Hotel.

After dinner had summoned his courage, Dan sauntered up an old street lined with Colonial and Victorian houses. Along the street big oak trees made an arch which was almost a canopy shutting out the skies and Dan thought this the most beautiful street he had ever seen.

Dan reached Inez's house. So surprised was the girl, all she could say was "hello."

Dan answered, "Hello."

But in his mind he knew this girl with her peaches and cream complexion was the most beautiful girl he had ever seen.

Dan met Inez's mother and her sisters, Aileen and Bertie. Mrs. Eley, as were many of the eastern Virginians, was a staunch Episcopalian. But her tendencies toward the church did not cause her to look with disfavor on the tall, handsome Baptist suitor who had come to call on her daughter.

The following morning Inez walked down to the wharf as Dan took the boat back to Norfolk. On this walk Daniel Cunningham and Inez Eley became engaged. The ride back on the rolling James didn't seem as if he were sailing on water to Dan. It was as if the boat had taken wings and was riding on the soft surface of billowing clouds. He forgot his love for history and didn't think about Bacon's Castle, near Smithfield, which was a stronghold for the rebels against Governor Berkeley in Royalist days, nor nearby Fort Boykin, built in 1836, where the brilliant Sidney Lanier played the flute on the embankments and wrote his earliest poetry. Perhaps if Dan thought of any poetry it was Pope's:

> "Ye Gods! annihilate but time and space
> And make two lovers happy!"

Inez was too young to marry. Dan still had his college career to finish; his pockets to line with a few dollars of spare currency on which to build his future. Marriage would have to wait.

Back at college Dan reported on the Y.M.C.A. conference to Lawrence Priddy, a student who was most interested in the Y's development, and who later became one of V.P.I.'s most active alumni in promoting the national reputation of Virginia Tech, as the school is often known.

The college year moved along until June "cramming time" arrived and Dan put a sign on his door reading, "Visitors are requested to place all communications under the door. The room across the hall will furnish all you want to borrow." After the examinations, came commencement exercises with the sham battle on the campus the afternoon prior to Final Ball. After graduation ceremonies, the entire student body entrained to Richmond, where the students were to parade at the reunion of the Confederate Veterans. Fellow students had described Dan as "And thou are long and lank and brown . . . as if the ribbed sea." Dressed for the parade in his high necked blue coat, white trousers and deep rounded white helmet, Dan looked perhaps long and lank, but at the same time every inch a soldier.

This trip gave Dan his first real opportunity to observe the great capital of the Old Dominion. The site of Richmond was visited by white men only a few weeks after the landing at Jamestown in 1607 and two years later Captain John Smith ordered a small fort, Fort West, established on the site. It wasn't until 1742 that Richmond—so named in 1737 for Richmond on the Thames—officially became a town. Its population was then 250. In 1779 Richmond was chosen the new capital of Virginia—formerly it had been at Williamsburg—and the following year most of the town's 700 population looked on while Governor Thomas Jefferson moved into a small rented house. The city, which had been planned by such people as the William Byrds—William Byrd I, William Byrd II, William Byrd III—had over 6,000 population by 1802 when the citizens turned down Benjamin Henfry's offer to light the streets by gas. So Richmond lost the opportunity to become the initial city in the United States to have planned street lighting. A year afterwards Richmonders were singing the praises of a visitor, Thomas Moore, famed Irish poet, who had not as then penned:

> "The harp that once through Tara's halls
> The soul of music shed
> Now hangs as mute as Tara's walls
> As if that soul were fled."

Nine years after Moore had visited Richmond, the Allans, John and Frances, wealthy Richmond people, adopted an orphan boy named Edgar Allen Poe, who later, made *The Southern Literary Messenger*, published in Richmond, one of the dominant periodicals in American literature, and became "the father of the American short story."

The railroad first came to Richmond in 1836 with the opening of the Richmond, Fredericksburg and Potomac, a line which carried passengers at the remarkable speed of ten miles per hour. Four years later the completion of the James River and Kanawha Canal brought Richmond additional commerce as it connected up the Tidewater and the Piedmont sections of the state.

At the time of the secession, Richmond was one of the foremost cities in the United States in commerce as well as culture. Some commentators on the national scene thought Richmond surpassed even Philadelphia and Baltimore for lavish entertaining, its patronage of the theatre—the initial theatre in America was built in Williamsburg in 1716—and in its general "well bred" background.

The morning following the big parade in Richmond, Dan felt a slap on his shoulder, whirled around, saw his old friend John Van Lew.

"I came up with the Roanoke Light Infantry of the Guard," explained John. "Let's go to breakfast."

Food always had its appeal to Dan, who agreed his friend's suggestion was an admirable one, but where would they eat, he queried.

John grinned, "You're my guest, Dan. I'm invited out to a famous woman's home. She's my aunt and she'll welcome anyone I bring along. You will recall Elizabeth Van Lew."

At the mention of the woman's name, Dan's face blanched and John laughed a bit self-consciously. John spoke, "Sure, Dan, she wasn't on our side of the 1861 fence, but she sets a mighty fine table, fellow."

Dan allowed that a mighty fine table might offset eating with a woman who had been a traitor in Confederate eyes, although she had been a heroine from the Union standpoint.

The men of the Confederacy and their sons had many heroines to recall from the days of war, but Elizabeth Van Lew was certainly not one of them: women such as Sally L. Tompkins, who established a hospital in an old mansion in Richmond after Bull Run, ruled with "a stick in one hand and a Bible in the other," and who was rewarded with a captain's commission in the Confederate cavalry; or Belle Boyd, most famous of all the war's female spies, who, starting out as a courier for Stonewall Jackson when she was seventeen, gave invaluable aid to the Confederacy; or Sally Partington, beautiful Richmond actress, who was the toast of Lee's men on leave from the battle fronts.

Among other women in the Confederate cause who were heroines to the young men were Mary Elizabeth Tynes and —to a lesser degree—Loreta Janeta Valesquez. "Molly" Tynes, the lovely young blonde daughter of Samuel Tynes, became the feminine "Paul Revere of the South" when, in the summer of 1863, she rode forty miles over dangerous mountain roads to warn the people of Wytheville that General Toland was leading Union cavalry on a raid to wreck the railroad. Stopping at every farmhouse, on the way from her home, Rocky Dell, Molly rallied boys and old men until the hastily assembled Home Guard was so strong it threw back Toland's regulars. Exotic Loreta Janeta Valesquez's exploits appealed to the more wildly adventurous and romantic young men, and perhaps, women. This young woman, of Cuban extraction, took the name of "Lieutenant Harry T. Buford," raised a battalion of Arkansas troops. "Lieutenant Buford" fought in many battles including Manassas, Ball's Bluff and Fort Donelson, was wounded at Shiloh. To be truthful, the girl did not confine her adventures to the battlefield, but did some of her best skirmishing on southern sofas and, as the handsome Confederate lieutenant, conquered the hearts of some susceptible Dixie girls.

As for Elizabeth Van Lew, there was probably no more hated woman in Richmond. Living in the capital of the Confederacy, she had remained true to the Washington government, acted as a Union spy, and aided in the escape of Federal prisoners. Her home was said to contain many secret passages which led to a tunnel under her garden and this, in turn, reached the river. This enabled her to get the escaping Yankees to a boat in which, with muffled oars, they would row past the Confederate gunboats. Her most famous exploit was on February 8, 1864, when she helped Colonel Thomas E. Rose and over 100 Northern soldiers escape from Libby Prison.

Elizabeth Van Lew's home was an impressive mansion on Church Hill overlooking the James. The two young men were greeted by Miss Van Lew after the colored butler had shown them in. Dan found her a small, wrinkled, white haired woman weighing perhaps ninety pounds. She looked about seventy years old. Her keen, steel gray eyes sparkled as she watched the boys consume a breakfast of waffles, baked shad and coffee.

After breakfast, Miss Van Lew took Dan and John to the second floor, opened a chest, took out a large Union flag. She said, "You will know that when justice triumphed and the villainous Jefferson Davis fled this city, U. S. Grant made me postmistress at Richmond; this, in appreciation of work as a supporter of the United States government. The great general also presented me with a flag. I flew this over the Post Office until President Grant left office and I retired. Shads sakes, but Richmond is full of Rebel flags these days of the Reunion. For me, you boys must hang out my flag. If I had my way, I'd tear down every one of those horrible Stars and Bars and throw them into the gutter!"

These were fighting words to Dan and John and, had it not been that Miss Van Lew was John's aunt, the boys would have turned on their heels, walked out of the house. As much as they hated to do it, they put out the Union flag, which was probably the only one flying from a private Richmond home.

Perhaps Miss Van Lew was testing out the visitors to

see if they were fit persons to stay in her home, as she smiled
when the breeze caught up the flag, said pertly, "You are
nice young men and I want you to be my guests tonight.
Out of honor to you for hanging out my flag, you will be
allowed to sleep in that big, heavy bed in this room. This
is the bed I reserved for badly wounded officers. Many of
them died in this very bed before I could nurse them back
to health so they could escape through a secret passageway."

Miss Van Lew walked over to the wall, pressed a hidden button. Instantly a section of the wall slid back revealing a dark, musty smelling passage. The boys peered
into its interior as their hostess continued, "One time those
dreadful Rebels searched my home when I had a seriously
ill Union colonel in the house. I hid him in this passageway
until the Rebels left. When I dragged the colonel out of
his hiding place, bless my soul, the poor man was dead."

At these words, Dan jumped away from the passage
as if he had all at once discovered the blue-uniformed body.

"See a ghost?" gibbed John.

"Maybe your friend did," cautioned Miss Van Lew.
"The colonel comes back ever so often. Sometimes I hear
him giving orders and can hear his sword clanking, yes,
even the swish of his sword as he draws it from his scab-
bard. Poor, poor colonel far from his home in Vermont
or Maine; that he should die almost where we stand was an
ill-deserved fate."

Dan decided that he had stood at the death spot of
the New Englander long enough, hastily suggested he and
John had pressing business downtown. Miss Van Lew graciously asked the boys to make certain they would return
in time for seven o'clock dinner.

"I'll be damned if I'll go back to your aunt's haunted
house," Dan remarked as the boys walked down the hill.

"Anyway we'll have to go back to take down the
flag," advised John. "Nevertheless, we can spend the afternoon getting down to that business you suggested."

The business was mainly one of consuming a number
of mint juleps. As the juleps went down, the boys' courage
went up. By the time seven o'clock approached, Dan and

his friend were in high spirits. Bolstered by the juice of the mint, they returned to the Van Lew home, took in the flag, and seated themselves at the dinner table. Oysters stewed in cream, oysters fried, soft shelled crabs, Smithfield ham and spoon bread drove the thoughts of ghosts from their minds.

Following dinner, Miss Van Lew sat with the two guests in the drawing room and soon dispersed the happy mood concocted by her exquisite food. The recurrent theme of her conversation was threaded with escaped Union troops and how she sometimes buried the dead soldiers in her garden.

With these nocturnal burial scenes in mind, the boys retired to their room. If it hadn't been that Dan's pride forbade him showing "the white feather" in front of his friend, he would have fled into the welcome night air. Instead he went to bed and found the secret panel a magnet dragging his eyes toward it.

Against his will Dan fell asleep only to awaken with a start as he heard the rattling of swords as if all the Vermont Yankees were coming on a phantom raid to avenge the dead colonel. Any minute Dan expected the miasmic colonel to appear out of the walls singing "We're coming Father Abraham."

John, too, had been awakened by the mysterious clank of swords and the bedmates took hope for a better morning in the mortal presence of each other. But there was no sleep for them the rest of the night as they awaited the chant of ghostly voices exhultating in "Marching Through Georgia."

Long before the colored butler was ready to summon them, the young men were dressed and ready for breakfast. After a repast of hot biscuits, fried eggs, and sliced fried ham, they again put out the flag as they imagined hands from Beyond were helping them. Their reward was an avalanche of smiles from their beaming hostess. She patted each of them affectionately on the cheek, said warmly, "My, my, such fine men. Tonight I'm going to have a really grand dinner. Then I'll give you a real treat. You are going to sleep in another room."

The forced smile on Dan's face turned into an actual one as he and John assured Miss Van Lew nothing would please them more than to change sleeping quarters.

"I'm happy you approve. You'll find tonight's room most interesting. You wouldn't believe it, but in the very bed where you will sleep, a Union general—yes, think of that, a general—unfortunately passed away."

That night Dan Cunningham and John Van Lew had a very pleasant sleep—on the straw covered floor of the Richmond Guard Armory!

When Elizabeth Van Lew died she was buried in Shockoe Hill cemetery in the shade of ancient elms and magnolias. Her companions in the cemetery were such people as Chief Justice John Marshall; Claude Crozet, first president of the V. M. I. Board of Visitors; the almost fabulous Peter Francisco, the "strongest man in the Revolutionary army;" and Jane Craig Stanard, who inspired Poe to write:

> "On deepest seas long wont to roam,
>   Thy hyacinth hair, thy classic face,
> Thy Naiad airs have brought me home
>   To the glory that was Greece
> And the grandeur that was Rome."

Even in her final resting place in Southern soil, Miss Van Lew wanted as little as possible of anything below the Mason-Dixon line. Her grave was marked by a New England quarried tombstone from Boston's Capitol Hill.

CHAPTER IX

*W*ITH the opening of the 1896 session at V. P. I., Dan found that he was almost out of money necessary to continue his college career and he was pondering on what to do when a letter arrived from Roanoke which ended Dan's college career. This letter, written by H. A. Gillis, general foreman of the Norfolk and Western shop, offered Dan a place as special apprentice.

This job was far superior to that of regular apprentice as it called for intensive training in all the departments of the railroad and such a position demanded a man with a college background. Dan felt this opportunity was not to be side-tracked, resigned from V. P. I. and again entered the Roanoke shop.

Training for a position as supervisor, Dan was sent on varied assignments. At Zuni, Virginia, a stand pipe had been installed to feed water to locomotive tenders. This was a comparatively new invention. One day President Henry J. Fink's special train pulled up to the stand pipe to take on water. The fireman could not shut off the stand pipe and the railroad track was washed out from under the private car of the Norfolk and Western's president. Naturally, the resultant explosion from the irritated official was heard over the entire system.

At Roanoke, H. A. Gillis walked through the shop asking for volunteers to repair the stand pipe. As no one would risk incurring the displeasure of the president, Dan, possibly because of his V. P. I. training, was drafted for the job. On the train to Zuni, which was across Virginia and on the edge of the Dismal Swamps, Dan did a lot of thinking. He knew nothing about a stand pipe and had not even heard of one previous to the accident. The only way he knew water could be put in a locomotive tender was from a wayside tank spout.

Midnight found Dan walking across a train trestle half a mile long—this ran through an arm of the Dismal

Swamp—on the way to Dwight, a siding where the badly behaved stand pipe was located. A sudden burst of wind blew out Dan's torch and he was unable to relight it. On the sides of the trestle he would hear the plop of snakes as they dropped from trees into the water. As the railroad line was a busy one, Dan knew should a train approach he would be forced to jump for his life into the snake-infested waters. He wisely decided the stand pipe could wait until morning, made his way in the darkness back over the trestle to Zuni.

Shortly after morning broke, Dan was down inside the box of the stand pipe. The pipe stood on a box about six by six which was five feet deep and in which were the valves regulating the flow of water from the pipe into the locomotive tender. To get into the box, Dan had dropped down through a man hole thirty inches square covered with a hinged door. This door Dan had left open.

Soon Dan found that one of the valves equalizing the pressure was leaking and with powdered emery he was grinding away on the valve when he had a feeling someone was watching him. He did not expect the president of the railroad to be looking on, but he was equally as surprised when he found the cause of his sensation. Not two feet from his face and hanging down from the trap door was three feet of snake weaving back and forth and sticking out an evil-looking tongue. Dan let out a howl that could be heard almost to Zuni. There was no way he could escape from his reptile caller.

The outburst did not disturb the snake which continued to observe the situation, but it did reach the ears of track workers, who rushed to the stand pipe and Dan, dripping in perspiration, almost fell over after his alleviation. Weakly he climbed from the box and found the snake —killed by the workers—was seven feet long and four inches in diameter.

The section hands, who looked sad over killing the monster, explained it was a non-poisonous water snake and doubtless it had entered the box imbued with a mixture of curiosity and friendliness; nevertheless, while Dan finished his repair task, a section man stood guard beside the trap door in case other such snakes in the vicinity were given to an intrusive nature.

Back at Roanoke, Dan was overwhelmed by the rush of shop workers who wanted to know all about the snake, asked nothing concerning Dan's success in fixing the stand pipe. Dan learned a Richmond newspaper had written up the story of the seven-foot companionable snake which had almost scared to death the six-foot-four railroad mechanic from Roanoke. And the Roanoke papers had copied the story of a local boy whose visions of a tremendous snake were not in dreams.

But Dan's success with the stand pipe was not unnoticed by the railroad's mechanical officers and soon he was called to go to Petersburg to repair a broken down gasoline engine used for running a centrifugal pump at a water tank. Dan had never seen a gasoline engine and all he knew was such a machine had two large flywheels on each end of the crankshaft. To start the engine one would put his foot on the bottom wheel-spoke and then pull the flywheel with his hands.

On Dan's arrival at Petersburg he tried to put this method into operation and was rewarded with no success. The engine remained dead. So he took it apart and reassembled it without finding any faulty part.

He tugged at the flywheel until he worked up an enormous appetite. Nothing happened. Finally Dan gave up, walked to the nearby home of the pumpman, and asked where he could eat lunch. The pumpman's hospitable wife said, "Right here, Mr. Cunningham, if you like turnip greens, hog jowl, string beans and sow belly, corn pone and buttermilk."

Fortified with this repast, Dan walked back to the broken engine with the intention of giving it one final whirl before he admitted he was licked. He grabbed the flywheel, gave it a yank, and the engine commenced working as if nothing had ever been wrong!

This feat put the name of Dan Cunningham up along with those of George Westinghouse and Thomas Edison in the eyes of the men of the Roanoke shop. Dan modestly told them all the credit belonged to his engineering professors at V. P. I. Yet to this very day, he has no idea what made the engine work!

Dan's engineering reputation was such a nephew of W. H. Lewis, superintendent of motive power, offered him a position to help develop an automobile engine. Only four years previously the first gasoline automobile in the United States was built by its inventor C. A. Duryea. This position would have required Dan to work at La Crosse, Wisconsin, and this seemed as far away as Kabul, Afghanistan, to Dan when he thought of his sweetheart in Smithfield. The job was refused. Later the young man, who had the idea for the new engine, was one of the developers of the Winton Six, a great automobile in its day.

Not all of Dan's time was taken up with his railroad work. His abrupt departure from V. P. I. had not lessened his love for football. Located at Roanoke was Alleghany Institute, a private school run by the Handy brothers; one was president and the other professor of mathematics and English. The Handys were desirous of a good football team for their school. At nearby Salem, Roanoke College, which had been incorporated in 1845 as Virginia Collegiate Institute, was fielding a team capable enough to win popularity.

Dan was asked to play on the Alleghany team as well as assist in coaching it with the V. P. I. plays. The Alleghany squad numbered among its players Joe Turner, later treasurer of Hollins College; Bob Streator, a 250-pound machinist from Roanoke shop; Corbin Glass, later a yardmaster for the N. & W.; young Coe, son of W. W. Coe, an N. & W. official. The team was managed by Fred Hippy, son of the general manager of the Norfolk and Western.

With this railroad background, the team was well supported by the student body and friends of Alleghany Institute and the railway people. Dan did not play the opening Alleghany game of the season as the team's foe was V. P. I. The Gobblers of Blacksburg triumphed 20-0. After this defeat, Dan entered the lineup, found his playing was somewhat handicapped by a bad left shoulder dislocated when he had been on the V. P. I. team. Joe Turner, who also suffered from a shoulder injury received in college football, wore a special harness and despite this protection, often time had to be called while teammates pulled Joe's dislocated shoulder back in its socket.

The Alleghany Institute team knew no bounds to its courage and like unafraid little Cumberland—which once lost to Georgia Tech 222-0 to become the worst beaten football team in college sports—would take on anybody.

Alleghany tackled W. & L. at Lexington only to find on the Roanoke team's arrival that the Minks remembered Dan had played for Blacksburg and protested his appearance in the lineup. When it was explained how pressed Alleghany was for experienced players, the Blue and White team allowed Dan to play, but, in turn, gave him a good going over while running up a Washington and Lee score approaching the astronomical.

The battered Alleghany team came right back to Lexington the following weekend to oppose Virginia Military Institute. Dan played right tackle—instead of left—so as to protect his bad shoulder. The Alleghany team put up a much harder fight than the Keydets anticipated. Cheers of the Washington and Lee students were behind Alleghany at the V.M.I. game. The W. & L. students had—and still have —a system in which they root against V. M. I. when the Tricolor takes on state opponents—except Virginia which is the main W. & L. rival—such as Hampden-Sydney, William and Mary, or Richmond. But let an out of state opponent such as Kentucky, Citadel, Maryland, Clemson, or Duke play V. M. I. and the W. & L. students shout themselves hoarse cheering for their neighbor.

So with the cheers of W. & L. behind them, Alleghany played over its head while the baffled Keydets became frantic. Among Dan's opponents was a V. M. I. cadet captain, who will be called "Cabell;" although this wasn't his name. Cabell, ordinarily a nice youngster, frequently would lose his temper completely in football games. During a time out, Dan was standing with his teammates when Cabell walked over, hit him on the jaw so hard Dan fell to the ground.

Dan might have been down, but he was not out. Getting to his feet, Dan ran toward Cabell, plunged head on into the V. M. I. player's stomach. The Lexington gridder went first to the ground and then to the hospital. As a former V. P. I. football player, Dan felt that the mildest thing the V. M. I. boys would do to him after the game would be to lynch him. This feeling was not eased on the final play of the game when Dan made a sensational tackle on the Alleghany five-yard-line to keep a teammate's fumble at mid-field from being converted into another V. M. I. score.

As the winning Keydets swarmed from the stands, Dan and his squad squared off for a brawl and prayed that some of the Minks would come to their aid. But the military students walked on past the Alleghany squad without any incident and some of them came up to Dan and told him there were no hard feelings as Cabell deserved the treatment he had received.

Alleghany's football team struggled on through the season; losing to the big college teams, winning games in its own class. A Bluefield team invaded Roanoke and Dan played against a big, strapping fellow named A. C. Needles, who had come to the Norfolk and Western as trainmaster from the Nickle Plate railroad. In 1924 this same man became president of the N. & W. and, often, on trips back to Roanoke from Salt Lake City, Dan would talk with him about their football days.

While Dan was playing for Alleghany, he took every opportunity to watch the V. P. I. football teams of 1896 and 1897 in action. These were the teams he would have played on had he stayed in college. The old V. A. M. C. Black and Gray colors had given away to the Orange and Maroon of V. P. I. and the new shout of Blacksburg was the now famous:

"Hokie, Hokie, Hokie Hi!
Techs! Techs! V. P.I.!
Sola-Rex; Sola-Rah!
Polytechs-Virginia!!
Rae! Ri! V. P. I.!!!"

In 1896 V. P. I., after winning from Alleghany, also won from Roanoke College, Hampden-Sydney and Maryville College. Virginia swamped the Techmen 42-0 and Tennessee edged them out 6-4, but North Carolina was held to a tie. The 1897 team, which would have been Dan's final one, won from King College, North Carolina, Roanoke, Richmond and Hampden-Sydney; lost to V. M. I. and Tennessee. As Dan watched the Gobblers, he was proud of his part in earliest Blacksburg football. The V. P. I. team was to rise in football power until by 1905 they were the Champions of the South, whipping mighty Virginia for the first time, 11-0, downing Army at West Point 16-6 and losing only to Navy 12-6 at Annapolis.

Dan had not forgotten the unexpected blow on the chin he had taken from Cabell at V. M. I. and he waited for a chance to take the first swing himself. One spring afternoon Roanoke sports fans turned out for the V. P. I.-V. M. I. baseball game at the city's ball park. The bleachers were blue-dotted with V. P. I. students and the grandstand took on a grayish hue from the uniformed spectators of V. M. I.

From his seat in the bleachers, Dan spotted a familiar figure playing baseball for V. M. I.; itched to get on the field as the Lexington player was none other than his old football opponent Cabell. For three innings the game progressed in scheduled fashion. Then Dan got his chance. In the fourth inning a V. M. I. player, perhaps inadvertently, spiked a V. P. I. runner. This touched off the bad feeling between the two student bodies. In a few seconds the diamond was a mass of fighting spectators, who had poured out of the stands, torn palings from the fence around the park.

Dan rushed at Cabell and, as he started to swing a haymaker at the V. M. I. player, a V. P. I. cadet raised a baseball bat with the intention of knocking out a Tricolor man. Instead the cadet knocked out one of his own supporters as Dan, who was in back of him, received the backswing of the bat on his bare head, woke up in a Roanoke hospital. A bump on Dan's head still remains as mute evidence of this baseball riot.

In time the bitter hatred between the two military schools moderated until the colleges became "friendly enemies" and the deplorable fights were a thing of the past. Perhaps the days when college trained soldiers from both V. P. I. and V. M. I. wrote history in World War I did more than anything else to bring about the esteem in which the schools hold each other.

Virginia Military Institute and Washington and Lee went through the same trying days in which raiders from the military campus would daub the white columns of W. & L. with red and yellow paint and the Minks would retaliate with night dashes over the long block separating W. & L. from V. M. I. to disfigure the Keydets' drill grounds and castle-like buildings. Feeling became so intense that following a riot after one sports contest between the two Lexington colleges all athletic relationships were cancelled. As a result, the unwarranted ill feeling gradually disappeared. In recent years when the West Point of the South goes north to play Army at West Point or Temple at Philadelphia, many of the supporters of the Keydets are W. & L. alumni urging on the invading team as they remember the lines of Confederate gray marching at Lexington.

Back in the Norfolk and Western shop, Dan had been elected to the shop Labor Committee and, if he had been made president of the N. & W., he would not have been more elated. Not long afterwards a machinists' grievance came up and Dan went up to the office of "the Old Man," the head of the mechanical department, and requested that he be allowed to see him.

"The Old Man" (W. H. Lewis) invited Dan in, motioned him to a seat, and said, "Will you please excuse me until I finish this letter I am dictating to my stenographer." When he was through, he asked Dan what was the trouble.

Dan explained his mission and was asked, "Do you represent all the machinists of the main shop?"

"Yes, sir, I do."

"Do you represent all the machinists over the entire railroad?"

"Yes, sir, I do."

"Well, Cunningham," the official said, "you go back to your people and tell them why in hell did they not send me a postal card!" He then proceeded to give Dan a strong talk on the problems of management as well as labor.

Some years later when Dan was superintendent of motive power of the Denver and Salt Lake railroad, he met "The Old Man" when both were attending the American Railway Master Mechanics' Convention at Atlantic City, New Jersey.

They had luncheon together and Dan said to him: "Do you remember when you ruined a good labor leader and made a superintendent of motive power? What you told me on that occasion was a big help when I sat across the table handling labor matters. You taught me to be fair and square with the men in the shop and on the road no matter on which side of the table I sat. As you know, men will usually do right if you will let them. I think one of the greatest compliments I have ever received was from a man I have known since I started out as an apprentice. He said 'Do you know old D. G. still wears the same size hat he wore when he was a worker in the shops.'

"When I became a railroad official and appointed a gang foreman or a lead man, I would have him watched and I would inquire from time to time to learn if his job had gone to his head. If it hadn't I would say there is hope for him, but if it had, I would set him back or change him out. Often men, when first advanced to an important spot by a railroad, try to show their authority by firing someone. They do not know this is following the line of least resistance. How much better it would be if they would develop a man, not fire him."

The summer of 1897 Inez came to Roanoke and visited her aunt, Mrs. R. B. Adams. Although she and Dan were engaged, the local lads considered such an engagement in the same light as diplomats do "scraps of paper" known formally as treaties. Dan's competition flocked to call on the Smithfield beauty. There were locomotive engineers who made $300 a month and sported diamonds as big as a headlight; the dapper boys from the General Offices of the Norfolk and Western, who spent their money on clothes and entertaining the girls and who felt as if they were the Beau Brummels of the city; and then there were the young doctors and lawyers fresh from Washington and Lee, Medical College of Virginia, Johns Hopkins, the University of Virginia and Hampden-Sydney.

Dan still wasn't making a very large wage with the Norfolk and Western, although he would pick up an occasional dollar or two from boomer machinists by setting valves for them.

Like Nathan Bedford Forrest, who allegedly made the much quoted remark about the way to win battles was "to git thar fustest with the mostest men"—Forrest actually said "to get there first with the most men"—Dan had a slogan of his own. In affairs of the heart, Dan's motto was "Get there first and stay late!" This method worked with Inez. The "Gay Nineties" dandies could not compete with Dan.

The "Gay Ninties" were not so gay speaking globally. In 1894 China and Japan had fought it out with the victory going to the Japanese and the treaty of Shimonoseki in April, 1895, gave Japan the Liaotung Peninsula, Formosa and the Pescadores. The same year as the Oriental treaty, the Cuban revolution began and a year later the Cuban military leader, General Antonio Maceo, was killed in action. Also in 1895 the Queen of Korea was murdered in her palace at Seoul and her oil soaked body was burned. Acquitted of implication in the crime was, of all people, the Japanese minister. In 1896 the Ethiopians under King Menelik routed the Italians at Adowa; set the background for Mussolini's campaign against Haille Selassie. In 1897 the Greeks and the Turks slugged it out in a private war of their own.

There was excitement in the United States, too. Such items as the Southern tornado which killed 3,000 people in 1893 and the march of "General" Coxey's army of 20,000 unemployed men from the midwest to Washington in 1894.

The big strikes by mine workers, the Pullman workers, and the American railroad strike called by Eugene V. Debs made news around the middle of the "Gay Ninties."

In 1897 the movement to "free Cuba" was sweeping the United States and at the Roanoke shop, Dan and his fellow machinists wrote "Free Cuba" on anything resembling a gun.

Perhaps inspired by the notion that some peace and harmony should be brought into the world, Dan decided to end his four-year engagement to Inez with marriage. Or perhaps Inez decided it. The perplexing question of whether it is the boy who pursues the girl or the girl who pursues the boy has never been answered.

The wedding took place on Dan's birthday anniversary, April 19, 1898, at the old Smithfield Baptist church. Ceremonies were at High Noon amid a setting of cut flowers and potted plants. Brother George, from whom Dan had borrowed fifty dollars to help finance the wedding, was best man and Bertie Eley was the maid of honor. The choir sang *Oh Promise Me* and the organist played the traditional wedding marches. After the couple had knelt on a large white rug and received the blessings of Dr. T. B. Shepherd, they marched out of the church and Dan chanced to think of the words of Sir Phillip Sydney, "He travels safe and not unpleasantly who is guarded by poverty and guided by love."

The groom, of course, had more of love than he had of poverty as the latter he had not experienced. Dan was dressed in a morning suit which looked very English with its long cutaway black coat, a white tie, striped trousers and patent leather shoes. After the wedding reception, he hurried back to the Smithfield Hotel to change into his regular business dress. The clerk looked admiringly at the handsome young man whose appearance was that of a fashion model in a magazine.

"Mr. Cunningham," he said, "if I didn't know who you were and if you wore a monocle, I would mistake you for a visiting English lord."

"Not for long," answered Dan. "I'm going up to my room and change clothes. We're going over to Norfolk and Richmond and I want to send this wedding suit back to Roanoke in my trunk."

The clerk flushed, stammered out, "Your trunk, Mr. Cunningham, with all your clothes in it has been sent by mistake on back to Roanoke."

Dan turned pale, "You mean all I've got to wear is this morning suit?"

"Unless you buy some new clothes, Mr. Cunningham."

"New clothes, eh?" Dan whirled around and walked out of the hotel. It was easy enough for the clerk to suggest new clothes, but Dan had no extra money for such an expenditure.

Soon Dan and Inez were on the boat bound for Newport News. An amusing incident which had taken place shortly before the marriage made them chuckle as they looked out over the water. Mrs. Eley had put her foot down on the couple's plan to take the midnight train back to Roanoke. As no train came into Smithfield, the couple planned to drive eighteen miles across the country to Suffolk and catch the Roanoke train there. But Mrs. Eley insisted they take the boat at Smithfield as "I won't have any daughter of mine riding eighteen miles in a buggy at night with a strange man."

The newly married pair got off the boat at Newport News and rode the trolley out to Old Point Comfort. Dan's morning suit was openly admired by some of the street car riders, who thought it quite democratic of a man in such attire to mix with the "common people" and their aside remarks were loud enough to reach Dan's ears.

Old Point Comfort had its social attraction, the famed Chamberlain, one of the most fashionable of the seacoast hotels. Also at Old Point Comfort was big Fort Monroe, where, in 1828, Edgar Allen Poe had been stationed when he was a private in the army and where, four years later, Chief Black Hawk and other Indian warriors were held after the conclusion of the Black Hawk war in the midwest. Old Point Comfort owed its rise in popularity to Chief Black Hawk as he was the feature which drew visitors in such numbers that Harrison Phoebus, proprietor of the little Hygeia Hotel, had to enlarge it. And so, inspired by a captive Indian chief, Old Point Comfort was on its way to social fame.

Dan found his morning suit quite in keeping with the uniforms which lent color to the hotel crowd. Commodore Schley's fleet was at anchor in Hampton Roads. The United States battleship *Maine* had been blown up at Havana Cuba, February 15, with a loss of 260 lives, and diplomatic relations with Spain were at the breaking point. Schley's fleet was destined to stay in Hampton Roads until May when *The Flying Squadron*, as it was called, sailed out and destroyed Admiral Cervera's fleet at Santiago, Cuba.

Unable to get accomodations at the Chamberlain because of the military influx, Dan and Inez caught the *Willougby Spit* for Norfolk. This boat was named for Willougby Spit, a narrow sand peninsula, formed in 1680 by a wind storm, when a certain Madame Willougby, who owned a home near the bay, found the wind had blown her 220 acres of what had theretofore been only water. In 1749 Fort George at Point Comfort had been hit by what the natives called "a great gust" and its double brick walls had tumbled.

The bridal couple learned for themselves the wind's power as, when crossing Hampton Roads, the boat was caught simultaneously in a heavy swell from the Atlantic and a violent wind storm. The combination almost collapsed the small coastal vessel and the newlyweds were happy to reach Norfolk without the aid of life boats or a cork life preserver. But Norfolk, too, was overcrowded with fleet personnel and Dan and Inez continued on to Richmond.

The next day Dan was thrilled to receive an invitation from Governor Fitzhugh Lee to a reception being given the beautiful Cuban refugee Evangeline Sisnaros, who had been confined in the Morro Castle in Cuba by the Spaniards.

Before the reception the couple spent their time sight seeing. First they went to the Confederate Museum, formerly the White House of the Confederacy, where they saw the swords and uniforms of Lee, Jackson, Stuart, and other Confederate heroes. This big house had been built in 1818 and was designed by Robert Mills, one of the country's first professional architects. After Lee's surrender, the building was used by the Federal government for some years, then turned into a school. Only a few years before Dan's visit, the former residence of Jefferson Davis had been rescued from ruin by the Confederate Memorial Literary Society and turned into a museum. One thing which caught the attention of the young couple was a Confederate artillery officer's beautiful uniform across the seat of which was sewn a patch of burlap sacking. Dan thought that no wonder Lee's army toward the close of the war was sometimes referred to as "Lee's Miserables" and often called the greatest fighting men the nation has produced.

Edward V. Valentine's Museum proved fascinating as the honeymooners visited the two story gray stuccoed house built in 1812 for John Wickham, attorney for Aaron Burr. Valentine was the sculptor for the exquisite white marble recumbent statue of General Lee which is in Lee Chapel at Washington and Lee University. General Lee, in field uniform, is lying as if he were stretched out for a few moments rest and a spread is thrown over his body. The story is told that a Northern man with his wife and child stood before the statue reverently. The man whispered, "How noble this work is and how lifelike is General Lee." Hearing the whispers, the child in a low tone of voice cautioned, "Daddy, hush, he is asleep."

Among the other sights Dan enjoyed were the Lee Monument, unveiled by General Joseph E. Johnston in 1890, and in which Lee is pictured bare headed on Traveller as Sculptor Jean Antoine Mercié thought Lee had a brow "too noble to be hidden under a hat" and so came about the first equistrian statue with the rider uncovered; the Hollywood cemetery where are buried John Randolph of Roanoke, Commodore Matthew Fontaine Maury, Presidents Monroe and Tyler, and Jefferson Davis; the Tredegar Ironworks, which had been operating since 1836 and where the plates were made which turned the Union warship *Merrimac* into the Confederate ironclad *Virginia;* and, of course, the Virginia

State Capitol, completed in 1792 and designed by Thomas Jefferson.

Shortly before time for Inez to return to the hotel to dress for the Governor's reception, the couple entered the garden of St. John's Church, the main part of which was built in 1741 on land donated by William Byrd and where, on March 20, 1775, the Second Virginia convention met and Patrick Henry said his immortal "Give me Liberty or give me Death!"

At the moment the couple walked into the churchyard, a negro hackman drove up with a load of tourists, pointed his whip to the church and said majestically, "Over dar am St. John's whar de great Patrick Henry said gimme Dis or gimme Dat!"

Out in the churchyard, Dan found a tombstone which intrigued him. He called Inez over and read the inscription to her:

> "Elizabeth Stuart. Age 16.
>   When I was young and in my prime,
>   It pleased the Lord to end my Time.
>   As I am now so you must be
>   Prepare for death and follow me."

Underneath this inscription someone had crudely chiselled additional words and Dan read:

> "To follow you I would not consent,
>   Unless I knew which way you went!"

After Governor Fitzhugh Lee's reception, Dan counted his money and found his bills were rapidly turning into change and he had barely enough left to get back to Roanoke. So he and Inez took a day coach, sat up all night, and onlookers must have blinked sleepy eyes at the tall young man in his morning suit and cane and thought that times were a bit hard "across the water" when an English lord couldn't afford a Pullman!

When Dan arrived unannounced at home, he found his brother Frank in the garden busy reading letters to a cousin, Brant Cunningham. The words had a familiar ring to Dan. Suddenly Dan realized that Frank was reading a collection of letters which Dan had received from girls while he was at college. Dan quickly seized the letters and said, "Frank, you were to burn these letters while I was away. That's what I paid you fifty cents for!" With these words Dan struck a match to the letters and watched them blaze.

Brant looked on sadly. He had paid Frank twenty-five cents to read the love letters to him!

Frank went back to reading Harry Castleman's *Frank on a Gunboat* and Dr. F. R. Goulding's great classic for boys, *The Young Marooners.*

Several days after Dan returned to Roanoke, the United States declaration of the Cuban blockade was followed by the outburst of war with Spain. In hardly more than a week Dewey had destroyed the Spanish fleet in Manila Bay. Volunteers were rushing out to join the United States forces supplementing the Regular Army of 57,000.

As Dan had served out his enlistment with the Roanoke Light Infantry, he was not taken into the service when the Virginia militia was absorbed by the United States army. Dan was torn by conflicting desires; to volunteer for service and join his old outfit; to stay with his wife; and to keep on his job on the surface table laying out work for the mechanics at the Norfolk and Western shop. The latter desires won out and in the final consequence Dan's decision proved most satisfactory as his old Virginia militia group got no further than Port Tampa, Florida, before the Spanish surrendered.

Some of the laborers around the shop were negroes and Dan was amused by their efforts to understand the railroad and its equipment. The memory of these negroes was recalled to him years afterward in a story told by Walt Medlock, long experienced with the D. & R. G. W. and who became master mechanic at Salt Lake City when Dan retired in January, 1943. Walt Medlock said:

"Once when I was general foreman at Kansas City on the Frisco Lines, the superintendent of motive power, P. O. Wood, said to me, 'Walt, come along and I'll take you down South and show you some of our larger power.' At the terminal at Thayer, Missouri, several spot engines were working out of there, so after looking them over, Wood called an old negro fireman over and said, 'Mose, this is Mr. Medlock. Tell him about your new engine.' Mose wiped the sweat off his face with a red handkerchief, said, 'Well, Mistah Medlock, they is the Cat's Whiskers. Dem Supreme Heaters gess burns 'em up.' (Meaning Superheater Units.) 'And dat monkey motion gess messes wid dem valves.' (Meaning Walscheart Valves.) 'And, boss, wheneber we hits de hills, I says to de Captain, ' "Wake up de little man." ' (Meaning the engineer to cut in the Booster.) "

When Dan learned his wife was to have a baby, he felt he should get a home so as not to burden Mam with the expected arrival. He raised enough money to buy a six room house with a curved stairway and inside blinds. After Dan had become an official on the Rio Grande railroad, he once said to a young mechanic who asked him if he should get married on his railroad wages:

"Young man, when I got married I didn't have enough money of my own to buy a box of West Virginia stogies. Today you boys and girls think you have to wait until the man has accumulated a small fortune to venture into matrimony. Remember, son, money in itself doesn't bring happiness. Which reminds me of a saying along that philosophy, 'A man with ten million dollars is no happier than a man with nine million dollars!' "

While Dan was expanding at Roanoke, so was the Norfolk and Western. In 1890 the N. & W. had taken over the Shenandoah Valley railroad extending from Hagerstown, Maryland, to Roanoke. Construction on this road had begun in 1870 near Front Royal, Virginia. Also that year the N. & W. acquired the Scioto Valley railroad extending from Columbus, Ohio, to Coal Grove, and first constructed in 1875. The Scioto Valley connected with the C. & O. at Ashland, Kentucky, by means of a train ferry over the Ohio river. In 1892 the N. & W. built the North Fork branch as well as the Bluestone extension.

Then in 1893 a serious business depression had hit the country and President Kimball of the N. & W. reported, "At no time in our company's history has business depression been so widespread and severe as the last half of the year 1893. All commercial and industrial interests are affected causing a decrease in the volume of passenger and freight traffic."

Efforts to keep the railroad out of receivership failed and this took place in 1895 due mainly to the continued business depression but, in part, brought on by the tremendous expansion of the railroad in developing the coal fields. The Norfolk and Western Railway Company (the present organization) came about in September, 1896, and the new company became the possessor of the old Norfolk and Western Railroad Company as well as other railroad properties, some of which were under lease to the old concern. So was acquired in 1896 the Roanoke and Southern, running between Winston-Salem and Roanoke and formed in 1887 from the Roanoke and Southern of Virginia and the Roanoke and Southern of North Carolina. This road had been leased to the N. & W. in 1892. The Lynchburg and Durham railroad, first operated in 1890, was bought by the new Norfolk and Western railway.

Far beyond the rails-end of the expanding Norfolk and Western, across mountain, river and prairie, deep past the middle of the nation, new rails were spider-webbing the west. Though this western railroad activity was beyond the far horizon of Virginia, it was no phantom at the end of the rainbow.

Dan Cunningham was to ride the rainbow into the west as the Alleghanies and the Blue Ridge disappeared behind the veil of distance.

CHAPTER X

"THE Devil must have combed Hell to find them and to Hell they will, of course, return after graduating from Cheyenne!"

So commented a visitor from the east when he came to Cheyenne a short time after the Union Pacific railroad had pushed its "Hell on Wheels"—as the railroad's track headquarters were known—into the newly founded Wyoming town.

Soldiers, Indians, dance hall whores, confidence men, gamblers, gunmen, real estate salesmen, sky pilots, doctors, lawyers, railroad gang workers, newspaper correspondents, cooks and dishwashers were all fused into the "rich man, poor man, beggar man, thief" population of the mushrooming frontier town.

General Granville M. Dodge, chief engineer of the Union Pacific, had founded the town in 1867 as the railroad terminus and he had named it Cheyenne after an Algonquin tribe of Plains Indians. A few months later a charter was adopted and by the end of November the first Union Pacific train arrived. The engineer climbed out of his cab, looked back at the cars piled high with furniture, tents, lumber for frame shacks, boxes which might have contained whiskey, clothes ranging from tights for the dancing girls to high silk hats, and railroad supplies. He wiped the sweat off his face, grinned, said to the welcoming committee, "Folks, I have brought you Julesburg!" Julesburg, Colorado, was 100 miles east and had been the previous end of the Union Pacific.

The Union Pacific was racing west at the same time the Central Pacific lanced eastward toward the planned junction of the two lines. Each railroad labored to lay as much rail as possible so as to get the government land subsidies. The actual building of the Union Pacific across Wyoming was completed in 1867-68. The U. P. route westward had been planned in part to open up new coal fields as all the coal used in pushing the railroad across the plains had to be brought from the midwest and cost as high as $48 a ton. As the work trains were subject to frequent attacks from hostile Indians, the tracks were laid under military protection.

Colonel Luke Martin was the first mayor of incorporated Cheyenne. He was a colorful figure who ruled that anyone who shot at a person within the town's limits would be fined $10 whether or not he hit the target. Colonel Martin was noted for his expensive thirst which he helped satisfy by a slight personal tax of twenty-five cents added to each fine he imposed. The mayor explained this was to cover the high cost of stimulants requisite to the competent administration of the law.

All this frontier recklessness might have been the reason Wyoming passed the first woman suffrage law in the United States and the territory won even further world renown when Wyoming introduced mixed juries. At first the frontier women would wear heavy veils to conceal their features while they were on jury duty. The suffrage actions inspired such varied reactions as a cable of congratulations from King William of Prussia to President Grant and countless newspaper verses an example of which is:

"Baby, baby, don't get in a fury.
Your mama's gone to sit on a jury!"

For about five years the Union Pacific was the only railroad in Wyoming. Then in 1873 John W. Young, a son of the Mormon leader, Brigham Young, launched the Utah and Northern which ran from Hamsfork, Wyoming, west to connect with the Northern Pacific. In 1886 the Colorado and Southern was built from Denver to Cheyenne and then north to Wendover and the same year saw the start of the Wyoming Central. In 1888 the Chicago and Northwestern extended its lines to Casper, Wyoming; and, in 1891, the Chicago, Burlington and Quincy increased its western mileage and came into Wyoming from Alliance, Nebraska.

Cheyenne survived the "boom days" of the Union Pacific and by 1875 was a great cattle center as the Cheyenne Plains had been well stocked by eastern and foreign financiers who became "cattle kings." Also around that time the

Dakota Black Hills gold fields were opened and this meant a tremendous new business for the railroads and stage lines. In 1890 Wyoming passed from a territory into a state and Cheyenne, which by 1900 was to have some 10,000 population, remained the capital.

Master Mechanic Manning looked at the July, 1900, calendar on the shop wall, then at the string bean machinist who stood before him in the Union Pacific shop at Cheyenne, "Want to get to Denver, eh? I'll bet your two boomer pals have talked you into asking me for half fare tickets. Can't blame you veterans of eleven days service here for wanting to get out. Sometimes fifteen or twenty men quit all at once. Since you've got a job on the Santa Fe at Albuquerque, don't see any reason why I shouldn't let you fellows go. Maybe the Santa Fe will send me a couple of boomers soon. But, Dan Cunningham, you're not getting half fare tickets. No, sir, I'm giving you full fare passes. And may the Good Lord help the Santa Fe when you get on that road!" Good natured Manning laughed and waved Dan aside as he went back to his work.

On May 10, 1900, Dan had kissed Inez and one-year-old Donna and had "hit the pike" to the west. With him were John Van Lew and Frank Wyman, who had completed their apprenticeship at the N. & W. shop. Dan had figured that it would be best for him if he went to work on a foreign road as if a young man remained in a shop where he had served his apprenticeship the proper promotions sometimes proved difficult to obtain. The old machinists were especially critical of the younger men and, when one would be promoted, the old timers would say, "Taught him everything he knows and now the damned squirt is trying to be boss!"

Yet it was a rare machinist who left the Roanoke shop to try to establish himself with another railroad. The Roanoke machinists, as opposed to the "boomer machinists," were known as the "Home Guards" because they chose to remain close to their regular work.

Dan, John and Frank set out with the intention not to accept work unless all three were hired in the same town. They had passes as far as Denver, Colorado, secured for them by W. H. Lewis, superintendent of motive power for the N. & W., but the men had no intentions of going that far west to get work. Actually Dan needed a change as he had been working night and day in the shop drop pit, which most of the time had water over its floor, and his health had suffered.

At Columbus, Ohio, John was offered a railroad place, but there wasn't any opening for Dan or Frank. "The Three Musketeers," as they called themselves, travelled on to Chicago, the railroad hub of the middle west. Surely they could find jobs on one of the many railways running into the Lake Michigan metropolis.

Dan did find a job at the Illinois Central shops, but, when Frank and John reported no success, he did not take the place.

Before they realized it, the young men had actually reached Denver in their search for jobs. At Denver the quest for the Holy Grail ended. All three machinists were hired by the Denver and Rio Grande railroad and sent to Burnham. There Dan drew the assignment to put the valve motion on a narrow gauge engine. The D. & R. G. had many narrow gauge engines at that time and the Virginians found most of their work was to be with the small locomotives. Whoever hired them forgot the fact the narrow gauge engines were undersized and Dan was oversized. The combination couldn't click as Dan was too big to get under the dwarf locomotives. Although the roundhouse boss suggested the solution would be to hook Dan on the head end and let him pull the narrow gauge coaches, the Roanokers resigned and returned to Denver.

Dan had all of $35 when he left Roanoke and the short stay at Burnham made no appreciable increase in his fortunes. Back at Denver, the men had the good fortune to run into some travelling machinists who showed them how to live on a small amount of money. A clean rooming house charged them 75 cents a night for beds. Certainly a quarter wasn't much to pay for a place to sleep, but would they be so lucky with the ever present desire to eat? The local boomers knew the answer. Ten cents bought coffee and hot

cakes for breakfast and ten cents provided a supper of coffee, a large piece of fish and two slices of bread served by a
sidewalk fish fry house. The same ten cents could be used,
should a change of diet be desired, for a large Irish stew,
coffee, and all the bread and butter wanted. Twenty cents,
therefore, bought two meals.

But what of lunch? This was no problem although it
required a bit of scouting around the saloons to find which
had the most attractive free lunch counter and the most
agreeable barkeepers. Once such a place was located, the out
of work machinists would push open the swinging doors,
order a five-cent glass of beer, and then move over to the
aromatic free lunch counter piled high with sardines, ham,
pork, beef, potatoes, cheese, frankfurters, pickles, onions,
white and rye bread. King Henry VIII never ate with more
gusto than the young men, who, when they felt an extra
nickle could be spared, would grandly order a second glass
of beer with as much spirit as a Browning Cavalier toasting
his monarch. Yet as Dan feasted on the free lunch, he and
John would recollect the meals they had enjoyed together
served by the colored butler at Elizabeth Van Lew's mansion
in Richmond. From a grand Virginia mansion to the free
lunch counter in a Rocky Mountain saloon, Dan wondered
if that was the meaning of a college education to an ambi-
tious machinist.

It wasn't. Years later at Salt Lake City and Denver when
Dan was a railroad official he would encounter some of the
boomers who had helped him when he was almost broke in
Denver. Dan saw that the boomers were taken on in the shops
as well as given a meal ticket to the railroad beanery. Although
the boomers would not remain very long under his wing, he
felt this was repaying them for the friendly interest they had
shown in the three boomers from the Norfolk and Western.

After two weeks of ten cent meals, the machinists learned
they could get on the shop force at Cheyenne and, at the same
time, keep putting out leads for something better. In less
than two weeks with the U. P., Dan had a letter from R. P.
Sanderson, assistant superintendent of motive power on the
Atcheson, Topeka and Santa Fe, telling them to pick up their

transportation at Denver as he had jobs for all three men in the Santa Fe shop at Albuquerque, New Mexico. Sanderson had taken a personal interest in the young men as they had served under him when he was master mechanic on the Norfolk and Western and he admired their courage in breaking away from the traditional "Home Guard."

Before train time, Dan walked out Cheyenne's paved streets—laid only a few years—to where General Dodge established Fort D. A. Russell, named in honor of Major General Russell, who was pierced through the heart by a piece of shell as he led his division of the United States Sixth Corps into battle above Winchester, Virginia, in September, 1864. Dan recalled his father had told him about this fierce struggle in which General Phil Sheridan had struck the first decisive blow against the South in his campaign to destroy the Shenandoah Valley, granary of supplies for the mobile Confederate army led by General Jubal Early, who had been fighting and marching rings around the Federals. At the battle's conclusion, Early's soldiers had been forced to withdraw, but the loss had been heavy on both sides. Generals didn't die in bed in the War Between the States. The North had lost Generals Russell and Mulligan, and the South Generals Rodes and Godwin. It was a month later that Early's men, stripped of even their canteens so no noise would betray their presence, made a surprise attack at Cedar Creek to regain Winchester. Only Sheridan's famous ride on his jet black war-charger Rienzi turned what Early had said was "Confederate glory enough for one day" into a Union victory. These thoughts of home and Virginia made Dan even more resolved to make a place for himself in the west and then, in time, perhaps some eastern or southern railroad would ask him to leave the west.

From Denver to Albuquerque, the men rode in a Pullman. This was the first time Dan had ever ridden in a sleeping car although such cars were originally introduced on the Cumberland Valley railroad (now a part of the Pennsylvania) in 1836. The initial sleeping car was a rebuilt day coach divided into four compartments built along the side of the car. Each compartment had three bunks, one atop the other. Twenty-three years later a passenger coach on the Chicago and Alton railroad made its first trip as a converted sleeping car from Bloomington to Chicago. This car had been reconstructed by a young Chicago contractor named George M. Pullman, whose dream was to build a real sleeping car rather than merely convert old coaches. Disregarding the fact that up to then the biggest amount ever spent to build a passenger coach was $5,000, George Pullman, in 1864, spent $20,200 on the first real sleeper and named it *The Pioneer*.

As Dan rode in the Pullman, the idea of sleeping in a fast moving train intrigued him, but the low ceiling and glass sides created the illusion to him that he was riding in a hearse.

Truly, Dan felt as if he might have awakened in a new world when he got off the train at Albuquerque. To the east he could see the Sandia Mountains rising 6,000 feet above the surrounding mesas and toward the west, beyond the Rio Grande river, rose snow-capped Cebolleta, which is nearly 12,000 feet high. Against the horizon Dan could see extinct volcanic cones. Here was a country as alien to the low Blue Ridge and Alleghanies as if Dan had suddenly taken a Jules Verne trip to the moon.

Dan and his companions were soon wandering through the old town which then numbered about 4,000 population. They learned that Albuquerque had first been seen by white men—troops of Coronado—in 1540 and Dan remembered this was sixty odd years before the settlement at Jamestown, Virginia. Don Francisco Cuervo y Valdes, in 1706, had picked up stones and grass, tossed them into the air with the words "Long Live the King!" and founded Albuquerque. The Rio Grande river was then known as Rio Bravo del Norte or "Fierce river of the north."

John Van Lew's reaction to the colorful Spanish-Mexican town was that here would have been a suitable living place for his aunt, Elizabeth Van Lew, who so hated anything resembling the Old South. Dan reminded John the War Between the States had stretched into New Mexican territory and that in 1862 General Henry Hopkins Sibley had captured Albuquerque for the Confederacy. West Pointer Sibley had resigned as a major of dragoons on duty in an Indian campaign in New Mexico at the outburst of the War of Secession to become commander of the Confederate army of New Mexico which numbered 4,000 men. The army's main objective was the conquest of California, but after early successes, the Confederates in New Mexico were forced into Texas and Sibley, instead of conquering California, commanded various Southern troops in Louisiana, and, following the war, went to Egypt where he built defenses for the Khedive. Fourteen years before Dan arrived in Albuquerque, Sibley died in Fredericksburg, Virginia.

The modern unique campus of the University of New Mexico constructed in the beautiful traditional Indian-type buildings so closely associated with New Mexico and Arizona was in 1900 a rather out of place collection of Gothic-Victorian structures. As the wide-eyed Virginians walked among the Indians and descendents of the Spanish and Mexican rulers of the territory, they felt as much a part of a stage play as if they were actors back on the stage of the Academy of Music at Roanoke. They saw the house where Lew Wallace, when he was governor of the New Mexican territory, wrote part of *Ben Hur* and Puccini did some of the scores for *La Boheme* and *Girl of the Golden West*.

The rapidly expanding Atcheson, Topeka and Santa Fe railroad had reached Albuquerque in 1880 after ground had been broken for the first construction of the line in November, 1868, at Topeka, Kansas; however, the initial plans for the railroad, originally organized as the Atcheson and Topeka in 1858, called for construction of a railroad only fifty miles long which would connect the two towns. Under the guidance of Cyrus K. Holliday, "the father of the Santa Fe," the new railroad was given a land grant of 6,400 acres per mile, but even at the low price of $1.25 an acre, Kansas land was not being over bought by speculators.

The land grant called for the completion of the railroad to the Kansas western border by June, 1873, and with less than a year remaining in which to fulfill the grant terms, the railroad had built 61 miles of track, had over 400 to complete. But construction was pushed so successfully that by the end of 1872 the Santa Fe had reached the Colorado boundary line and had over 500 miles of track in operation.

Then the panic of 1873—which cost Billy Mahone the A. M. & O.—cut short the expansion of the Santa Fe until 1877 when William B. Strong, a Vermonter who had begun railroad work as a station agent and telegrapher at Milton, Wisconsin, left the Burlington to become the general manager of the Santa Fe. When Strong, who had risen to president in 1881, left the Santa Fe in 1889, the railroad had become transcontinental with 7,000 miles of track and terminals at Chicago, San Diego, Los Angeles, Denver, Galveston, El Paso, and Guaymas, Mexico. Strong had been capably aided by the Santa Fe's chief engineer, A. A. Robinson.

The saga of the mighty Santa Fe has been heralded in story and song. If ever a railroad ripped open the frontier to progress, the Santa Fe did it. Today as the crack trains of the Santa Fe fan throughout the southwest, they carry on the heritage of a proud past.

Albuquerque, thought the boomer machinists, would prove a most interesting place to live. The next day they were to start work in the Santa Fe old "back shop" and, after the first Santa Fe checks had been cashed, they would wire their families in Virginia to come to this wonderland.

Saturday morning the men commenced their promising careers at Albuquerque with the Santa Fe railroad. They had finished their noon lunch when General Foreman Wincheck came up to the men and said, "How would you like to go to California to work?"

Visions of oranges and palm trees and sunny California came to the machinists. As much as they were attracted to Albuquerque, the lure of almost legendary California was far greater. So at eight o'clock that night they were on the California-bound train.

The high altitude at Flagstaff, Arizona, caused Dan to get a serious nose-bleed and he practically ruined the sheets in his berth. Embarrassed, he dressed, went to the day coach so as not to face the Pullman porter. But Frank Wyman, who learned of Dan's trouble, explained to the porter that Dan was going to California for his health and to be mighty good to him. The porter came up to the day coach, took Dan back to the Pullman and treated him with a touch not exceeded by a most loving mother.

When the train pulled into Kingman, Arizona, the porter started lowering the car windows and Dan asked him why, with the heat so intense, he was doing this.

"Boss," answered the porter, "you ain't felt nothing not yet. The sun shines down on dem rocks and the winds comes swoopin' along and blows that thar hot air in like it was a blast from a furnace. Dat's why I got to keep them windows closed. Boss, you sure looks hot and I feels kinda sorry for you 'cause just wait 'til we gets to the place whar we has dinner."

Dan felt that if he looked at himself in a mirror, all he would see was the reflection of a giant sponge dripping in its own perspiration. He asked where the train made the dinner stop.

"Boss, it's a little red hot bit of Hell itself. Place called Needles."

"Needles!" For a supposedly sick man Dan let out a powerful cry. "Needles is hotter than this? Damnit, man, that's where I'm going. What about all the palm trees and oranges and beautiful California?"

So for the first time Dan learned what the general foreman at Albuquerque had neglected to say: Needles was right across the Arizona line and was the beginning of the vast Mojave desert. California as Dan pictured it was several hundred miles further west along the Santa Fe tracks.

When the porter helped Dan off the train and shook his head in sympathy, all the railroader could see was sun, sand and rocks. He walked over to the Harvey House and looked at a thermometer on the wall. "Good God!" Dan bellowed, "it's 160 degrees!" The bellow reached the ears of an onlooker who remarked, "Yes, stranger, this is certainly one swell day after yesterday. Hit 170 degrees then."

Dan reached into his pocket. One ten dollar gold piece clung to the wet cloth. That was all the money he had and Roanoke was several thousand miles away. Dan swears that if he had been the possessor of another ten dollar gold piece he would have forsaken his resolution to make good in the west and caught the next train east.

But the terrific heat at Needles was partially offset by the friendly railroad men who welcomed the new machinists; Fred Havil, master mechanic; Jack Records, division foreman; Jimmy Lawler, roundhouse foreman; and George Fluhr, chief clerk.

The Virginians noticed the absence of women and learned that in the summer months most of the women and children were sent to the coast where there were palm trees and orange groves and that kind of California the publicists painted as all of California.

Needles took its name from sharp-pointed peaks near the railroad crossing of the Colorado river. It had perhaps 2,000 population which had assembled in the days since 1883 when Needles had been established as a way station by the Santa Fe. Today Needles is a modern town and its streets are shaded with palms, cottonwoods, tamarisks and pepper trees and the fascination of the desert is chronicled by the Needles *Nugget* one of the pioneer newspapers of the California desert.

Dan and his companions had thought of the desert in the terms of pictures they had seen in their geography school books which showed the Sahara or the Gobi. Soon they realized the Mojave was not like any desert they had ever imagined. The sandy expanses of the Mojave were well dotted with vegetation; saltbrush, pearlwood, and the olive green creosote brush which was impervious to the hottest sun. Strange shaped trees of the desert were the Yucca, called the Joshua tree by the Mormon pioneers, and the reproduction of which was carried on by a tiny white moth which infested its blossoms.

When once the extreme heat had become matter of fact, the former N. & W. men felt the strong spell of this land with its rich past. The Mojave desert had been covered at least twice in ancient geological time by the incroaching ocean, later had thrust itself to a precipitous land of needle-like crags and deep chasms. Volcanic ash, mud, lava and erosion filled the lands. Chains of small warm water lakes supported a life of tropical verdure and gargantuan animals which would have made King Kong almost a lap pet. Yet as the years tumbled by—thousand upon thousand—the mountain ranges rose around the land as if they were the Great Wall of China and the Mojave became a closed in desert. From the Mojave's ancient soil have been excavated fossils of the Oligocene and Miocene epochs, which were deposited over 25,-000,000 years ago.

With the Brobdingnagian animals vanished in years almost inconceivably distant, Dan found the desert was alive with sidewinder rattlesnakes, tortoise and horned toads. The desert was not silent for the night brought its small sounds from the Lilliputians of the animal world, mere minikins of an ancient age.

After settling down to work at 42 cents an hour at the Santa Fe shop, Dan wrote Inez to bring the baby and come west as he felt this would be their home for at least several years. When Dan received the wire that she and Donna were on their way, he could hardly wait for the days to pass until they reached Needles.

Shortly before the time for Inez's train to come in, Dan opened a wire from Las Vegas, New Mexico, read Inez's message that she was delayed by a washout which had stranded the Santa Fe train. What Dan didn't learn until Inez arrived was that, when the railroad bridge had been found washed away, Inez had carried Donna across a footbridge one plank wide with no hand guards thrown over water tearing along at millrace speed. As Dan mentally pictured his wife and baby crossing the slim span, he felt as dizzy as if he had been seized with a sunstroke.

Inez must have felt somewhat as if she had a right to indulge in a fainting spell herself when she saw Needles. What Cheyenne had been in its earlier railroad days, Needles was experiencing. Every other building on the main street was a saloon and gambling house where patrons threw away their time and money with the card sharks operating for the house, or the painted ladies, who drank with the men and then entertained them in a more intimate fashion. The slap of playing cards on wooden tables mixed with the click of poker chips and the whirling noise of the roulette wheels as money changed hands in games of stud poker, crap, black jack, fan tan, and the old pastime of matching for the high card. At some tables, alert players held their cards in one hand and a gun in the other ready to shoot at the slightest tendency of their opponents to edge a card from the bottom of the deck.

Tenderfeet joked with the dance hall hostesses and kept an eye on the well travelled stairway leading to the upstairs rooms where women—not as pretty as the "come on" tarts in the dance hall—used their bodies to shake down a paying guest for whatever he had from gold dust to gold-backed currency.

Not all the railroad men detoured past the houses of sin. Conductors would stop by, and, after parting with a considerable portion of their pay, would continue home where their wives would inquire why the month's pay was so small. Many a conductor's wife knew her husband's reputed pay was far short of what the conductor made on the opposite run. But her protest would bring a ready explanation from her husband who hadn't done all his riding of late on the Santa Fe. "Why, darling, that bastard conductor who makes all the money stands in with the Chief Dispatcher. Buys him whiskey by the quart. So what happens? The Dispatcher has me hauling empties most of the time and the other conductor gets all the good paying runs. Now, sweet, you wouldn't want me to spend our money buying that son of a bitch Dispatcher whiskey, would you, sugar plum?"

Wives of other railroad employees who filled the flesh pots with their earnings would get similar fables. Engineers would tell their wives the pay was short because they had pulled a bunch of drawbars; firemen would explain that they made a poor fuel run; and switchmen would protest they had been penalized because they lost a switch key or went through a switch. The "little woman" would get sugared words, but the whores would get the "sugar."

Some of the shop men would cash their Santa Fe checks, go over to the sporting houses, and, within an hour, be so broke they would return to the railroad payroll office and borrow against their wages so they could pay room rent. The sole reason that some of them didn't starve to death— providing that the bought love wasn't enough to fill their appetite—was the railroad would issue them meal books charged against their pay.

Dan cautioned those of his men who were given to eye strain from looking at red lights which weren't railroad signals by telling them there was no way to beat the game. One day he changed his tactics, told one of his laborers, who was a frequent oar-puller in a Needles love-boat, he had found a way to beat the game. Dan said, "Go over to the Bloody Shirt and give the owner half your pay. Put the other half in your pocket. Walk out. You will be in half your wages. That is the only way you can beat the game!"

The logic was wasted.

The Santa Fe tracks were the unofficial dividing line between the social class of Needles and the common folk. The railroad shops, the homes of the Indians, and the houses of the prostitutes were below the tracks and next to the Colorado river. On the other side of the tracks and up towards the hills lived the more aristocratic element. Atop one hill was a church and a schoolhouse and on the other hill was the cemetery bare and bleak, marked with small rocks protecting the graves to keep the wind from blowing the sand covering from the wooden overcoat of some unknown resident. Occasionally some prostitute would climb up the hill to shed a few tears and a few weeks later she, too, would be making the horizontal journey with her ticket a bullet some jealous lover had pumped into her insides.

Many of the Indian inhabitants of the country in and around Needles were working for the Santa Fe. These Indians proved a great curiosity to the people from the east. Most of the Indians were Mojaves. This tribe came from the Yuman stock as did the Havasupal, the Maricopa, the Walapai, and the Yumas. Most numerous of the Indians in Arizona were the Navajo tribesmen. These, as well as the Apaches, had their Indian blood considerably mixed with Spanish ancestry. Sometimes Dan would encounter Paiute Indians, noted "because they steadily resisted the vices of civilization," or members of the Moqui or Hopi tribe. No Indians were more friendly than the Papago natives who were fairly numerous.

As the new Santa Fe men could speak no Indian and most of the Indians would speak no English, the two worked together through a system of grunts and signs. Dan soon picked up a few Mojave phrases to aid him. He learned that "Na wha ha" meant "Good morning" and "Mut na wha ha" meant "Good morning, how are you?" In listening to the Indians converse, Dan heard the frequent repetition of a word which sounded like "somerdick." As he wondered if this were some special tribal word, he asked the Indians what it meant, but he got the same answer from all of them, "I don't know."

Dan had a helper named Penewha, who knew more English than most of his tribesmen. Dan asked Penewha to reveal to him the meaning of the mysterious word. "Mister Supertend," explained Penewha, "somerdick means 'I don't know.' "

As with all Southerners, Dan was interested in family background and he asked Penewha about his people. Penewha answered, "Mister Supertend, not long ago I was a small papoose. Mother say no good. No work. No like. Then she go away and leave me. I almost starve. Then I grow up. Then I get job, work hard and have nice mud house. Then my mother come back and say 'Big Buck workum good. She stay with me. I no like. One day she get sick. She die. Then I am damned glad of it!"

That ended Dan's excursion into Penewha's background.

Ochee, Penewha's wife, was a slender, pretty Indian girl who had been educated at the Fort Mojave Indian school. Around Dan she was very bashful and would answer all questions with a meaningless grunt. Dan realized that she could speak English and he wondered how he could break down her bashfulness. One day he realized that he could never recall having flattered her, as good a way to break down a woman's reserve as any man has conceived. So Dan called her "Wallia," meaning "Old Woman," a mark of distinction among the Indians. This Indian flattery did the unbending and from that time on she talked to Dan in perfect English.

Dan was careful, nevertheless, not to adapt the Indian term of flattery to his white feminine acquaintances.

Despite her school training, Ochee would often revert to her native habits, color her face with green, red, yellow and white paint, which, to the white man, did not heighten her natural beauty. She would put on a long dress that touched her feet and cover her head with a mantle made of four red bandana handkerchiefs. Sometimes she would make a "tamocooche" by tying the ends of the mantle over her forehead. This she would use as a sack or bundle carrier and it was a substitute market basket when she went to the railroad store.

On May 30, 1901, Dan dropped all Santa Fe matters, hurried home from the railroad shop. He had a most adequate reason for this action. Inez had presented him with a new daughter. Dan reached home to find the front yard filled with Indians; bucks with full feather head dress and painted faces and squaws dressed in their most colorful rainbow-hued clothes. The Indians had turned out to honor the "white papoose" belonging to the railroad boss. After Dan had seen Inez and the baby, he brought out his little papoose and the Indians filed by, gave an approving grunt, and silently walked away. Soon afterwards the Indians sent a messenger saying the papoose had the full approval of the Indians and they had given her an Indian name meaning "Young Pale Face Not Afraid."

Dan and Inez named the girl baby Margaret Susan.

Although the white men sometimes had a bit of trouble with the Indians, certainly the Indians, in turn, had their annoyances with the white men. This was singularly true when applied to the attractive young Indian girls. The youthful squaws being educated by the government at the Fort Mojave Indian school would come to Needles to visit their homes. Soon these girls had changed from their blue school uniforms to colorful dresses. The combination of a pretty Indian girl, a thin dress, and the Needles heat was too overpowering for the unrestrained blood of the railroad brakemen. Some brakemen would take great delight in chasing with evil intent the Indian maidens across the sand and, as the Indian girls could not outspeed the men, often they would get caught and once again the poor redskins bit the dust. But not all of the pretty Indian girls cared to be caught by the over amorous brakemen and, when they realized that escape from violent attention was impossible, they would squat down, throw sand on themselves, thereby rendering of no use that part of their anatomy which the brakemen sought. So did the sands of the desert protect the virtuous daughters of Hiawatha and Dan said even if the sands of the desert never grew cold, the Indian maidens did!

Many of the Indian squaws wore a dress resembling a one-piece smock. Bertie Eley, Inez's sister, had come to visit when Margaret was born, and Dan took her to see the Indians. Bertie was skeptical about Dan's ability to carry on a conversation with the redskins.

"Brother Dan," Bertie suggested, "say something to the Indians." Dan turned to a fat squaw, said, "Muchike?" Immediately the squaw lifted her single garment over her head. Bertie and Inez were embarrassed by the display of bare Indian figure.

"What in the world did you ask her?" Bertie queried as they hastened away from the Indian rapid-fire strip tease.

Dan laughed. "I merely asked her if she was hungry. All she did was answer by lifting her dress over her head to show us she didn't have any wrinkles in her stomach. This meant that she was well stuffed and not hungry."

Bertie from then on was well satisfied that Brother Dan was acquainted with the Indians and asked no more questions.

Ochee was most friendly with Inez and seemed to worship her. An Indian girl, who was a friend of Ochee's died, and Dan and Inez sent their regrets. A short time afterwards, they heard a commotion outside their house, saw a party of Indians building a funeral pyre of wood. As Dan and Inez watched, the Indians put the body of the dead girl on the pyre, placed all the girl's clothes, shoes and personal belongings on top of the pyre, and then set fire to the wood. The Indians formed a circle around the flames and danced until wood, girl, clothes and all were reduced to ashes. The ashes were carefully raked into the dirt. An Indian led up a horse. Dan knew what was coming and Inez went into the house at his insistence. The Indians killed the horse and had a feast.

The funeral pyre had been built close to Inez's house at Ochee's orders as a mark of affection, but that exhibition was "ahote," or "enough," for Inez and she requested diplomatically that if any more of Ochee's friends were to go to the happy hunting ground the ceremonies be kept strictly to the Indian section.

The Cunningham family laundry was done by an old squaw who came to the house. On one occasion the squaw brought along her husband, who slept on a couch on the front porch while his pony ate the bermuda grass in the front yard. The old squaw turned to Inez and said, "Where your Buck?" Inez explained that her Buck was working at the Santa Fe shop. The Indian looked at the young girl fresh from Virginia and, with a look of sympathy for a fellow woman, said, "You pretty girl. Too bad your Buck no good. Now my Buck no work. He fine Buck!"

The squaw turned back to her washing; her "fine Buck" continued to sleep on the porch; and the Indian pony contentedly nibbled the bermuda grass.

Bertie Eley met a Santa Fe trainman from Ohio, Otto J. Ballenger, and the two fell in love. Since Bertie was an Episcopalian, she insisted they be married by an Episcopalian minister. As Needles had no such minister, the nearest one located was at San Bernardino, county seat of vast San Bernardino county, 250 miles away.

After the marriage, the minister, Father Hickman, decided properly enough that his long journey warranted more than performing a marriage ceremony. He began a survey of Needles to ascertain the practicability of starting a church there. On his rounds, Father Hickman knocked at the door of a little frame house, inquired of the woman who answered, if there were any Episcopalians around. The woman looked sharply at the minister, said, "Episcopalians? Well, I don't know, mister, but yesterday my boy John killed a varmint of some kind and—if you want to—you might look at it out in the wood shed 'cause it might be one of them."

CHAPTER XI

"*Y*OU son of a bitch, I don't like the way you are facing that valve!" Dan turned from the passenger engine on which he was working to see who had shouted at him. He saw the speaker was one of the assistant foremen, and we'll call the assistant foreman, Joe Long.

"What did you say to me?" Dan asked.

Joe Long scowled at Dan and in a disgusted tone of voice repeated, "You son of a bitch, I don't like the way you are facing that valve!"

"That's what I thought you said," Dan replied as his face grew red in anger, "and I just wanted to make sure before I threw you out!" With these words Dan seized Joe by the nap of his neck and the seat of his pants and, as Joe shrieked for help, Dan pitched him through a roundhouse window. Glass splattered all over the place as Joe's body took out the window glass in its inglorious exit.

Dan wiped his hands, went to his locker and dressed. Then he entered Jack Records' office and spoke, "I'm leaving the Santa Fe."

The official looked surprised, "You're kidding, Dan. What in the world is the matter?"

"I know fighting during working hours on company premises is prohibited and a dischargeable offense. Well, I just threw Joe Long right through a roundhouse window."

"Why, Dan?"

"He called me a son of a bitch. Where I come from anybody who calls me that has a fight on his hands."

Jack Records started laughing, then said, "You damned hot-headed Virginians, no wonder you started a war. The wonder is that you ever lost it. Now, my boy, forget about breaking the rules. All I hope is that you did a good job of throwing Joe out. I've wanted to get rid of Joe Long for months as he wasn't a good assistant foreman. Now all I have to do is fire him for creating a disturbance in the shop

as he certainly didn't know how to address one son of a bitch
—of a good machinist!"

As a result of Long's leaving, there was a shift around in
the Needles setup and Dan was promoted to assistant roundhouse foreman. This incident had taken place less than a
year after Dan had arrived in Needles. So throwing an assistant foreman through a window, brought Dan his first
promotion out of the ranks in railroading.

In the fall of 1901, Dan found a new machinist working on the lathe next to his. This man was a former boomer
named Herbert S. Wall, later to become one of the best
known men in west coast railroading and for many years
mechanical superintendent of the Coast Lines of the Santa
Fe until his retirement June 30, 1943.

Born in Hamilton, Canada, Wall had come from a railroad family as his father had been an engineer on the Cana-
dian National and the Union Pacific. After attending St.
Mary's School, Laramie, Wyoming, Wall had entered railroading as a machinist apprentice on the Colorado and
Southern and then was a boomer machinist on the Union
Pacific, the Santa Fe and the Kansas City Southern. He soon
became roundhouse foreman at Needles and shortly was promoted to general foreman. He was then transferred to
Barstow as division foreman and Dan succeeded him as general foreman at Needles.

Herbert Wall was a picturesque railroader at Needles
as revealed in this description of him taken from *The Saga
of Herbert S. Wall,* a booklet by this author:

"To an amazed worker on the Santa Fe railroad, who
had just arrived in Needles, Wyatt Earp, or a character out
of the picturesque tales of Owen Wister or Clarence Mul-
ford, had materialized from the bright blue Arizona skies,
stepped across the border to Needles as if a mirage from the
heat. But the bubbling of the arrowing mercury in the
thermometer was not any alchemy brewed by the Gods of
the Mojaves. The heat—and the character—were real.

"The strange worker, who stared at the approaching
tall, slender man handsome in his western boots and his frontier attire, thought to himself what a picture of the west

this man is; of the novelist's conception of the sheriff or marshal who could quail you with his steel grey eyes without drawing his .45.

"But the stranger soon learned that this man was neither sheriff nor marshal; that instead of spending his time watching the boys from the ranches gather for a game of faro, or looking over pictures of desperadoes on whose head the United States Government had placed a liberal reward, the tall slim man spent his evenings at home reading mechanical literature and books about the railroads.

"The story-book sheriff was Herbert S. Wall, the 26-year-old general foreman for the Atcheson, Topeka and Santa Fe railroad at Needles!"

At Barstow, Herbert Wall ran into some unique problems which he hadn't encountered at Needles. Perhaps the most amusing one is recounted in the above mentioned booklet:

"When the new division foreman entered on his work, the local head official of the railroad or industry supporting the community was the chief of law and order. So at Barstow, in the absence of constable, doctor or undertaker, the division foreman assumed leadership. Death had come to an itinerant laborer who was without any known relatives. Herbert Wall phoned the coroner at San Bernardino for instructions. The coroner's reply was to stretch the corpse out on a board and put weights on the eyelids. This being the first such case at Barstow, a sort of board arrangement was fixed for the body with a crosspiece for the arms. This done the body was stretched out with arms and hands held down in an outward position with a bell cord and, with a rope on the feet, a heavy weight was suspended. So the corpse was stretched. It was weighed with a ¾-inch nut placed on each eye. The report from the coroner was that a good job of stretching was done!"

By the time Dan was made general foreman, a fair-sized group of Virginians worked at Needles. Sometimes J. M. Barr came through on an inspection trip. He had been for a short time an official of the Norfolk and Western and had left to become vice president and general manager of the Santa

Fe. It was Barr who had brought R. P. Sanderson out west from the N. & W. as assistant superintendent of motive power for the A. T. & S. F.

Until the former Norfolk and Western shopmen had arrived at Needles, the roundhouse was ruled, in the main, by men from Topeka, Kansas. The shopmen would joshingly ask, "Where is the capital of the United States?" and then before anyone could answer they would say, "The capital is Topeka, Kansas. And who is president of the United States? Jack Records, by God!"

After Dan had become general foreman, the shopmen changed the formula slightly by saying, "The capital of the United States is Roanoke, Virginia. And who is president of the United States? Dan Cunningham, by God!"

Frank Wyman and John Van Lew had brought their families out to Needles. One day George Fluhr, chief clerk to the master mechanic, came into Dan's office and said, "Need a boy to help me make up the payrolls, Dan. Got anybody on your force who can use a typewriter?"

"Not on the force, George, but in a few minutes I'll have a business college graduate for you," Dan answered as he walked out of the office. He soon returned with a pretty girl and said to the chief clerk, "Here's the answer to your problem, George; she's Helen Van Lew, John's sister. She is as good a typist as ever tackled a machine in the state of Virginia. And Helen's a fast worker."

"But, Dan," protested George, "I asked for a boy and you brought me a girl!"

Nevertheless, Helen was hired and George got a fast worker in more ways than one. About two months afterward, George Fluhr and Helen Van Lew were married. A short time later Fluhr was transferred to the Transportation Department and rose until he was superintendent of the San Bernardino Division.

One summer when the Santa Fe men's womenfolk had gone to the Pacific coast to escape the heat, Frank Wyman and John Van Lew came to stay with Dan at his home. The first night Frank was bitten by something and, in the lamp light, the men saw the offender, a black bug about an inch long which had queer looking pinchers in front resembling ice tongs. Immediately the discussion arose as to whether the insect was of a poisonous variety as its looks would have been enough to frighten a person half to death. As there was no authority to consult, Dan said he knew how to settle the problem. All Frank had to do was to go back to sleep and if he woke up in the morning, the insect was non-poisonous. Frank decided this was good logic and went back to sleep.

The question was decided in the morning. Frank awoke.

When Dan was roundhouse foreman and later general foreman, the main trouble he encountered was keeping an adequate shop force in operation. The experienced machinists were often migratory like the birds. They would come in the fall and leave in the spring as the summer heat was too much for a man who could get a job at Wadsworth, Nevada, on the Southern Pacific; or La Junta, Colorado, or Raton, New Mexico, on the Santa Fe.

Some of the inexperienced help tried out couldn't last a full working day and the condition at Needles was later brought back to Dan's mind by a favorite story told by W. J. Tapp, fuel engineer for the Denver and Rio Grande Western:

"Fred Eusey, who was one of the most popular engineers on the D. & R. G., and a brakeman were up at Cañon City, Colorado, switching cars and the brakeman gave Eusey a very violent back-up signal into the house track and Fred was not sure whether or not he should take the signal. As he hesitated, the brakeman ran up to the head end and shouted at Eusey, 'I'd like to be superintendent here for about three minutes. I'd show you stubborn hoghead where to head in!' Fred looked down from his cab and said with a snort, 'That's about as long as you'd last—three minutes!' "

At Needles Dan felt that three minutes should be about as long as some of his so-called help remained on the payroll.

The boomers, of course, knew their work. One fall Dan watched such a boomer, Gus Huber, leave the roundhouse, dig a hole in the sand near a tree, come in and ask for his time as he wanted to hit the pike. Gus was paid off.

Months later in the spring Dan looked up from his desk to see Gus standing before him. The wanderer had returned.

"What engine shall I work on, sir?" Gus inquired. He hadn't bothered to ask if he could have back his old job.

"Gus, reduce the back end main brass rods on Engine 3280," replied Dan.

Gus turned, walked out and, after a few moments, Dan followed him. He saw Gus go over to a tree, dig up his tools, and start back to work at Needles.

Some of the boomer machinists settled down in later years to become the "Home Guard" on western railroads. Some rose to be officials of the railroads. One shop employee Dan hired at Needles was named Charles Ray. Later Charles Ray went to California and became one of the foremost motion picture stars of his time along with Douglas Fairbanks, Milton Sills and Wallace Reid. When Charles Ray died several years ago, his fortune had vanished and he was vainly fighting to re-establish himself in Hollywood. Dan wondered when he read of Ray's death if perhaps Charles Ray wouldn't have enjoyed a happier life if he had stayed on the Santa Fe.

Orders came through for Dan to transport an engine to the Searchlight Mining Company railroad at Searchlight, Nevada. The H. K. Porter engine arrived at Needles in two gondola cars and was dismantled except for the frames and boiler. Laborers loaded the boiler onto two large dollies. The road to the Nevada mining town crossed mountain ranges and in pulling the dismantled engine over the road, Dan used sixty horses and mules, most of which he had rented from the Death Valley Borax company. Thirty mules were needed to pull the frame and cylinders, and the rest of the horses pulled the heavy ore trucks filled with boxes containing the engine parts. The mountain road was so narrow only four horses could be used abreast and Dan was relieved when his safari reached Searchlight without an accident.

The mining railroad—subsequently discontinued after the Santa Fe reached Searchlight—was only 15 miles long and ran from Searchlight to the Colorado river where the mills and smelters were located. Dan found Searchlight equally as wild a town as Needles. Once it had been the site of a battle between wild burros arranged by gamblers and it was told that a quarter of a million dollar claim changed hands for a quart of rot-gut whiskey. The story is that Searchlight received its name from a box of Searchlight matches prospectors found at the spot where the town was subsequently located.

Dan's hauling the locomotive over the mountains made him a hero with the mining people, who urgently needed the services of the little H. K. Porter. But Dan told the mining executives his task hadn't been anything spectacular and he related the facts of a really amazing railroad locomotive haul.

This haul took place at Martinsburg, West Virginia, when the Baltimore and Ohio yards were captured in 1861 by cavalry under Colonel Thomas Sharp, acting under orders from Stonewall Jackson and Jeb Stuart. The first B. & O. locomotive had come into Martinsburg in 1842 and, by the time of the war, it was an important rail yard which boasted a new railroad bridge. The raiding Confederates burned the bridge and destroyed thirty-five locomotives, but spared fourteen engines.

The Southerners made board ties for the wheels of these engines and with thirty-two horses pulling each engine set off on the highway for the Confederate railroad center forty miles away at Strasburg, Virginia. The camel-back locomotives with cabs atop the boiler rolled up the Shenandoah Valley Pike as the ash cans, used for holding coal, rattled in the hoppers. Confederate cavalrymen guarded the procession's flanks against any Union attack.

Wide-eyed citizens of Martinsburg were certain the Confederates could not make the Iron Horses travel the highway. It was with mixed emotions the populace had watched the engines leave, for Martinsburg couldn't make up its mind which cause to support, Washington or Richmond. As a result, the citizens had formed a Home Guard which was in the service and loyal to only Martinsburg, West Virginia. This attempt to remain neutral failed as the Home Guard was soon spying on—the Home Guard.

But Colonel Sharp was more successful with his plan and his prize of fourteen Baltimore and Ohio engines arrived safely in Strasburg. John W. Garnett, the president of the B. & O., was astounded when he heard of Sharp's feat in filching the locomotives and, after Appomattox, Sharp was made master of transportation for the Baltimore and Ohio at Garnett's suggestion. Of course, wily Garnett, it was alleged by his foes, was hoping to get the Virginia railroads under the B. & O. control, and perhaps he figured that Sharp might be able to drag some of Billy Mahone's locomotives out of Virginia!

A message came into Dan's office, after he had returned from Searchlight, requesting an engine watchman for a work train engine tied up at Kleinfelten, a few miles west of Needles. Dan had no experienced men available at that moment and wondered where he could locate a watchman. A few minutes later a cowhand wandered into the shop.

"Look around and see how you like the place," Dan said to the cowhand.

The cowhand explained that the outfit he had been with had laid off a lot of hands and he thought maybe the railroad was hiring men.

Here was the answer to Dan's problem, if the fellow knew any thing about railroading. "Can you watch an engine?" queried Dan.

"You damn right I can watch engines," replied the cowboy.

"You are damn right on the Santa Fe payroll now," Dan spoke. The cowboy whooped, hit his legs with his big Stetson. Soon Dan had him on a freight with orders to the train crew to drop him off at the work engine. Dan promptly forgot all about the matter.

Several hours later Dan's phone rang. It was the conductor of the work train calling and he told Dan to get over to the train as soon as possible as there was all hell to pay. With that the conductor hung up.

Dan called Jasper Wood, the bridge and buildings foreman, and they started out for Kleinfelten on Wood's track speedster. When the two men reached there, they found all the workmen on a hill overlooking the locomotive. The workmen motioned to the new arrivals to take it easy and be careful.

Dan and Jasper jumped off the speedster, slowly walked up behind the engine. Somebody shouted "whoa!" and the men stopped. By the front of the engine stood the cowboy with his rifle. He was behind a barricade of track ties which he had built alongside the cowcatcher. The cowboy put his rifle down when he saw Dan. "Boss," he explained, "I got plenty of trouble, but I'm holding the fort."

"What the hell have you done?" Dan thundered.

"Boss," replied the cowboy, "you hired me to watch this engine and, so help me, those guys up there on the hill have been trying to take it away from me. Almost had to plug a couple of them railroad rustlers!"

So Dan took the cowboy in hand, ordered the barricade torn down, and while the frightened workmen seeped in from the hillside, Dan told the cowboy to climb aboard the locomotive and explained to him how to put water in the boiler and the rest of the duties of an "engine watchman."

The cowboy caught on quickly and decided to stick with railroading. Today he is a prominent western railroad transportation official and he often tells about the time he "held the fort" for Dan Cunningham.

Several months after the cowboy had been a railroad Bronco Bill Anderson (the first cowboy movie star prior to the William S. Hart era) Dan received word that the president of the United States, Theodore Roosevelt, was coming through Needles on his special train. At Needles, the Santa Fe was to change engines, inspect the train, and get Teddy on his way as quickly as possible.

Fortunately Dan had a large Baldwin engine all painted and shined up as is the custom in all roundhouses in order to outshine the Division sending in the arriving locomotive. So proud was Dan of his beautiful Baldwin, he was certain Solomon in all his glory was never as richly arrayed. He ordered the hostler to take her out so the Needles people gathering to meet the train would have ample time to admire her.

While Dan watched the hostler going across the turntable, the smoke in the Baldwin's stack turned yellow indicating the fire had gone out. The hostler jumped from the cab, said, "The emergency valve in the oil tank is disconnected." As the tank would have to be drained, and steamed out to eliminate the oil and gas before a man could go inside to connect up the emergency valve, this meant the engine would be out of service for several days.

Dan's watch showed he still had time to get another engine ready for the presidential special, even though the beautiful engine was out of commission. He told the hostler to set out the 3682, a large Richmond fast freight engine. The hostler must have been upset over the fate of the Baldwin as, in moving the engine off the turntable, he got the rear trucks on the ground and, wildly running the engine ahead, tore the rear trucks from under the engine.

Dan felt that he could almost hear Roosevelt's train coming into Needles as he raced to the enginehouse to order a Pittsburgh engine fired up. He had stopped this locomotive for flues as he thought by having them reworked he could get another trip out of her.

As Dan got opposite the gangway, a boilermaker crawled out of the firebox door and said, "I have the beads cut off the flues and will soon get them out, but it's a lucky thing you don't want this engine today, Boss."

Not bothering to explain to the boilermaker that this engine was his last hope for the president's train, Dan was madly running to the train dispatcher's office when a young woman stopped him and said sweetly, "Are you the call boy?"

"No, madam," Dan answered, "I'm the boss of this damned place. I'm the roundhouse foreman. But how I wish I was the call boy!"

The dispatcher had a message from the special's engineer saying his locomotive was leaking so badly he was having difficulty keeping the train on schedule, but he would make Needles all right in time for the switch in engines.

So there was Dan with no locomotive and the presidential engine about ready to give out.

At the Santa Fe station, the Indian band from Fort Mojave was assembling under its leader Ho Marka Ma Sava, which meant "Big White Baby." Dan knew if the train could be kept at Needles a few minutes longer than scheduled, he might be able to fix the locomotive leak and the president wouldn't realize that anything was wrong. The Indian

band was the answer. Yes, Big White Baby could do a great
favor for the Great White Father approaching Needles.

This Indian band had on previous occasions given "con-
certs" at Needles and Dan knew he could reason with its
leader. Attired in full southwest Indian splendor, Ho Marka
Ma Sava greeted Dan warmly as the Indian had a marked
respect for the man who bossed the Iron Horse.

Dan spoke, "Ho Marka Ma Sava, the Great White Father
will be highly honored by your band coming to play for him.
Now I want you to make him happy and I know he has one
favorite tune. You forget about all the other pieces and play
only *The Star Spangled Banner*. I'll be up on the engine and,
after the president has finished speaking, break into *The Star
Spangled Banner* and keep on playing it until I give you the
signal to stop."

Although the Indian leader might have been disappointed
that such action would not show off the musical versatility of
his players, he agreed that if the president liked *The Star
Spangled Banner* the Indians would see that he got it.

All of Needles was out to roar a welcome to Teddy
Roosevelt, the hero of San Juan Hill, when the Santa Fe train
pulled into the station. The Indian band formed around the
observation car platform, and the crowd, comprised of railroad workers, Indians from a scattering of tribes, the leading
citizens of Needles, a few Chinese, cowboys from the surrounding ranches, and miners who had left their desert holes,
all gathered in back of the band.

But Dan wasn't there to greet the president. He was
climbing on the ailing locomotive.

Teddy flashed his wide smile and showed his teeth. He
commenced what was obviously a very short comment on
how delighted he was at this welcome in Needles. Soon he had
concluded. The crowd cheered. A few exhuberant cowboys
fired their pistols into the air. Ho Marka Ma Sava raised his
baton and the Indian band blared into *The Star Spangled
Banner*. Teddy Roosevelt and his staff stood stiffly at attention; perhaps even more stiffly than usual to impress the wild
west with the dignity of the government.

Meanwhile Dan was still on the locomotive feeding sawdust through the syphon on the injector in hopes this would stop the engine leak. At that time the railroad shop had no electric welders to repair the leaks.

The Indian band finished the national anthem and the dignitaries on the observation car relaxed only to snap back to attention when Ho Marka Ma Sava started his players into a repetition of the number.

As the sawdust flowed on the head end of the train, so the music flowed on the rear end. The Indians played as if all the great Indian warriors of the past—Sitting Bull, Tecumseh, Red Cloud, Black Hawk, Chief Joseph of the Nez Perces, Osceola, Geronimo—were in the audience. Teddy's moustache began to drip perspiration from the Needles heat and the stiff collars of the military aides were limp with moisture.

Up ahead Dan knew that if the sawdust failed, the train would have to be held up until an engine could be rushed from Barstow, the next Division terminal toward San Bernardino.

As the band went into its third rendition of *The Star Spangled Banner,* Dan felt that Teddy Roosevelt must have regretted the night Francis Scott Key watched the British bombard Fort McHenry and was inspired to write the immortal words. Yet Dan knew that as long as the Indian band played on, the president and his staff would stand at attention.

Just as the Indians were swinging into the final bars, Dan swung off the engine, signalled Ho Marka Ma Sava to stop his players; the conductor gave the engineer a "highball"; Roosevelt and his staff slumped into their seats in the observation car, and the special was on its way.

If Roosevelt had actually carried that "big stick" he continually talked about, doubtless he would have gladly rapped it over the head of Ho Marka Ma Sava!

After thanking Ho Marka Ma Sava for his splendid cooperation and assuring him that the Great White Father had never been more impressed than with the three renditions of *The Star Spangled Banner,* Dan went into the dispatcher's office and watched him check off station after station until the special reached Barstow where a new engine was awaiting the train.

The reputation of the Needles roundhouse of the Santa Fe had been saved by a combination of a Virginia roundhouse foreman, a bucket of sawdust and an Indian band!

When the Santa Fe strike hit the Needles roundhouse in 1904, this meant the end of the Virginia dynasty. Most of the former Virginia workers returned to the Norfolk and Western. John Van Lew was one of them and, after marrying Louise Boswell, he stayed in the Roanoke shop until his retirement and, until his death in 1945, lived on a small farm in between Roanoke and Salem. Frank Wyman, nevertheless, said he would stick it out in the west and he found a place with the Tonopah and Goldfield railroad in Nevada. His path was to cross Dan's ten years later at Salt Lake City.

As to Dan, he had said when he came west that he would never go back east unless a railroad offered him a better position than he had. The offer of a bigger position came from Dan's old railroad, the Norfolk and Western. The former special apprentice had done so well with the Santa Fe at Needles, the N. & W. asked him to take the job of general foreman at the large railroad shops in Portsmouth, Ohio.

Alfred Tennyson wrote in *Locksley Hall Sixty Years After*, "Follow you a star that lights a desert pathway, yours or mine." Dan's star had shifted its light from the Mojave desert to the hills and rivers of verdant Ohio.

CHAPTER XII

*I*N April, 1904, Dan stood on the high hills around Portsmouth and looked over the Scioto and Ohio valleys and toward the Kentucky uplands in the distance. He could see the confluence of the Scioto and Ohio rivers and he thought of the bygone days when Portsmouth was a river town and steamboats such as the *Lady Franklin* and the *Belvidere*, built in Portsmouth, had plied their trade along the waters.

Unlike some Ohio river towns, Portsmouth had dropped its picturesque past and swung over to its fast-growing place in the industrial picture. The city had been founded in 1803 by a Virginia land speculator, Major Henry Massie, and by 1815, when it was incorporated, Portsmouth had a population totalling all of 300; many of these people had been brought to the town by the advent of the first steamboat to call at Portsmouth four years previously. By 1832 the Ohio and Erie canal had reached Portsmouth, and it became the southern outlet for the entire Ohio valley as goods flowed down the river. In a few years Portsmouth began producing iron and clayware; the quarries were busy turning out material for brick while small charcoal furnaces were like mammoth fireflies resting in the river night.

The Scioto Valley railroad, Dan recalled, reached Portsmouth from Columbus in 1875 and the Norfolk and Western had taken it over in 1890. Portsmouth industries were making stoves, paper boxes and shoes. In fact, Portsmouth was one of the great shoe producing cities of the United States and Dan thought what a business the shoe people could have done in Needles if they had salesmen capable of convincing the redskins shoes were not only a necessity but a pleasure.

Dan couldn't find as much interesting history around Portsmouth—outside of the tales of the old river folk—as he had in the west. He visited the old house on Front street where Julia Marlowe had lived from the time she was seven until she was twelve. Then Julia, born in England in 1865, had left the saloon run by her mother, joined a Gilbert and Sullivan troupe, and, in time, became the great Shakespearean actress.

As the general roundhouse foreman for the N. & W., Dan found he had a new shop under his control. The story went that the shop was to have been built at small Kenova, West Virginia, but a smallpox epidemic in the immediate section of Ohio, West Virginia and Kentucky, had resulted in the frightened folk of Kenova requesting the N. & W. not to stop its trains in their hamlet. In turn, the miffed railroad officials switched their building plans to Portsmouth, which welcomed the new industry. A fifty stall roundhouse and a large back shop were constructed and the railroad business brought millions of dollars to Portsmouth in payrolls and material. Kenova, now a town of some 3,600 has a running repair shop maintained by the N. & W.; however, it missed its chance at major railroad industry when the inhabitants were afraid some germs were raw-hiding on the Norfolk and Western!

Dan found his old railroad had expanded tremendously while he was at Needles in a way that would have pleased Billy Mahone. The great railroad builder had died in Washington in 1895 and had been buried in Blandford Cemetery as had been his request when he said, "Bury me in Blandford Cemetery among my old soldiers. At Judgment Day I'll call up those ragged rebels and we'll charge the Devil!"

Yes, the successor to Mahone's A. M. & O., was booming. In 1901 the Cincinnati, Portsmouth and Virginia railroad was acquired by the N. & W. This gave the Norfolk and Western a line aimed at Chicago and the vast commerce originating there as well as in the shipments coming in from the mighty lake fleets. The N. & W. was already getting heavy commerce from Columbus through what had been the Scioto Valley railroad. The Columbus and Cincinnati lines converged at Portsmouth to make a tremendous influx of rail traffic.

The Cincinnati, Portsmouth and Virginia had experienced a rather hectic background before being purchased by the N. & W. It had started out as the Cincinnati, Batavia and Williamsburg railroad in 1876, but in a short time it was the Cincinnati and Eastern and operated to Winchester, Ohio, as a narrow gauge. The C. & E. reached Portsmouth in August, 1884, after being blocked by the Scioto Valley which wanted no rival line. To stop the C. & E., the Scioto Valley had raised its tracks six feet so that the rival road could not cross them. Although the C. & E. won its fight to enter Portsmouth, it was not so successful with its creditors and went into receivership in 1885 and became the Ohio and Northwestern. This line, too, went into receivership in a few years and, in 1891, the newly formed Cincinnati, Portsmouth and Virginia took over the O. & N. operations.

The same year the N. & W. acquired the C. P. & V., it built a branch up Crane Creek from the Bluestone Extension. The following year, 1902, witnessed many additions to the N. & W. The line took over the Hillsboro railroad, founded in Ohio in 1869 as the Hillsboro Short Line; and also the Iaeger and Southern railway in West Virginia. The N. & W. started its Tug Fork Branch the same year as well as commenced building the Kenova and Big Sandy railroad with seven tunnels on its line from Naugatuck to Kenova.

At Portsmouth Dan found he was in "damnyankee" territory. The Buckeyes, whose fathers had fought for the Union in the War Between the States, were antagonistic to anything from Virginia or even West Virginia. If there was any remnant of the old Ohio "Copperhead" (supporters of the South in the midwest) movement, Dan didn't run across it. Southerners were still "damned rebels" and "negro beating aristocrats" to the Ohio folk, who still thought *Uncle Tom's Cabin* ranked alongside the Bible. It was said that the spot where Eliza crossed the ice with the bloodhounds on her trail was below Portsmouth.

Dan's winning personality broke the ice of the Buckeyes and he was prudent enough not to flaunt his admiration of the great Confederate military leaders, especially when he viewed the captured Confederate battle-flags at the State Capitol in Columbus. He joined the Knights of Pythias and soon was a captain in the uniformed ranks of the organization. On Decoration Day he was selected to be the Chief Marshal who led the parade out to the cemetery to decorate the graves of the Union dead.

Dan realized that the Federal soldiers had fought bravely and well and he felt honor should be paid to them; nevertheless, many former soldiers of Grant marched back of Dan in the parade and he felt, if the veterans had known that a son of George Cunningham, C. S. A., was leading them, they would have doubtless seen to the election of a new Chief Marshal.

When the Knights of Pythias met to elect a new colonel, Dan went to Gallipolis, Ohio. He found the sleepy, picturesque river town his idea of the places dotting the shores of the beautiful Ohio. Unlike Portsmouth, Gallipolis had not thrown off its past. At that time Gallipolis was known chiefly for its hoary French background and the fact it was the third settlement in the state. First postmaster of the "City of the Gauls" had been Francois D'Hebecourt, who often told of his friendship with a schoolmate at military college. Together they had planned to come to the United States to establish a political refuge, such as Sir Thomas More's *Utopia*. Only D'Hebecourt came to this country as the schoolmate found his activity in Europe a bit too pressing to allow extensive travel, although he did take a trip as far as Russia. You see, he was Napoleon Bonaparte.

One young man's face was missing around the community when Dan visited Gallipolis; this was the smiling countenance of Oscar Odd McIntyre. Oscar Odd had been brought to Gallipolis when he was five years old from Hannibal, Missouri, and from 1889 on was reared by his grandmother. The ever inquisitive young man had left Gallipolis to work on the East Liverpool *Tribune*, the Dayton *Herald* and the Cincinnati *Post*. Back in McIntyre's mind was a desire to write something other than tales of the brick house in Gallipolis built in 1819 and in which Lafayette had stayed in 1825 and Jenny Lind in 1851. When O. O. McIntyre died in 1938, he was one of the nation's greatest newspaper columnists and his *New York Day by Day* ran in over 500 newspapers with a total circulation of 15,000,000. He had beaten the lean years, after going to New York in 1912—he was first associate editor of *Hampton's* and then dramatic editor of the *Evening Mail*—in which his idea for a column met with little response. Ever in the years until his death "O. O." wrote about the joys of life in Gallipolis until the little Ohio river town became as well known as William Allen White's Emporia, Kansas, or Sherwood Anderson's Marion, Virginia. Yet as much as McIntyre extolled the charm of life in Gallipolis, it took death to bring him back to the shores of the Ohio.

Dan soon learned his railroad work at Portsmouth required a participation in fire-fighting and flood control. When a fire in a small town on the Cincinnati Division threatened to flame beyond the control of the volunteers, Dan loaded up a Portsmouth Fire Department engine and hose wagon on flat cars, and, with the locomotive hitting the curves at a speed which terrified Dan, the emergency train arrived in time to save the town. The visiting firemen were amply rewarded with food and drink by the town fathers.

On another occasion, as high waters menaced Portsmouth, Dan sent a locomotive into the city to pump seepage from the levy. Portsmouth has always been menaced by the fast rising river water, but today it has unique flood control protection. It is the only city in the United States surrounded by a concrete wall.

In those days, a general roundhouse foreman sometimes had to take matters in his own hand. When a passenger engine arriving from Cincinnati failed outside Portsmouth, Dan commandeered Charlie Petengill, one of his clerks, took out a locomotive to reach the stalled train. At the time the locomotive was approaching the stalled train, Dan asked Charlie to take off the white flags flying on the locomotive. This would save time. Two things happened at the same time: Charlie bravely climbed out on the running board; an unsuspecting cow decided her place in life was on the railroad tracks in front of the locomotive. Dan threw the air brake valve into emergency; shuddered the engine to a quick stop practically at the cow's nose. He looked for Charlie. There was no one on the running board. But from a swamp came frightful screams.

When the engine had stopped, Charlie had commenced moving through no desire of his own. He had been pitched headlong into a swamp which was fortunately along the road bed. Quickly Dan fished his friend out with a clinker hook and felt in the future he would send no more clerks to take off white flags. At least not in cow country.

Many years later Dan was reminded of the time he took

the matter in his own hands when F. W. Lampton, sales manager of the Hunt-Spiller Manufacturing Corporation, told him this story:

"One evening at a railroad station in the Panhandle of Texas, I boarded a train. For twenty minutes the train didn't move and, being an ex-railroad man, I became curious as to what might be the trouble. Going forward to the engine, I found a large group of men. This group, I learned later, was made up of a crew of the passenger engine, a crew of the freight train which had taken siding, as well as several of the town's loafers and wise men.

"When I neared the engine, I heard a terrific noise caused by steam escaping from the cab. Picking out a man in the crowd, who looked as though he had more intelligence than the others, I asked him if he knew what was causing the trouble. He informed me there was a broken steam pipe in the cab and when asked what they were going to do about it, he said they would take the freight engine from the freight train to tow the passenger engine to the terminal for repairs.

"After hearing this, and being in a hurry to make a connection at the other end of my trip, I asked the fireman if I could go into the cab to determine the trouble. He said, 'O.K., if you know what you are doing.' I assured him I did and the two of us entered the cab. I knocked the wick out of the torch about two inches, and then asked the fireman to get the scoop shovel. With the aid of the torch and scoop shovel, I discovered the steam pipe to the flange oil lubricator had broken off about six inches above the spud that screws directly into the boiler, which had no shut-off valve. After one look at the pipe, I knew the leak could be stopped by flattening the pipe with a hammer.

"Because of the terrific heat in the cab, the fireman and I went down to the platform for a minute. After shedding my topcoat and hat, I borrowed a jumper, cap and gloves from one of the crewmen and said to the fireman, 'Come on, let's get the engine going.' Reluctantly he agreed and, as requested, he got the shaker bar and hammer. I placed the shaker bar where I wanted him to hold it, and with a few licks of the hammer I succeeded in closing the copper pipe, thus stopping the leak. All of this took possibly three or four minutes.

"In the meantime, the conductor of the passenger train had contacted the dispatcher and they had arranged to change engines. When I had stopped the leak, one of the crewmen ran down the platform and told the conductor some stranger had fixed the engine and it was ready to go. Naturally, when I took the job upon myself, I heard some very unkind remarks about the damned fool who would doubtless be killed by going into the cab.

"I exchanged my wearing apparel with the man on the platform and the old engineer came up to me and thanked me for getting them out of their predicament. Frankly, I was disgusted with the crew for not trying to help themselves and I told the engineer I hoped he would get going for if the train was late I would miss my connection at the next terminal.

"The train started in a very few minutes and the conductor came up, thanked me profusely and asked my name as he had a very fine superintendent, who wouldn't have much regard for him if he was unable to find out who had repaired the engine. I explained I was not a railroad man, just an ordinary peddler, and gave him one of my business cards.

"I don't think I ever had such a ride, Dan. The engineer had taken me at my word and he was seeing to it I wouldn't miss the connection. The engineer made up all his lost time with the exception of about five minutes and I was able to catch the other train.

"Back at my office, I found a letter from the railroad's superintendent thanking me for my voluntary help. The superintendent realized that the engine men should have taken it upon themselves to remedy the condition and not given up so quickly. It was really not a dangerous job if one knew how to handle the situation."

Speaking of situations, while Dan was at Portsmouth his young brother, Frank, arrived from Roanoke to live at his home and work in the Norfolk and Western shops. Dan's house was soon crowded with Ohio girls, who came to call on the youthful handsome apprentice. Dan and Inez enjoyed the young people, but, as Inez did not want Frank to throw his money away on the girls, she took all his wages for room and board except one dollar a week. How Frank handled the situation and kept his pretty Ohio admirers satisfied on a dollar a week he has never revealed.

Frank sometimes hinted he would like an extra dollar; especially the time the circus came to town. The two brothers hurried down to the parade and got the thrill of having the Queen of Sheba—a highly painted circus beauty—wink at them.

It took Inez a week to bring them to their senses.

As the Portsmouth shop expanded, not always could Dan get really experienced workers. And the same problem faced the other branches of the railroad. Dan was with the road foreman of equipment once when he was examining a new fireman. Included in the examination was the item of economy, especially of oil and waste. Safety was, of course, stressed. The road foreman asked the young fireman what he would do if he was running fifty miles per hour on a single track and saw another train approaching. Remembering the safety and economy angle, the fireman replied, "Why, I would grab the oil can and a bunch of waste and jump off!"

Then the N. & W. had a new brakeman who went back to flag and all at once he appeared back at the caboose. The conductor asked, "Why did you come in? The engineer did not blow in his flag." The brakeman, who was almost out of breath from running, replied, "I had to come in. I saw a mountain lion right in the middle of the track." The conductor thought a moment, queried, "Where did he go?" The brakeman shook his head in wonderment and answered, "Sir, if that lion moved as fast as I did by this time he is passing Dayton, Ohio!"

One of the boomer brakemen coming into Portsmouth made his first trip on the N. & W. At the bottom of a heavy grade was a water tank. Frequently it was empty because of a scarcity of water at that point. When the engine crew drove up to the tank and the fireman went back to take water, he signalled the engineer the tank was empty. When the fireman got back to the cab, the engineer winked at him and asked him if he had "the makings" for a cigarette. The fire-

man replied that he didn't have any and the engineer turned
to the boomer and asked him if he had any. When the boomer
answered that he was out of makings, the engineer roared,
"Cut me loose from the train. I'm not going to pull this
train another damned mile until I get some tobacco!" When
the engine got to the top of the hill, the engineer said to his
fireman, "I'm going into the eating house here and get my
tobacco." The fireman knew that the reason the engine came
to the crest of the hill was for water. But the boomer wasn't
in on the joke. He shouted, "I've railroaded on the Southern
Pacific. And I've railroaded on the Texas Pacific. I've been
a brakeman on the Louisville and Nashville and the New
York Central. By God, I've railroaded all over the United
States. I've seen engines run for coal and run for water. This
is the end. I'm quitting when I get in for I'll not work for
any damned pike where they leave a train on a side track and
run for tobacco!"

A Norfolk and Western train was pulling one of the
steep West Virginia grades, and it had almost stalled. The perplexed engineer felt as if every time the wheels turned that
would be the final revolution. Finally creeping into the terminal at the top of the mountain, the engineer gave a sigh of
relief as the engine made the grade. Shortly the new brakeman
came up to him and said, "You sure had a hard time making
the mountain. Lucky thing I thought to save the day for you
by setting some hand brakes to keep you from slipping back."

Not always did the student workers or the boomers pull
the only boners. One of the railroad's younger officers upon
being told a train had slipped down because of a bad rail,
wanted to know why the bad rail had not been renewed and
who was responsible for leaving it in. This same young official put out a bulletin advising he wanted the snow plow
kept on the side of the mountain that had the snow trouble
so that it would be handy and not have to move so far when
it snowed or there was a blizzard or snow slide. He must have
thought the railroad could control snow storms just as King
Canute commanded the waves; or, for that matter the fire
chief in a small Ohio city who ordered the fire engine fired up
thirty minutes before each alarm.

The boomer brakemen at Portsmouth, as with all boomers, had a language of their own. If called out on a passenger run, they would say they were taking out "The Glass Cars." If the run were on a cattle train, the boomers would say they were hauling "Hoofs and Horns."

Boomers never called a division by its official name. Some of the favorites were "The Punkin Vine," "The Pea Vine," and "The Tad Pole." One division was known to the boomers as "The Feeble-Minded Division." While Dan was at Portsmouth, a young superintendent decided all men should call the division he was in charge of by its right name and he would fire anybody who called it "The Tad Pole." One day the superintendent was riding in a caboose when he heard the brakeman mention "The Tad Pole." When the train pulled into the terminal, the superintendent sent a message to the brakeman requesting his immediate presence in his office. When the brakeman arrived the superintendent turned to him and said, "Against my specific orders, I heard you refer to this division as 'The Tad Pole.' You know anyone who does this is liable to be fired." For an hour the superintendent harangued the brakeman and then told him he would not be fired this time, but he must watch his language in the future. The brakeman said, "Yes, sir, I understand fully. From now on I will never call this division anything but its right name." As he went out the door, he looked back at the superintendent and commented, "Well, it sure will be good getting out on 'The Tad Pole' tonight."

The superintendent didn't comment. Eventually he gave up his notion in despair and before he was promoted he, too, was saying "The Tad Pole Division."

When Frank Cunningham had finished his apprenticeship at Portsmouth, Inez took him down to the bank. She showed him a bank book and told him the money was his. All the time he had paid her for room and board, she had saved his money and put it in a special account. Frank had wanted to go to V. P. I. to study engineering, but he didn't have enough money. When he saw how much money Inez had saved for him, he at last realized why she had let him spend only a dollar a week. Too, he was glad he hadn't squandered his

money on the Portsmouth girls. Frank returned to Roanoke
before entering Blacksburg along with his cousin Brant. He
wrote Dan he had arrived home in time to see a Virginian
railroad train first enter the city. On this train had been the
great Mark Twain. The gay orange painted passenger cars
of the Virginian were long one of the sights in Virginia
railroading.

In March, 1907, Dan received a notice he was being
promoted and his new position was general foreman at
Williamson, West Virginia. Dan was not too happy over
the promotion as he felt being sent to Williamson was like
being exiled to the salt mines of Siberia.

"We'll miss you, Dan," Charlie Petengill said. "You
won't find Williamson a city like Portsmouth. Williamson's
down in the wild mountaineer country. Why it was just a
cornfield when the N. & W. first went through it in 1891.
Twenty-seven people lived there."

"Williamson's big enough to be the Mingo county seat,"
Dan said defensively.

"Sure. And you know how Mingo county was formed?
Moonshine whiskey did it, Dan. About 1890 an arrested
moonshiner said Logan county had no authority over him
because his still was really located in Lincoln county. Seems
the moonshiner thought his still was in Lincoln county for
the simple reason he paid taxes to that county. So it came
out that Lincoln county for years had been collecting taxes
on a part of Logan and nobody had known the difference. So
in time big Logan county was split up and in 1895 Mingo
county was created and Williamson became the county seat.

"Yessir, Dan, you'll be right down there on the Tug Fork
and you'll probably wish you were back at Portsmouth or even
on that far away Santa Fe railroad at Needles. The Tug
river tells the whole story of that country, fellow. Major
Andrew Lewis led an expedition against the Ohio Indians in
1756 and the whole shebang got fouled up by the weather and
ran so short of supplies the men boiled the tugs of their boots
—and ate 'em. So they named the river they were on the Tug."

The joshing was all in a good-natured vein as Dan's
friends at Portsmouth wished him the best of luck with his

new position on the Norfolk and Western. To show him they meant it, the shop employees gave him an expensive watch.

"Remember at Williamson," they told Dan, "you'll be working on Ohio time!"

ᴊOSSING his hat on a hook, Dan sat down in his office at the Norfolk and Western shop at Williamson to start off his first day. No sooner was he seated than a shop employee rushed in, shouted, "You Mr. Cunningham, the new general foreman?" Dan nodded affirmatively, answered, "And take it easy, fellow, I'm not deaf."

"Boss, I got a reason for shouting. The turntable engine with its housing has just toppled over into the turntable pit!"

With the aid of a steam derrick, the turntable engine was restored, and by the end of the day locomotives were again being moved so that train traffic was no longer tied up at the busy terminal.

The Norfolk and Western had built a new roundhouse at Williamson, but it hadn't been put in use. Dan figured as the old roundhouse was almost falling apart, the time had come to put the new building into service. So orders were issued transferring activities the next day to the new building.

Before Dan left his office at the end of his first day, Chief Charlie Wingo, boilermaker foreman, entered. The "Chief" was named for a non-existent Indian tribe; took great pride in his title.

Wingo carefully explained he had one long cherished ambition; when the new roundhouse opened, he wanted to be the first man to run an engine into it. Knowing that Wingo was one of the best liked men at the shop and that granting such a request would please the workers, Dan assured Wingo the honor would be his.

When word got around the Chief was to run the engine, an onlooker would have thought from the excitement the president of the United States had been chosen. The shop men fixed Wingo a big Indian war bonnet and decorated the feathers with the red paint always found in railroad shops.

The time arrived for running the initial engine from the old roundhouse. Chief Wingo climbed into the cab, pulled the throttle, and the engine moved slowly along the track accompanied by cheers which would have rivalled those at

Promontory Point, Utah, May 10, 1869, when the Golden Spike was driven as the Union Pacific and the Central Pacific met in a junction which linked together the continent by rail.

All along the short route between the roundhouses, the excited onlookers acclaimed the locomotive and its entranced pilot. Wingo rode as if, in the words of Shakespeare, he had "touched the highest point of all my greatness." Hannibal could have had no more satisfaction etched on his face after he had crossed the Alps, than did the Chief as he leaned out of the cab of his locomotive. The "engineer for a day" must have felt he could go on like that until the end of time.

And he tried it!

As the locomotive puffed into the new enginehouse, it kept right on going to the end of the track, knocked aside the bumper, and like some Frankenstein monster, plowed through the wall!

Unhurt, Wingo finally got his hand off the throttle and the engine churned to a rough stop. The Chief impassively looked around at the new brick and windows he had spread over the countryside, climbed out of the cab, headed for his post in the boiler shop. Never again did he ask to drive a locomotive.

So ended Dan's second day at Williamson.

The next day Dan was in his office checking reports when an Italian workman burst open the door and fell exhausted at Dan's feet. Dan thought warring workers had commenced a vendetta. While Dan was wondering which would be the better course; to crawl under his desk, or to find a gun and start shooting, himself, the workman found his breath and explained what had happened.

It seems the laborer, Tony Milano, had been working in the cinder pit when two parked coal cars had somehow become released from their hand brakes and, gathering momentum, were plunging toward the pit. At that moment Tony happened to look up. As if the Devil were chasing him out of the depths of Hell, Tony raced out of the pit, headed for the Tug river and kept going until he was into Hatfield territory. No sooner had he drawn a few breaths of Kentucky air, than he heard the ping of a bullet. After a few seconds, other bullets came by and kicked up the dirt from his feet. Tony had enough of Kentucky. Back across the Tug he beat his mad retreat and sought sanctuary in the bossman's office.

The fourth day was highlighted by a wreck in the yards in the early morning. This wreck practically called a halt to all shop work for the day as the wrecked cars had been loaded with beer and the chance to drink up "on the house" was eagerly taken by the laborers.

By this time Dan was certain nothing else could happen unless, perchance, some uniformed men came in and stated the shop had been taken over for the use of the state of West Virginia as an insane asylum.

Dan was wrong.

The Tug rose up like lather in a shaving mug and, by the following morning, had washed away the railroad's water pumphouse along the river banks. With the help of Clyde Raines, the roundhouse foreman, Dan rushed out appeals for help all along the railroad line. From Columbus, Ohio, to Norfolk, Virginia, the Norfolk and Western hastened pumps to Williamson. Soon the West Virginia bank of the Tug was lined with an array of pumps big, little and middle-sized; some worked and some didn't; and some were spitting as much muddy water into the air as into the water system.

Alexander Kearney, superintendent of motive power, hurried to Williamson to survey the water situation. He looked at the carnival of pumps and shook his head in wonderment. Something had to be done to assure an adequate water supply for Williamson. The only water for the shop and the town came from the Tug and this river was practically a drainage stream from Keystone. As a result, the water was so foul and dirty it was impossible to keep workmen at the Williamson shop. The shop force was held to such a small number that— except for light repairs—bad order cars had to be sent to Portsmouth or Bluefield.

The Norfolk and Western ordered a new powerhouse built for Williamson. This was constructed mostly under- ground on concrete pilings as the sandy soil went down many feet. This powerhouse was equipped with two 150 horsepower centrifugal pumps placed in a well twenty by forty feet deep;

a tunnel ran out into the river and connected with twelve inch perforated cook brass pipes placed in an H shape and covered with six feet of gravel and sand which acted as a filter. Whenever these perforations became clogged with silt, the operator would shut down the pump, open a valve from the high three hundred gallon service tank. The pressure would flow back through the pipes and clear the perforations so the water could resume its flow into the system.

As the sand and gravel provided an ideal swimming hole for the Williamson boys, they began to come out for a plunge. One day, while a group of the lads was in swimming, the system became clogged and the powerhouse operator opened the back pressure valve. Up went the bottom of the river ten feet in the air! Out of the water sprinted the frightened boys who thought the river had exploded and some, shaken by their experience, charged down the road for home without bothering to put on shoes, clothes, or even a wet towel!

Consequently there was no more swimming in the pump part of the Tug, much to the relief of the ladies of the town, who had blushed at the onrush of naked boys.

Under Dan's direction the improvements on the water supply continued. The shop built a water tower fifty feet high with two 25,000 gallon redwood tanks one above the other. On the top tank was built a galvanized iron pipe coil rectifier. Live steam was passed through this condenser and cold water, running over the coil, condensed the steam into water. As this resulted in distilled water with a flat taste, when the water passed to the bottom tank it was aerated with a jet of air and a small amout of lithia was released by a trap. The water was piped through the ice house and presently the citizens of Williamson were coming out to the shop with jugs and bottles to get the sparkling drinking water.

Shop employees would take home containers full of water each night and soon the water situation at Williamson had ceased to exist. In a short time the payroll jumped from eight thousand dollars a month to eighty thousand dollars. No longer were bad order cars sent elsewhere for repairs; the shop force became so large that it could work on locomotives. Too, the general health of the population of Williamson improved so vastly the water project became news and the United States Department of the Interior sent an investigator to Williamson.

With the official report in Washington, the Congress of the United States passed a resolution of thanks to Dan Cunningham and his men for the work they had accomplished in saving the lives and improving the health of the West Virginia townspeople.

When the work on improving the water supply had commenced, Dan had brought his family from Roanoke to Williamson. During the first dinner in their new home, Inez noticed a large rat sitting on some packing boxes outside the window. Without a word she walked over to the buffet, picked up a revolver and fired two rapid shots at the rat. Dinner was resumed. Before the Cunninghams had taken more than a few bites of their "snaps" and sweet potatoes, the noise of a fire engine was heard and, in a few moments, the fire chief came running into the dining room asking "Where's the fire?"

Dan explained that the chief must have the wrong house, as there wasn't any fire, and was told, in reply, two shots had been fired in rapid succession from his home; this was the fire signal in Williamson. Embarrassed, Dan explained what had taken place, asked why two shots were necessary. Why wasn't one shot enough for the fire signal?

The amiable chief poured out a big glass of buttermilk, picked up a piece of corn pone. "Mr. Cunningham," he said, "you are kind of new round here. Sometimes we have a little shooting when the Hatfields or the McCoys wander over here. You know, Mr. Cunningham, when one of those mountain fellows shoots—he has to shoot just once!"

Later when Dan was made Honorary Chief of the Salt Lake City Fire Department, he recalled his visit from the Williamson chief and also one of the favorite stories of William J. Jenks, the present president of the Norfolk and Western.

When Jenks was living in Bluefield, West Virginia, around the turn of the century, the first fire department in the town was organized by an N. & W. shop employee, "Uncle Billy" Munroe. Despite Munroe's impassioned plea to the

town council for money he insisted was necessary to buy
additional fire hose, the Bluefield "city fathers" turned him
down and, instead, voted money for new horns for the town's
brass band. Shortly thereafter, the home of Bluefield's mayor
was ablaze and the fire fighters found the hose too short to
reach the burning structure. Perplexed firemen looked to
Uncle Billy for advice, received a resigned nod of the head
followed by the triumphant exclamation: "Call out the band,
boys! Let 'em blow it out with their damned new horns!"

On Christmas Eve, 1909, Dan sat in his office by a warm
stove and congratulated himself on a job well done. A few
hours previously he had been flashed a warning on the railroad
telegraph to take the necessary precautions as a bad cold wave
was moving down on Williamson. This Dan did immediately.
Materials were set for fires around the stand pipes and on the
cinder pits and Dan was confident neither men nor machines
would freeze at the Williamson shop.

Already the storm had sent its advance forces into
Williamson and the howling wind blew traces of snow into
the office through cracks around the door and windows. As
Dan meditated on how delightful to be by a red-bellied iron
stove while the elements performed outside, the phone rang.
Dan picked up the receiver. From over the wire came the
words, "Portsmouth calling. This is General Superintendent
Johnson speaking. How're you fixed for the cold spell that's
getting worse all the time?"

Dan assured Johnson everything at Williamson was under
control and there was no need to worry about the shop. Dan
could hear Johnson exhale in deliverance from worry. Then
a flood of words tumbled out of the phone, "Good going, D. C.
That's great. Since everything is so damned well under control
at Williamson, you better get the hell out of there. I wish
you would get an engine and caboose and come west on the
Kenova District. Lots of pumps and stand pipes have been
allowed to freeze and are out of commission. They need to
be thawed out. Traffic is tied up. Our trains are standing
still. I'm afraid the locomotives will run out of water. Leave
right away if you can. . . . And Merry Christmas!"

When Dan put the receiver down the storm seemed to

have doubled its intensity. He summoned the able car foreman, W. V. McNamara, and told him to have the call boy
round up an engine crew while Dan had a caboose stocked
with food from the commissary on the wrecker.

Within an hour the engine and caboose pulled away from
the shop. All along the line between Kenova and Williamson
pumps were thawed out and repaired, frozen engines were put
back into service as day and night Dan and his men kept busy.
The storm lasted so long the men spent the entire Christmas
holidays on the rails and had little time to think of the Yuletide except when they glimpsed the decorated trees in the
small homes of the miners or heard the explosion of fire-
crackers set off by children.

The repair crew knew they were carrying on a Norfolk
and Western tradition and keeping up the record of the "old
line that stands so well for good transportation" as Dan
phrased it. Yet in sticking by their task, the men felt in their
hearts they had really missed Christmas and rather groused a
bit at the ill luck which kept them away from their families.

When the weary crew returned to Williamson, one of
the machinists told them to accompany Dan to his office. As
the bleary-eyed, exhausted men entered the office, they were
greeted with the sight of a big Christmas tree brought in from
the hills. Under it were piled presents for the whole crew;
jugs of wine from the Italian workers, crocks of corn liquor
sent over by the Kentucky mountaineers; roast hams and
turkeys donated by the fire department; and a varied assort-
ment of ties, socks and shirts. The joy these gifts brought to
his co-workers recalled to Dan the words of the Old Testa-
ment, "A gift is as a precious stone in the eyes of him that
hath it."

Dan found that the United States Marshal for Kentucky
was named Dan Cunningham and one day, when the rail-
roader stopped by the fire house, the chief told him how Devil
Anse Hatfield, powerhouse of the Hatfield clan, had sworn
to shoot Cunningham on sight. Devil Anse, Captain Anderson
Hatfield, had been one of the top leaders in the Hatfield-
McCoy mountain feud from the days of 1882 when Johnse
Hatfield had attempted to elope with Rosanna McCoy. The

resultant ambushes by both clans brought death to both Hatfields and McCoys and the feud became the most prominent in mountaineer history.

Later Dan met Marshal Cunningham, a one-man army who was quick on the draw when necessity demanded it, and therefore, one of the most respected and well liked men in the region. Marshal Cunningham related to Dan the time he met Devil Anse in Williamson and Hatfield did not recognize him. As the marshal had to make his arrest in Kentucky, he asked Hatfield if he could cross the Tug in the same rowboat. Soon Devil Anse was rowing his hated enemy across the river. All went well until a quick burst of wind whipped back the marshal's coat. Devil Anse saw the officer's badge and, without a moment's hesitation, leaped from the boat, turned it over and spilled the Kentucky marshal into the river. Hatfield made his way back to the West Virginia bank and Cunningham reached the Kentucky shore.

Devil Anse had a way of meeting up with trouble. Soon he was involved in a fight with a Williamson policeman and was promptly slapped in jail. Word flew across the Tug to the Kentucky hills and the Hatfield clan warned that, if Devil Anse wasn't released by morning, they would come over to Williamson and blow up the jail.

The next morning Dan went down to the jail to look at the captive mountaineer leader. He found a crowd around the jail with the object of interest a hole in the wall where two bricks had been knocked out.

"That where the Hatfields are going to throw in the powder stick?" Dan humorously asked an onlooker.

"Nope," replied the man, "didn't you know that Devil Anse broke outa the calaboose last night and 'pears that's the hole he crawled through. Yep, all six feet plus of the rascal and him weighing over 250 pounds. Jailer says must have been a tight squeeze for Devil Anse. But I ain't seen none o' his skin stickin' on them bricks!"

All the stories about Captain Hatfield aroused Dan's desire to meet the colorful mountaineer chief. Finding out one of his shop men knew Devil Anse, Dan's persuasion soon had the man agreeing to take him to the Hatfield home.

On a Sunday morning, the two men crossed the Tug, borrowed horses and commenced riding into the mountains. As they rode along, Dan's friend said, "Boss, you better watch your step when you meet Devil Anse. Likely as not first thing he'll do is offer you a drink of corn likker. He's mighty proud of his own corn and any criticism of it is just inviting yourself to be the center of attention at an early funeral."

When the horsemen reached the Hatfield house, Devil Anse arose from the stump on which he had been seated, held up the rifle he was cleaning until he recognized his friend. Dan could see that Devil Anse was a large man with a beak nose like an eagle, bushy eye brows and ice gray eyes. Those cold eyes were on Dan as he dismounted.

"Who be that long critter with you?" asked Captain Hatfield. The friend answered, "He's the railroad boss over at Williamson. Mighty great admirer of yours, Devil Anse. Says he'd bet his last dollar you could plug a squirrel on the highest tree in any o' these hills." This compliment relaxed Devil Anse until the speaker said, "Yep, Captain Hatfield, this is Dan Cunningham."

"Dan Cunningham!" Devil Anse brought his rifle up to his waist. "Son, you any kin to that skunk of a United States Marshal, that polecat what stinks up the Kentucky hills?"

Assured that Dan was not even remotely related to the Kentucky marshal, Devil Anse put down his rifle, grabbed Dan's hand and gave it a grasp which practically crushed the four fingers into one lump of bruised flesh.

As predicted, Devil Anse invited his visitors over to the still, which was in a dense wood beside a small mountain stream and so camouflaged that revenue officers could have walked right past it without noticing any evidence of illicit liquor making.

With no cups or glasses on hand, Hatfield picked up a gourd—such as mountain people use to dip in springs—put it under the worm of the still and let about a pint of corn run into it. Dan took the out-thrust container, held his breath for a moment, and then poured a drink into his mouth. If he had bitten down on the red hot hinges of Hell, the sensation would have been no greater.

For a moment all Time stood still and Dan felt as if at any moment he would go up in a billow of smoke and flame and enter a Better Land where all corn liquor was aged before being drunk.

Devil Anse looked mighty serious as if he were his Satanic Majesty passing judgment on the damned. Dan smacked his aching lips which felt as if he were slapping together raw steaks. The hills seemed to echo back his over loud words "Good! Best corn likker! Good! Good!"

Dan's companion, used to the deadly concoction, swallowed his drink with evident pleasure. Devil Anse grasped the gourd, still almost full, and drank its contents down as if he were gulping mountain spring water.

After that Devil Anse invited the men to his house for a possum dinner and when, following the meal, the men were leaving, Devil Anse said, "Mighty fine having you over. Reckon though I was a mite disappointed you wasn't that other Dan Cunningham. Would have made this a mighty fine Sunday just to shoot him!"

Apparently Captain Hatfield was impressed by Dan's visit as several weeks later a giant man came into the shop saying that Devil Anse was his cousin; had told him to get a job from the all right railroad boss across the river. Noting the vigorous build of the man, Dan put him on his track force. Three days later the Hatfield worker entered Dan's office and demanded his pay. Dan explained he would have to wait until payday. The mountaineer shook his head, started taking off his coat, and said, "Young fellow, you uns done hired me and you uns pay me right now!"

Dan reached into his pocket.

Devil Anse still surveys the mountains. A life size statue stands on a hill near Omar, about thirteen miles from Logan, West Virginia. Captain Hatfield, bare-headed and bearded, is atop a four foot granite base. The figure, made at a cost of $3,000, came from Italy. Devil Anse is pictured with his hands at his side. It would have been more life-like if the sculptor had put Hatfield's fingers around his rifle.

On the back of the base is inscribed, "Capt. Anderson Hatfield 1839-1921. Levicy Chafin, His Wife, 1842-1929. On the other side the inscription is, "Johnson, William A., Robert L., Nancy, Elliot R., Mary Elizabeth, Elias, Troy, Joseph D., Rose, Willis E., Tennis S.; Their Children."

In the years which Dan spent at Williamson he made a number of acquaintances among the mountain people. One of the farmers asked Dan over to his place to see a coffin he had made of curly poplar which he had cut and seasoned himself.

Dan had no desire to look at the coffin until the farmer mentioned he also possessed some smooth corn liquor which had been well aged by peach pits. The appeal of a generous sample of really fine corn, offset the thought of the coffin or even a farmhouse stacked to the ceiling with coffins.

So, on arrival at the farmer's home, Dan quaffed the corn, and was prepared for the vision of the farmer's final resting place. The mountaineer took Dan to his bedroom and from under a handsome four poster bed pulled out his coffin. Even though the coffin was made from such a beautiful piece of wood, Dan couldn't understand how anyone could sleep over such an object; however, he was informed this was customary among many natives. The well-to-do farmers were proud of the fine coffins they made for themselves. But they never made elaborate coffins for their wives. Wives would have to be satisfied with the thought that the master of the house would be well "put away."

Dan attended the funeral of a mountain woman, whose husband had worked for him at the shop, and who told Dan he couldn't understand what caused his wife's death. He explained she had certainly been healthy that day as she had plowed five acres of ground, cut a cord of wood, put out the washing for the family of ten children, butchered a hog and cleaned it, and then was getting supper when she sat down and died.

Halfway through the funeral, the preacher stopped, said, "Now I will pause to give the friends and relatives a chance to mourn." Never had Dan heard such weird shouts and chants as the mountain people cried out for their dead. His spine tingled at the eerie noises. Abruptly all was quiet. The preacher resumed his sermon.

A week after the funeral, the bereaved husband called by Dan's office to inform him he had a new wife. Although the man was nearly sixty, he had married a girl about sixteen years old. Several days after the funeral, he went to a neighbor's house on a nearby hillside, explained since the death of his wife he needed someone to keep house and look after his patch of ground. The neighbor obligingly called out his six girls and told the friend to take his pick. Naturally the prettiest one was selected. The couple stopped by a Justice of the Peace; went home to a one room log cabin where the bride and groom slept along with the ten children. Later Dan learned that the man was raising children by his new wife so apparently the crowded room was no detriment.

When Dan wasn't getting local color from the mountaineers, he was being amused by Chief Wingo's activities. Chief Wingo's contribution to the opening of the new roundhouse had become a classic story along the Norfolk and Western. Wingo was asked to attend a company meeting at Roanoke and, on his return to Williamson, Dan inquired what Wingo had learned in Roanoke.

Chief Wingo replied he had finally found out what made electric lights burn. At Roanoke Wingo had seen an electrician pouring oil into a transformer and had asked the reason for it. The explanation was that after oil had been poured into the transformer, a man in the powerhouse pumped oil out through the electric wires and this made the electric lights burn.

Among Chief Wingo's various activities was the Redmen, an organization in which he was grand factotum. On one occasion the Redmen dressed up in Indian regalia for an initiation at a schoolhouse near Williamson. The initiation's high spot was when the new member was tied to a stake. With the use of red powder for flames, the paleface was "burned alive" in the best Indian tradition. Precisely as the Redmen broke into their war dance around the stake-bound victim, a band of older natives of Mingo county, who had encountered **real** Indians in previous years, charged the initiation **party** with rifles ready for action. The natives thought real Indians had again hit the warpath.

Chief Wingo and his make-believe Indians fled for their lives.

Dan appeared at this same schoolhouse later when he was a candidate for the West Virginia legislature on the Democratic ticket. As his work in getting the new water supply for Williamson and his position with the railroad had won him many friends, Dan was persuaded to run for the office. Following a campaign speech at the school, he was shaking hands with his audience when a long-whiskered hill-billy approached him. Greeting him in his best professional manner, Dan inquired, "Who are you for, friend?"

The hill-billy hit the center of an empty tomato can with a squirt of amber, wiped the tobacco juice off his whis-kers with the side of his hand, said crisply, "Stranger, I'm fer anybody who is agin the government!"

This West Virginia region was normally Republican and Dan found he had a hard fight on his hands. Too, the campaign was proving costly as money was flowing freely on both sides. One negro came up to Dan and said he'd like to vote for him, but first he'd have to be "boughten off" with some money.

"Uncle, who paid you to vote in the last election?" asked Dan.

"The Republicans gimme ten dollars," replied the darkie.

"Is that all you got?"

The colored man grinned, "Well, suh, the Democrats gimme five dollars."

"So you got ten dollars from the Republicans and five dollars from the Democrats for your vote. I suppose, Uncle, you voted the Republican ticket."

Dan looked amused at the negro who thought a moment before he replied, "No, suh, Boss, you is all wrong. I'se voted for the Democrats as I figured they 'twas the party what was the least corrupt."

Before election day was reached, the campaign grew so heated the Norfolk and Western officials in the main office asked Dan to withdraw as they felt the contest had reached a point where it would interfere with his railroad work, and, too, the political situation was fraught with dynamite for a railroad man. Dan complied with the request.

Whereas Dan liked Williamson and the men with whom he worked, he had tired of living in the coal fields. Williamson was built along the mountains and the roofs of the houses— four stories high in front—would touch the mountain in back. One day Donna, then eight years of age, fell out of the front yard and broke her arm. The incline of the country was so steep that once when Dan inquired why a passenger train was late he found a cow had fallen out of her pasture on-to the top of the baggage car of the train. Coal was so prevalent that all Williamson residents had to do to get fuel was to dig it out of their basement floors. Too, with the increase of the Norfolk and Western coal traffic, Williamson was a very hard shop to run. Around 130 locomotives, mostly Mallets, were turned every day.

Dan felt after three or four years at Williamson he deserved a change and appealed to Superintendent of Motive Power Alexander Kearney for a better location. He suggested if the Norfolk and Western couldn't find him such a position perhaps some other railroad might offer him a job. Kearney laughed and told Dan he had made such a fine record the company would have a most difficult time locating a man to replace him and, as for a foreign railroad offer, "you had better forget it, Dan, as in Williamson you are buried from the outside world."

While Dan was at Williamson, he had received many letters from his brother, Frank, who had entered V. P. I. in 1907 and followed Dan's footsteps by playing in the line on the freshman team. That season the varsity team won the state championship, downed Georgetown and George Washington, but lost to Davidson and Navy. Dan hoped his brother would play for the V. P. I. varsity in his sophomore year; however, Frank, smaller built than Dan, was too light to make the squad.

When Frank left Blacksburg, he returned to work for the Norfolk and Western at Roanoke and was soon in charge of testing mechanical stokers on the railroad. This meant that he was continually riding engines. Walking to the roundhouse in the dark of an early morning, Frank turned his ankle on a broken place in the wooden sidewalks and was forced to return home and miss his assignment to ride a test. The locomotive went out without him and shortly thereafter blew up killing the crew. Dan spent a sleepless night when he learned how close he had come to losing his younger brother. A few years later Frank, who had married Ruby Grayson Lawrence, of Martinsville, Virginia, left the Norfolk and Western to become assistant general manager of the Standard Stoker Company, Erie, Pennsylvania.

Dan had an outside caller one afternoon at Williamson. Dan looked at the business card sent to him and read "W. W. Lemen, Sales Representative, Ingersall Rand Company." He knew then that his visitor had come to the wrong railroad office. Yet on an impulse, he asked the visitor in. In a few moments he was shaking hands with a thin, sickly looking young man, who appeared as if he should be calling on a doctor rather than at the roundhouse.

The young salesman managed to twist a wan smile on his face, said, "Mr. Cunningham, I'll tell you the truth. I'm up against it for orders. Two weeks ago I got this job with Ingersall Rand and ten days ago I came through Williamson and landed in my hotel with yellow jaundice. Hell, I haven't been able to make a call and my expenses are piling up. If you can give me an air tool order—I don't care how small it is—I can send it in to my company and maybe they won't fire me."

"Sorry, Mr. Lemen," Dan answered as he toyed with a paper weight, "but I can't do a thing. This isn't a buying office. I couldn't even put in an order for this thingamabob. Everything is ordered out of the main office at Roanoke."

The caller looked so depressed Dan, feeling sorry for him, commented, "Now it cannot be as bad as all that. I don't think your company will fire you. They'll realize the lack of orders from you is some bad luck on your part. You'll be getting business as soon as you hit the railroads' purchasing departments."

These words failed to console the salesman and he was

such a picture of dejection Dan racked his brain to think of any possible companies in Williamson which might be interested in air tools. Finally he remembered Colonel Bob Williamson and the Williamson Coal and Coke Company. Sometime back Colonel Bob had asked him if he knew of a good air compressor. Dan picked up the phone and, after a few minutes conversation replaced the receiver. "We're going to take a long walk, Lemen," he said, "and maybe you'll feel better. I called a company in the market for a new air compressor and the president said to bring you over."

The coal company office was two miles away from the roundhouse and the path led over a mountain trail. Lemen, suffering from the aftermath of the illness, stumbled often and Dan helped him over the rough spots.

Bob Williamson looked at Lemen's pictures of the air compressor, asked, "Dan Cunningham, is this young man's compressor a good one?"

"It's as good as any in America," Dan answered.

"Dan, if you recommend it that is good enough for me," the colonel replied. He took out his pen and began to fill the order blank.

In half an hour Dan and Lemen started back along the mountain path and Lemen needed little help this time. His health had improved rapidly for he had in his pocket an order for a five thousand foot air compressor costing $38,000.

Before the grateful salesman left the Norfolk and Western shop, he asked Dan if he could do anything for him in return for his landing the big business. Dan laughed and said, "Nothing, Lemen. Nothing at all except let me know how you come out with your company." Later Dan had a message from Lemen telling him on the strength of the order he had been given an excellent territory in Canada as district manager.

Regularity of life at Williamson was broken by some trouble with the residents of Little Italy. One of the occupants of the Italian settlement went on a rampage against his neighbors and burned a box car used as living quarters. The offender was speedily taken into court where Dan had to testify the box car was on railroad property.

The judge knew unless some drastic action was taken the Italians would continue their spasmodic outbursts and later on serious trouble might break out endangering the lives of many people. He found the worker guilty of arson and said it looked as if the only thing possible was a stiff sentence, perhaps ninety-nine years. The prisoner was asked if he had anything to say.

"Judge," the Italian said, "I got nothing to say except about my friend, Dan Cunningham, the beeg boss. Maybe I be gone for awhile. Maybe I be gone away from home for ninety-nine years. Beeg boss is one damned fine fellow. So please, Mister Judge, will you tell the beeg boss he musta look after my wife until I get back after the ninety-nine years."

Dan, after hearing these words, looked at the Italian's wife. She was well over 200 pounds and looked as if she could eat her weight in ravioli every night. As the judge was a friend of Dan's, the "beeg boss" stepped up to the bench, spoke a few words into the judge's ear.

After the judge had chuckled awhile, he turned to the prisoner, "The beeg boss has said some very influential words in your favor and he has told me how unfair it is to separate you and your loving wife. On the condition that you never get in trouble again, I'm going to suspend your sentence. Case dismissed."

That night all of Little Italy celebrated and Dan had to join in with his Italian workers and drink copiously of "dago red" wine. He was the new Garibaldi of the Italian population of Williamson and, from then on, he had no real trouble with the friendly Italian workers. Dan often wondered what he would have done with the *signora* had her husband been sent away "for awhile."

The Williamson shop had its characters whom Dan still remembers. There was the Italian, Sam Siallis, whose job was to babbit (put lead in) "croschets," as he called the locomotive crossheads and, who, it is said, spent practically his whole working life in wrecking shells as there were nearly always some engines in the Scioto Division to be repaired. Len D. Gillett, loquacious master mechanic, told some of the tallest stories along the lines and he became famous throughout the South for his tale of being the designer and builder of the great Virginia Natural Bridge, the 90 foot stone bridge across a 210 foot gorge, cut by Cedar Creek, between Buchanan and Lexington. That Thomas Jefferson in July, 1775, came into possession of the Natural Bridge and some 150 adjoining acres for a payment of 20 shillings, did not make one iota of difference to Gillett. In conversation no matter what famous railroad man was brought up, for example, Daniel Willard, president of the Baltimore and Ohio, Len would always say, "Why I taught Dan Willard how to fire and run a locomotive." If some railroader would bring up the fact that Willard left Massachusetts Agricultural College in 1879 to begin his railroad career on the Vermont Central; a few months afterwards was a fireman and engineer on the Connecticut and Passumpsic River railroad, Len would immediately take on such a New England background he could pass for one of the Green Mountain boys. Or should someone mention George Blow Elliott, then assistant general counsel for the Atlantic Coast Line—he became president of the A. C. L. in 1928—Len would remark, "Yeah, taught him how to fire right after he got out of V. M. I.," disregarding the fact Elliott did not start his career in railroading in the cab of a locomotive.

Another Williamson shop character was Henry Nye, a shop laborer, always known as Coxie. He held a unique "Division Championship"; the "most fired man on the division." Coxie had a set routine. He would get his paycheck, get it cashed, get drunk, get fired, get remorse, and get his job back. Everytime Coxie became intoxicated, although he never caused trouble, Dan vowed he would not rehire him, but the big tears in Coxie's eyes, as he swore off "the Devil's brew," would soften Dan's heart.

Dan was superintendent of a small mission Sunday School and, prior to class time, he went to his railroad office to check over business. One Sabbath morning Dan walked by the freight station and found Coxie cold-sober sitting on a rail.

"Good morning, Boss," greeted Coxie.

"Good morning, Coxie," answered Dan. "I'll be back

from my office in an hour and, since you are in fine shape, I want you to go to Sunday School at the mission with me."

Coxie's face fell. This was no reward for his good behavior. He looked at his faded blue shirt and shook his head, "Sorry, sir, but I ain't dressed up well enough to go to church."

Dan assured him that the Lord would welcome him even in the old blue shirt and he would pick him up. After Dan had finished at the railroad, he walked back by the freight station. He could see Coxie all "fussed up" in his best "going to meeting" outfit. Finally the old soak had religion thought Dan. But, as Dan neared Coxie, he found the true situation a bit different. Apparently the worker had found his dressed up clothes too much a concession to Sunday and had offset his softening of attitude with a quick over indulgence in alcohol.

The sight of Dan brought Coxie staggering to his feet. He fumbled with a loose button on his coat, said thickly, "I knew the Lord wouldn't want to see me, Boss, until I felt happy. Let's be off to the damned meeting house!"

One of Dan's best friends at Williamson was Russel Henley, the night roundhouse foreman. Dan predicted that Henley had a brilliant future with the railroad and the prediction came true. Today Russel Henley is the general superintendent of motive power for the Norfolk and Western.

Walking past the Western Union office one March day in 1912, Dan was stopped by Operator Vaughn, who thrust a telegram into his hands. The wire read, "You have been recommended by W. W. Lemen for position as Superintendent of Salt Lake City Shops, Denver and Rio Grande railroad." Dan looked at the signature to the wire "J. F. Enright, superintendent of motive power, Denver and Rio Grande railroad, Denver, Colorado."

So from distant Denver came a wire to a railroader "buried" in Williamson, West Virginia. W. W. Lemen hadn't forgotten the man who had landed the $38,000 order for him!

The reaction to the offer at the Cunningham home was favorable. Inez was happy she could take the girls away from the coal fields. Dan was happy as the offer meant a considerable increase in salary. After lunch, Dan wired his resignation to Roanoke and his acceptance to Denver. Later he learned

President L. E. Johnson was very disturbed when he found out an N. & W. man would quit to work for any other railroad in the country. Dan stayed at Williamson until the N. & W., after several weeks, sent down a replacement, A. E. Willard, who had been the roundhouse foreman at Portsmouth.

When the time came for his departure, Dan was given a party at the railroad Y. M. C. A. at East Williamson. A special train was run from Williamson to carry his friends. There was a big banquet, toasts were drunk and speeches made. All Williamson shared the honor of having been discovered by a railroad "way out west." Presents were passed out and Dan found himself with a new silver service and a fitted travelling bag. Inez looked admiringly at her new matching travelling bag. In Little Italy the workers talked of the sad departure of the "beeg boss" for a land filled with Indians and buffalo and some people called Mormons and they thought Dan was a little bit crazy to leave such a fine place as Williamson.

Across the Tug, the friendly Kentucky mountaineers smacked their lips over their corn liquor and swore that the railroad's boss man would never "drink likker like this in them wilds o' Utah!"

$\mathcal{D}$AN CUNNINGHAM climbed into the cab of a Ten Wheeler locomotive at Helper, Utah. With him was W. J. Bennett, D. & R. G. master mechanic for the Salt Lake and Green River Division, who had come up from Salt Lake City to meet the new superintendent of shops, who had stopped over at Denver on his way west from Williamson, West Virginia. Bennett, an Englishman experienced on the Chicago, Indianapolis and Louisville railroad (the Monon), introduced Dan to Fred Cowan, the engineer on the 740.

"All our locomotives are as good as the 740," Bennett explained and Cowan, who knew the fine power the Norfolk and Western had, winked at Dan. The 740, with its big sixty-seven inch wheels, let out a few puffs as if Bennett's praise had reached its ears and, trying to cover up for its deficiencies, the 740 was adding some exclamations of its own. With four engines aiding the 740, the ten car train commenced ascending the 4 per cent grade to Soldier Summit.

On main lines throughout the country the predominating grades are from 0.01 per cent to 1.00 per cent. Some mountain territory requires grades of 2.2 per cent. All grades over 2.2 per cent on main lines are not common. The steepest grade on a standard steam line in the United States (1940 survey) is at Madison, Indiana, where the Pennsylvania ascends the Ohio river and the grade is 5.89 per cent. On a main line of a railroad, the steepest known grade is at Saluda Hill, in the Blue Ridge mountains of North Carolina. The grade of the Southern railroad there is 4.7 per cent. Perhaps the most difficult grade of all was on the Uintah railway in Garfield county, Colorado, abandoned around 1938. Dan, years later, heard yarns of this railroad from his friend Lucian C. Sprague, its vice president and general manager. Sprague is now president of the Minneapolis and St. Louis railroad. The 72 mile Uintah had a five mile 7.5 per cent grade between Atchee and Baxter Pass. Incidentally, this narrow gauge railroad had a curve at Morrow Castle which was originally 80 degrees although standard gauge curves reaching as high as 11 degrees are rare. The

Uintah had 233 curves over a thirteen mile stretch. In 1912, the Denver and Rio Grande railroad probably had more steep grade track in proportion to its total miles, than any major line in the United States.

Slowly climbing, the 740 and its cars reached Soldier Summit, the top of the Wasatch range; the helper engines were released and sent on to Tucker at the foot of the 4 per cent descent. There these engines would meet the east bound trains which had made the 2 per cent grade from Thistle Junction and add their power to the push-pull combination necessary to make the climb up to Soldier Summit.

As the train started down toward Salt Lake City, Dan could see the track was relatively straight with very few curves. It seemed to Dan as if Cowan was holding back the 740 to keep the train from any chance of a runaway. Dan looked at Bennett, "Say, Mr. Bennett, it's not that I'm unaccustomed to mountain railroading in the east, but this is one damned steep descent and what if somehow a train would get out of control?"

Bennett chuckled. "We've thought of that, Mr. Cunningham. You wait a few minutes and you'll see the answer."

Not long afterward, the 740 ground to a halt and Cowan blew his whistle for a switch stop. After a few moments, Fred widened the throttle and the train resumed its descent.

At Bennett's instructions, Dan peered out of the cab and soon saw the train run by a side track upgrading into the hills. Bennett explained, "That's the runaway track. When Fred blew for a switch stop, the switch tender knew the train was under control, so he threw the switch for the main line instead of the runaway spur. If the train had not been under control, we would have run up the spur and come to a standstill. Then we'd have called for help from Soldier Summit or Tucker to shove us back on the main line."

"This is one helluva way to get down a mountain," Dan commented. But Fred kept his Ten Wheeler out of trouble and the descent was made without resorting to the runaway tracks. But at Springville, the 740 lost a spring and going through American Fork the locomotive parted with one of its four guide bars. Just as the train pulled into Salt Lake City, a cylinder head was knocked out. Nevertheless, the 740 rolled into the terminal on time and Bennett proudly exclaimed, "My boy, see what good power can do!"

Dan felt the credit was perhaps due to Cowan's handling of mediocre power, but he remained silent on the subject. After the first class power on the N. & W. Dan was surprised at the type of engines sometimes used by the D. & R. G. in conquering the high mountains.

But Dan's real astonishment came the next day when he first entered the Salt Lake shops of the Denver and Rio Grande March 19, 1912. Knowing the railroad had excellent shops at Burnham, Colorado, and under General Foreman F. T. Owens were turning out superior work, he wasn't prepared for the situation at Salt Lake City.

The Salt Lake roundhouse had eight stalls built out of corrugated iron, no heat, and with dirty pits full of water. In addition there were eighteen stalls in a reconverted narrow gauge roundhouse and the roof of this was so low locomotives could not be headed in as the smoke stacks would hit the top. The pits had not been set out properly and it made certain repairs difficult. Between the turntable and the erecting shop were lead tracks jammed with dead and disabled locomotives; and, to get an engine out of the back shop, sometimes a day had to be wasted moving the bad power. The following day the lead tracks would be full again.

Dan watched Japanese laborers changing tires. Locomotives had to be wheeled and unwheeled on an antiquated hoist. After the tires were heated over a wood fire, the Nipponese gathered up old sacks and handled the hot steel locomotive tires. This usually meant somebody got badly burned.

Walking up to such a group of Japs, Dan said, "Look, no use killing yourselves. I'll show you how to use a crane in changing tires. It's an easier and safer method." Dan reasoned that perhaps the Orientals' philosophy had something alien to the use of cranes. Such was not the case. The shop had no crane for this purpose and depended on the muscles of the Japanese.

Soon Dan had the men rig up a small jib crane for handling wheels and tires; the Japs were highly pleased with the new method and the railroad doctor was kept less busy applying salves.

The more Dan saw of the Salt Lake shops the first day, the more discouraged he became. After the shops of the Norfolk and Western and even the under-manned shops of the Santa Fe at Needles, this was the worst mess he had encountered. In the afternoon, while Dan was still in a perplexed frame of mind over the condition of the shops, a committee from the Union entered his office.

"Mr. Cunningham, have you got a Union card?" queried the committee spokesman. Dan remembered when he had been a spokesman for the Union machinists at Roanoke.

"Gentlemen, I am the superintendent of shops, an official of the Rio Grande, and, as such, I don't need a card. What else can I do for you?" Actually Dan had a card. When he was promoted to a foreman at Needles, he had been given his withdrawal card from the International Association of Machinists. The Union had done this as it did not think it rational for former machinists, when promoted, to sit in on the Union transactions.

The shop committee went into a quick huddle and announced its decision. "Mr. Cunningham, you can do something for us. We will give you just thirty minutes to get your card—or we'll run you out of this shop!"

This bombastic statement let out Dan's feelings. "Listen, you damned bunch of bastards, I don't intend to get a card while I'm on the job and all of you can go to the devil. And, furthermore, I'll be an official at Salt Lake when all of you are pounding back doors begging for a handout. Get out of my office!"

The shop committee made a quick exit and no more was heard from them. Dan's words came true as far as he was concerned for he was to remain an officer of the Rio Grande—with the exception of the little over a year he was superintendent of motive power on the Denver and Salt Lake railroad—until his retirement some 31 years later.

At the Salt Lake shop, the men soon found out they had a boss, but one who was in all matters square with them as Dan realized the problems of labor from the experience as

a machinist on the Norfolk and Western and the Santa Fe.
Nevertheless, Dan realized had he allowed the arrogant shop
committee to bluff him, it doubtless would have weakened
his position as an official.

Machinery in the shop, Dan found, was with few excep-
tions old and worn out. This made it almost impossible for
the machinists to keep the locomotives in good shape and the
result was thirty or forty engine failures a day. Sometimes
engine crews were on the sixteen hour law before the trains
got fifty miles out of Salt Lake City. "Dog catchers," as the
relief crews were called, had to be sent out to replace the
regular crews. The engineers and firemen on the Salt Lake
Division won Dan's respect for their capable handling of
unreliable power.

The machinists at the shop, when a journal ran hot and
cut the brass out, instead of dropping the wheels and fixing
the journal, slipped in a new crown brass which would run
hot as the journal was rough. Such a practice led to potential
engine failures.

Several days after Dan arrived on his new job, he received a report that Engine 1151 would not steam and was
useless as a helper engine. This engine had a short time previously been turned out of the Salt Lake shop with heavy
repairs and was a regular passenger helper in the mountains.
Dan ordered the 1151 back.

When the engine reentered the shops, Dan found the
cylinders were one half inch out of round, the bull rings were
one inch smaller than the cylinders and the valves were out.
Dan instructed his erecting shop foreman to see new bull
rings were made and to get a boring bar and see that the
cylinders were rebored. The foreman informed Dan there
was no boring bar and, in his year at Salt Lake, not a cylinder
had been rebored.

Despite the foreman's statement, Dan was certain that
at one time the shop must have had a boring bar and searching among the scrap, he found parts of an old bar in the
tool room. Missing parts were made in the shop and soon
Dan had the 1151 rebored and in good shape.

The boring bar was on a twenty-four hour shift as Dan

The famed *Shou-wa-no,* first freight locomotive on the Denver and Rio Grande, in all her shiny splendor as she enters service in 1871. Photo credit: *Rio Grande*

First standard gauge Rio Grande Western train to leave the Salt Lake City station, 1890. Photo credit: *Rio Grande*

Indomitable GENERAL WILLIAM JACKSON PALMER, founder of the Rio
Grande Railroad: his daring dream of a transportation empire materialized in a
land of rugged mountain fastness.   Photo credit: *Rio Grande*

Poster proclaiming the conquest of the Rockies.   Photo credit: *Rio Grande* used it on all engines of the same class as the 1151. This move was prompted by news from the railroad central office they were going to build a coal wharf at Provo as the locomotives such as the 1151 could only take forty empties to Provo, 48 miles away, and then run light to Thistle for coal. Dan thought these engines could give far better performances and the lack of efficiency was because of the out of round cylinders. He requested the management to hold off until he could run a test.

This test, if successful, would show the Rio Grande top officers the railroad hadn't made a mistake in sending all the way back to the N. & W. to get a superintendent of shops. On the way out from Williamson, Dan had stopped at Denver and there he met W. W. Lemen, who had recommended him. Lemen was with the Galena Oil Company and had the contract for lubricating the D. & R. G. Dan had no intention of letting Lemen down.

With the locomotives in shape, Dan ran a test train to Thistle and back with six tons of coal left. This round trip run was made in eight hours with eighty cars against the former time of sixteen hours to Provo with only forty cars.

At Denver, the transportation department was well pleased with the progress initiated by their new Salt Lake shop superintendent. And as reward, they rushed through Dan's requisition for a new boring bar and told him from then on he could rebore cylinders to his heart's content.

Dan noticed the workmen in the car department of the shop seemed to move at a slower gait than the southern mechanics. It was as if their tempo followed some unseen instruction. This disturbed Dan as he reasoned more work could be turned out if the men picked up their pace. Yet he knew if he tried to push the men, the reaction might be negative.

Investigation revealed the source of the slow gait. In the car department was a large low speed stationary engine with a fifteen foot flywheel which made approximately sixty revolutions a minute. As soon as convenient, Dan had this slow engine replaced with a high speed Buckeye engine which made sixteen hundred revolutions a minute.

Subconsciously the workmen readjusted their working pace with the fast Buckeye and their output increased by almost thirty per cent. Dan swears the men stepped faster and had more energy as the change in engines had the same effect as increasing the tempo of the music at a dance.

Nevertheless, one of the major men in the Denver mechanical department wasn't satisfied with the advances made at Salt Lake and when Dan told him, "I think the situation while still bad is improving as we cannot change the manner of work overnight when outmoded machinery has hampered the workmen for years," the official flared up with, "You were brought here from the N. & W. to do good work and now you admit the work isn't good. I'd have a happy job if the Rio Grande stopped at Grand Junction, Colorado. I wish the Salt Lake shops were in Hell and you were in the deepest part of torment under a steam hammer!"

This remark struck Dan so funny he burst out laughing and, when reprimanded by the visiting official, Dan replied, "Maybe you think I should cry instead of laugh. Well, there's not a job in the United States I'd cry over, and I certainly don't intend to weep over this matter when I'm doing a fine job with the material available."

The official returned to Denver where he reported to E. L. Brown, president of the Denver and Rio Grande, "If damned Dan Cunningham at Salt Lake fell into a cesspool, he'd come up with a bunch of bananas in one hand, a new suit of clothes in the other, and saying, 'I'm doing fine!' " This report, although not so intended, made Big Dan a friend of the D. & R. G. president until Brown's death.

When Dan recounted his trouble with the mechanical department official, Frank Ainsworth, who in September, 1902, had become air brake superintendent for the D. & R. G. and later went with Westinghouse Air Brake Company, countered with this interesting story of the difficulties he had getting automatic air on the Rio Grande narrow gauge lines. Said Ainsworth:

"On a trip over the Rio Grande in 1902 in connection with air conditions and brake maintenance, I introduced myself as general air brake instructor so as to get the best cooperation. This gave me an opportunity to talk with a great number of employees, especially engineers.

"At Gunnison the leading topic of conversation was the hazardous operation of loaded freight trains over Marshall Pass, the top of the Continental Divide, and at an altitude of 10,950 feet, as well as over many narrow gauge sections of the road where heavy grades existed. I was told of many instances where railroad employees were picked up in baskets after train runaways. The long winter season was the most hazardous as the snow piled so high the trainmen, in jumping from the runaway trains, could not clear the equipment and were drawn under the wheels. Most men stated the brakes controlled the wheels while intact, but if for some reason the brake pipe hose parted, they were turned loose on the grade with only the hand brakes which were wholly inadequate if the train gained momentum. The opinion among employees was that if automatic air was installed on the rolling stock, they would even more likely be killed, as none of them thought automatic air brakes could safely control the loaded trains on the long 4 per cent descending grades. This conviction of the employees was strengthened mostly by the engineers who had never worked with automatic air—not even on the Rio Grande's standard gauge lines which used automatic air brakes—and who had seen twenty or more years service on the narrow gauge.

"Disregarding the mortal fear on the part of the narrow gauge engineers—as well as some of the trainmen—on my return to Denver I called on the management with an urgent recommendation to modernize the brake equipment of the whole road. I heard nothing more of this for about a month at which time a loaded narrow gauge train ran away and derailed on the Marshall Pass grade, killing the engineer and seriously injuring the fireman. The engine went down in a canyon about 1,000 feet from the track and some of the cars followed it. After the conductor had walked two miles to Poncha Junction to report the wreck, he returned and found coyotes howling around the dead and injured. The fire still smoldering in the firebox glared through the open furnace door and kept the animals at a distance from the bodies which they came to mutilate. This accident caused great consternation among the Rio Grande management, and a Westinghouse Air Brake representative was called in and my previous recommendations approved.

"The conversion to the automatic brake equipment consumed approximately one year, although some test runs were made with selected automatic equipment during the transition period. On one of my test runs, the regular engineer refused to handle his train and went back to the way car. A road foreman from the standard gauge lines agreed to handle the train, and, on leaving Marshall Pass, the road foreman went through a snowdrift which came up to the base of the smoke stack. Those narrow gauge engines were wonderful in holding the rails in deep snow.

"When the air controlled train arrived at Salida, I met a bunch of engineers who were quite hostile, saying possibly the automatic air might hold the trains on Marshall Pass, but they could not control the trains on Villa Grove Branch which served the iron mines of the C. F. & I. and was a 4 per cent or better descending grade. Their contention was also automatic air brakes wouldn't work on the Monarch Branch where the altitude reached 11,650 feet and the grade ran from 4 to 6 per cent. But without the use of hand brakes—and with the trainmen certain all of us would be dashed to death—I ran the air brake tests successfully. Soon even the die-hard engineers on the Rio Grande narrow gauge lines were won over to automatic air brakes."

In connection with air brakes, it is interesting to note the rate of emergency brake action with the "AB" brake is 930 feet a second. On a mile long train, brakes can be applied in less than six seconds. In the early days of railroading no satisfactory brake was developed although over 300 patents had been granted for railroad brakes prior to George Westinghouse's invention of the straight air-brake in 1868. The original Westinghouse brake was only partially satisfactory, but in 1872 Westinghouse developed an automatic triple-valve air brake which was a vast improvement over his original brake and by 1884 practically all passenger trains in this country were equipped with Westinghouse brakes. Adoption of the brake for freight service was slower as the development of an efficient freight brake was more difficult. Improvement on brakes was studied in a railroad laboratory at Altoona, Pennsylvania, in 1893 and after two years the laboratory was transferred to Purdue University and continual tests there and elsewhere have resulted in numerous brake improvements. From 1929 to 1932 road tests led to the adoption of the modern "AB" air-brake for freight service. When one considers the importance of brakes in any moving vehicle, perhaps the skepticism of the narrow gauge trainmen in "risking their lives" with the automatic air cannot be too harshly criticized.

At Salt Lake City Dan learned the remarkable story of General William Jackson Palmer, who had meant as much to Rocky Mountain railroad pioneering as "Billy" Mahone had to Southern rail progress.

"General Palmer, it's no use. You can never carry freight and passengers up and over those mountains to any benefit. It's not worthwhile and it's impossible to carry out your plans to advantage." So said scientific and civil engineers, gathered in a railroad headquarters tent in the Rocky Mountains of Colorado, to General William Jackson Palmer.

The verdict of the engineers was answered by Palmer, who jumped up, hit his fist on a table and said, "Gentlemen, the decision is made. It is going to be done. We will build the railroad!" General Palmer had helped push the Pennsylvania railroad over the Appalachians. He was determined to conquer the mighty Rockies. Behind him was the east and its heritage of railroad progress.

Born on a farm in Kent county, Delaware, September 17, 1836, William J. Palmer commenced his railroading career at the age of 17 as an engineer laying out the Hampfield railroad in Pennsylvania. While on this project he wrote Isaac H. Clothier, later one of Philadephia's great merchants:

"I am in the field nearly all the time from early morning until late in the evening, tramping over hills and across valleys, through woods and through fields of grain. Nothing stops us for a railroad line must be a straight one—a locomotive is not proficient in turning corners."

The above opinion was reversed later when Palmer sent
his adventurous narrow gauge trains spiraling up the Colorado
and Utah mountains on cork-screwing rails over which engineers said no trains could run.

When the War Between the States broke out, Palmer
resigned as private secretary to J. Edgar Thomson, president
of the Pennsylvania railroad, and organized and led, as captain, a cavalry troop attached to Anderson's Union command.
Perhaps Palmer's most exciting experience in the war was
when—as a spy in civilian clothes and under an assumed name
—he was captured by Southern troops in Virginia and im-
prisoned in Castle Thunder, the former tobacco factory used
as a prison in Richmond.

Palmer needed the aid of no Elizabeth Van Lew in getting out of prison. Northern authorities immediately sought
to exchange Palmer as he was in danger of being shot under
conditions of warfare as he had been captured out of uniform.
Before this exchange could be brought about, a group of
Confederate officers entered the prison. One walked by Palmer and said in a low voice, "There is a vessel coming down the
James River. This is the former Union *Merrimac* converted
into a mighty ironclad by the Confederates and is called the
Virginia. It will attack the United States fleet at Hampton
Roads. When you reach Washington, tell President Lincoln."
The Confederate officer was himself a Northern spy. Palmer
was shortly thereafter exchanged. It would have meant a
great deal to the success of the Confederacy if the Southerners
had executed Palmer. It is said Palmer warned the North of
the *Merrimac's* mission in time for the Federals to rush the
Monitor against the Confederate ironclad and save the wooden
Yankee fleet and possibly the Union itself. General George H.
Thomas, known as "the Rock of Chickamauga," later commented, "The coolness displayed by Captain Palmer, when he
was captured by the enemy as a spy and during his captivity,
undoubtedly saved his life, under God, for such a man was
never born to die until his work was accomplished."

With the war's close, Palmer, by then a brigadier general,
was soon in charge of the construction of the Kansas Pacific
railroad (now a part of the Union Pacific) from Kit Carson

to Denver. When Palmer took over this task, he had no material in sight; yet he had the road graded, rails laid and bridges built in 150 days for the final 150 miles. And in 1870 the first railroad from the east entered Denver. Thirty-four year-old Palmer was also instrumental in bringing into Denver the Denver and Cheyenne railroad.

But the most important contribution of Palmer to railroading was still an idea in the young man's mind. He saw that while Denver, a town of about 5,000 population, had railroads to the north and running west to reach the mining camps, the expansive area of Colorado to the south was served by no rail lines. Palmer knew this potentially rich land would expand commercially with traffic facilities and, with the help of Dr. William A. Ball, an Englishman, established important financial contacts in England. Palmer hoped to run his railroad all the way to the Mexican border at El Paso, Texas. Commented General Palmer later:

"At that time no railway west of the Missouri was projected or thought possible without government subsidy in bonds or lands. The organizers of the Denver and Rio Grande Railway Company, however, had faith in the natural resources of the country, and in their correctness of their plan for railroads for their development, and asked only of Congress a grant of a right of way 200 feet in width for the roads named in its charter—a general North and South trunk line with side lines connecting the base of the mountains with the mines, this forming a self-supporting railroad."

Construction of the D. & R. G. began in 1871 with narrow gauge tracks. Because of this the Rio Grande was soon known as the "baby railroad." It was built narrow gauge because, for one reason, the construction could be reduced thirty-seven per cent. This was at the beginning of the "narrow gauge fever" in railroading and by 1880 there were 148 narrow gauge companies in thirty-four states with a total of 4,200 miles of narrow gauge track, most of which was three-foot track as contrasted with the standard gauge of 4 feet 8½ inches; a gauge which goes back to the time of ancient Rome when chariots were built with a similar clearance between wheels. This width was first used by the English

locomotives and adopted as standard in the United States by
1887. Up to then the gauge had varied from three feet to six
feet. It was around then the N. & W. changed its gauge to
standard as most of the Southern railroads used a wider gauge
than the Northern ones, and, in a remarkable accomplishment
of co-ordinated activity, made the switch over on its entire
lines—408 miles—in one day.

Today about 99.4 per cent of all railroad track is standard gauge. The narrowest gauge, as reported around 1940,
was the two foot track used by two railroads in Maine, the
Monson and the Bridgton and Harrison. The D. & R. G. W.
(the Denver and Rio Grande became the Denver and Rio
Grande Western in 1921) still operates narrow gauge lines
successfully in the mining country of Colorado and in northern New Mexico.

At the time the decision was made to build the Denver
and Rio Grande narrow gauge, General Palmer said:

"The Denver and Rio Grande . . . would inevitably have
many branches frequently running up through narrow and
tortuous valleys to the gold and silver mines, parks, forests
of lumber, coal mines, etc., in the adjoining mountains. . . .
They would of necessity be required to be narrow gauge as
their construction of broad gauge would involve tunneling,
rock cutting, and so forth so expensive as to be impractical. . .
It was desirable that the gauge of the D. & R. G. should be
as narrow as consistent with efficiency."

The important part played by the small gauge lines in
the development of Colorado resources justified that conclusion, and, also, the success of the narrow gauge enabled the
railroad to establish standard gauge on its main lines. By 1882
the D. & R. G. had 1,282 miles of track in Colorado.

With the Denver and Rio Grande project within Colorado well on its way, General Palmer ended his direct connection with the railroad and organized the Rio Grande Western
which by 1883 was constructed from the Colorado boundary
to Salt Lake City and Ogden and which developed the Utah
mining wealth along the same principle as the D. & R. G.
in Colorado. In 1901 President Palmer sold the Rio Grande
Western to his old Denver and Rio Grande at a profit said to

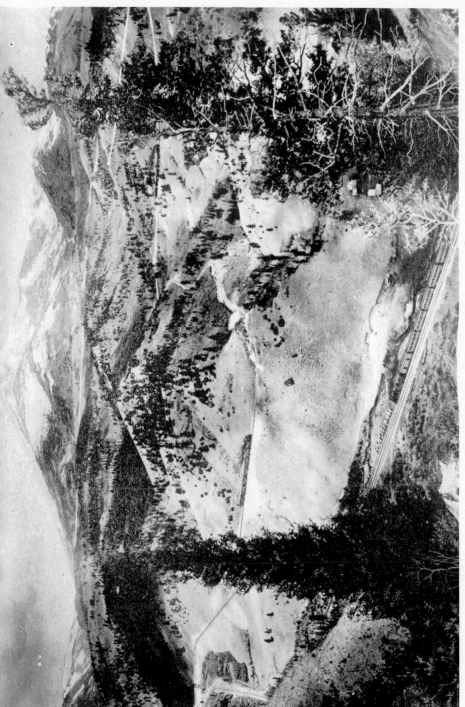

MARSHALL PASS

Five car freight with a total capacity of 100 tons on the slopes of Marshall
Pass in the early 80's.   Photo credit: *Rio Grande*

When wood was king. Old narrow gauge on trestle over Lake Fork.
                                                              Photo credit: *Rio Grande*

have reached $3,000,000. Benevolent Palmer divided $1,000,-
000 of this amount among the Rio Grande Western employees
ranging from officers to section hands. It is stated that many
a section hand received as much as $5,000. The passenger
agent at Salt Lake City, a Mr. Babcock, received, for example,
$25,000.

During this time Palmer had made a survey through the
Feather River Canyon with an idea of extending his railroad
to the coast (this was stopped by the economic tendencies of
the time) and this route was later used by the Western Pacific
railroad. And, thinking in terms of empire, General Palmer
was one of the principal constructors of the original lines of
the National Railway of Mexico.

Outside of his railroad interests, Palmer founded large
Rocky Mountain industries, fathered Colorado Springs at the
foot of Pike's Peak in 1871 with this message, "My theory is
. . . it should be made the most attractive place for homes in
the west . . . a place for schools, colleges, literature, science,
first-class newspapers, and everything that the above imply.
I would not lower the standard under the pressure of temporary poverty." Four years later, General Palmer helped
establish Colorado College.

While horse-back riding in 1906 at his estate, Glen Eyrie,
near Colorado Springs, General Palmer was thrown and suffered a broken neck. Never fully recovering from this accident, this courageous developer of the Rocky Mountain region
died two years later. But the puffing of the Denver and Rio
Grande Western engines over the mountains and flatlands
of Colorado, Utah and New Mexico will ever signal the
success of General William Jackson Palmer, "Pathfinder and
Builder."

Most of the shopmen at Salt Lake City were members
of the Church of Jesus Christ of Latter-day Saints, known
more familiarly as Mormons as their Bible is *The Book of Mormon*. The Mormons were, in Dan's words, "friendly, sober,
industrious, and very attentive to their work. They were
fine citizens, went to church regularly, paid 10 per cent of
what they earned as tithing to the church, many had been on
church missions and they were good musicians and singers."

Dan's initial social contact with the Mormons came shortly after he had reached Salt Lake City. He was invited to the home of O. B. Evans, who had returned from a Latter-day Saints mission to New Zealand. Dan's feeling of being an "outsider" was soon dispelled by the hospitality of his newly found Mormon friends. In a discussion of railroading with O. B. Evans, Dan learned the story of the Utah Central railroad, the unique project carried through by the Mormons in Utah.

Brigham Young, President and Chief Apostle of the Latter-day Saints, when the Mormons in 1847 sought a haven from persecution in the midwest by migrating to Utah in one of the greatest and most courageous pioneer movements in American history, desired the future development of railroad transportation into what was then Mexican territory. It is reliably stated that some 20,000 Mormons perished on the way west in their treks by wagon trains and hand-carts over mountain and desert.

At the time of the driving of the spike of California gold and one of Nevada silver at Promontory Point, Utah, on May 10, 1869, signalling the meeting of the Union Pacific and the Central Pacific, Brigham Young was far out of hearing of the whistles, bells and gunfire. The Chief Apostle, Vermont born, was at beautiful little St. George, his beloved spot in southern Utah. Brigham Young was irked at the Union Pacific because it had by-passed Salt Lake City and instead entered Ogden.

Previously, the Union Pacific had appealed to the Mormons for aid in building the railroad in Utah and the fiery Young answered with, "Point out the path and we'll tear down the rocks, fill the valleys and make a pathway for the iron horse." When one recalls how the Mormons had even then developed their State of Deseret, as Utah was first termed, this was no idle statement. Brigham Young called out his workers and the path for the U. P. was cleared. Then the railroad, which had not promised to enter Salt Lake City, went into Ogden and, on that very day, Brigham Young organized the Utah Central railroad to connect Salt Lake City and Ogden.

Hard pressed for funds, the Union Pacific, which had agreed to pay over $2,000,000 to Young for his construction contract, repaid part of it with approximately $650,000 in railroad equipment for the Utah Central. After church official George Smith had dedicated the land, Brigham Young, in high hat, black coat and polished boots, swung the first pick at Ogden May 17, 1869. So the Mormons commenced work on a co-operatively built railroad, the initial such line in the west.

With rails from the U. P., ties cut from wood slashed out of the Wasatch mountains, the Mormons—who had survived in a land which had been desert a thousand miles from the fringes of civilization and surrounded by Indians—because they realized the value of teamwork flocked to build their railroad. Often this work was done on a "promise to pay" even as Southern workmen had rebuilt the shattered Virginia railroads for Mahone after the War Between the States.

By January, 1870, the Utah Central was completed and all of Salt Lake City spear-headed the Utah celebration with fireworks and bonfires as well as the usual speech-making and band music. Brigham Young thanked the Union Pacific and the Central Pacific for their aid and a U. P. speaker returned the praise by saying, "You can publish to the world that the working men of Utah built their own railroad!"

Oddly enough, the first train to run from Ogden to Salt Lake City carried cars labeled 'Central Pacific R. R. of California" and "Union Pacific R. R." as the Utah Central hadn't the opportunity to stock its railroad with its own cars. The big Union Pacific sent the Utah Central two new locomotives; Brigham Young had an elaborate private car built in line with his position in the church; and the Utah Central prospered so well in 1870 the Utah Southern was commenced. Later the Utah Southern and the Utah Central merged and the Utah Central in 1900 became a part of the San Pedro, Los Angeles and Salt Lake railroad. Later, when the Union Pacific absorbed the latter railroad, commonly known as "the Salt Lake route," the dream of Brigham Young, who had died in 1877, was realized. Salt Lake City was on a main line of the Union Pacific.

The development of modern Utah can be traced to its penetration by the railroads. Wrote John Henry Evans, in 1933, "Before the arrival of the steam horse, there was no trade to speak of, mining languished, and there was little contact, either social or intellectual, with the outsider . . . but the railroads changed all that."

Dan's Mormon friends saw to it that he met Heber J. Grant, later the distinguished president of the Church of Jesus Christ of Latter-day Saints, who assumed office in 1918. President Grant told Dan how he had ridden the first passenger train over the Denver and Rio Grande into Salt Lake City, the locomotive of which was driven by James T. Beless, beloved veteran engineer.

The brilliant Mormon leader and the newcomer from Virginia took an immediate liking to each other and this mutual admiration lasted until Heber J. Grant's death in the early part of 1945.

At one of their early meetings, President Grant told Dan the following graphic story of a trip he made in 1882 when Utah was still a territory; Utah went from the State of Deseret and its provisional government to a territorial government, still under the leadership of Brigham Young, in 1850, and became the 45th state in the Union in 1896.

In December, 1882, (said Heber J. Grant) I left in company with Brigham Young, Jr., to visit the settlements in San Luis Valley, Colorado, and also to visit the people located on the San Juan river, Bluff City being the principal town. We held meetings in two or three towns in San Luis Valley and then went by narrow gauge railroad—in fact, all the D. & R. G. lines were narrow gauge at that time—to Durango. They had failed to get word that we would be there, and we had to wait three or four days before a team came for us to take us to Bluff City. Then Brother Luther Burnham came to take us to Bluff City in an open wagon.

The first day we drove to Fort Lewis. This was a military fort and there were no buildings there whatever except those belonging to the Fort; however, there were a lot of fireplaces for campers. We expected to sleep on the ground, but an officer came from the Fort and said, "I understand there is a brother of my classmate, who was graduated with me at West Point, going to sleep on the ground here." Brother Young spoke up, "I am a brother of Willard Young." The officer invited our party to the military headquarters. We had a pleasant evening. That night the thermometer went down to 26 below zero. Maybe if we had slept on the ground, we would not have awakened the next morning.

Brother Burnham tried two or three times in the morning to hitch up his horses, and it was so cold he froze his fingers. Along towards noon we started and had gone about twenty feet when our friend, the officer, shouted, "Stop!" We halted and he came out of headquarters with a big buffalo overcoat and a fur cap and insisted on my wearing them. He said that we would not reach our destination, which was Pond's ranch, before I, thin as I was, weighing only 140 pounds and being over six feet tall, would be frozen to death. I told him I thought with my big overcoat I would be all right. He replied, "I know what I'm talking about." So I put on the buffalo overcoat over my heavy coat. Even with this protection I got out and walked once or twice because of the cold before we reached Pond's ranch.

Arriving there we had a hot supper and were offered coffee which we declined. The ranch owner said, "Well, you know, there were a couple of men here about two years ago who would not drink coffee, the first we ever had at our ranch." I said, "Was one of them a very large man with a florid face and light hair? And did they have a single buggy with a span of cream colored horses? They did? Well, that would be a man by the name of Francis M. Lyman and the other would be John Gillespie; they took a trip down here two years ago."

The next night we camped on the San Juan river. We made our bed in the wagon and it was so cold we got out on the ground. The next morning we cut 16 inches of ice on the San Juan river which seldom freezes over. Then we visited Bluff City, held meeting with the saints there, and then returned to San Luis Valley.

We then went south to the end of the D. & R. G. at Espinola. We had first telegraphed and engaged beds in a tent, but when we got there it was claimed we had no reservations and therefore no beds. Brigham and I had to sleep in the freight house at the depot on top of a table. There were two gambling halls nearby in tents and in the night there was some shooting. One bullet struck the platform outside the station. Brigham said, "Well, Heber, it is just as safe here as outside and just as safe lying down as standing up."

The next morning, after breakfast, as we had telegraphed ahead and engaged our passage on the stage to Santa Fe, we went back to the depot and got our valises and were standing waiting for the stage to call. It came up with the horses trotting, and the station agent threw in a small bag of mail. The stage went right on. There we were stranded and the thought of staying another day was anything but pleasant. Pretty soon a wagon came along, the team driven by a Mexican. I asked the Mexican where he was going and he said, "Santa Fe." I asked, "What are you getting for carrying those big trunks for the drummers?" He replied, "I'm getting all of eight dollars." I then said, "You carry this gentleman and myself to Santa Fe and we'll pay you ten dollars for both of us." This was agreeable to the driver so the trunks were unloaded and we climbed in the wagon. I might mention that the drummers, who owned the trunks, were the ones who had stolen our lodging in the tent and who later had taken our reservations on the stage. Off we rode toward Santa Fe.

While in San Luis Valley and on the San Juan river and at Bluff City I had heard people speaking of a burro being able to do more work than a horse or a mule and that it ate only one-third as much. I asked Brother Young how to spell the word burro. He told me and I tried all down the line to get a dictionary to find out what a burro was. I disliked the idea of a man being 26 years old and not knowing this domestic animal when one of the brethren had twelve of them. I was determined not to show my ignorance.

As we were driving to Santa Fe we saw a lot of burros loaded down, carrying fully twice as much as their own weight. Brigham spoke up, "Men ought to be prosecuted for loading poor little burros down that way." I thought, "So that's it. For Heaven's sake! A burro is a jackass!"

Upon arriving in Santa Fe, I bought an evening paper and it told of a tenderfoot from Boston who was a conductor on an Atcheson, Topeka and Santa Fe mixed train—freight and passenger. He said, "I cannot check out my baggage. I am a jackass over and a burro short." If I had read this joke sooner, I would have known what a burro was.

We soon ran into the drummers who asked if we had passed a wagon coming from Espinola. We told them we hadn't as, of course, was the truth. The next morning the trunks hadn't arrived and the salesmen did some profaning, went to the depot and got their reservations on the sleeper in hopes the trunks would show up at the hotel in time to be delivered at the station.

As the train started out with Brigham and myself aboard, I saw the harried drummers standing on the platform still waiting for their trunks. I raised the window, waved my hand to the drummers and said, "Good day, gentlemen, I hope your trunks will arrive sometime in the near future." The drummers commenced swearing and I said, "He laughs best, my friends, who laughs last."

From Santa Fe we went to Sunset, where Lot Smith presided, and also visited Mesa City, St. Johns, and Snowflake, Arizona, where Bert Jesse W. Smith was president, and the stakes located in that section of the country. We then returned to San Luis Valley and up to Denver, catching the first train to Salt Lake City on the D. & R. G. railroad. We thoroughly enjoyed the scenery on the Denver and Rio Grande and the Rio Grande Western. When we arrived home, the first Sunday I preached in the Tabernacle I praised the wonderful scenery on the Denver and Rio Grande and suggested that any person travelling east ought to go or return by that route so as to see the fine scenery; that, through the Grand Canyon of the Arkansas, nothing but a bird or fish had traveled until the railroad builders had blasted away the rocks into the river making possible the famed Royal Gorge route of the Denver and Rio Grande.

*   *   *   *

Not long after his meeting with illustrious Heber J. Grant, Dan found himself writing Inez about the wonders of Salt Lake City. Inez had stayed in Roanoke with the girls, Donna, Margaret and Dorothy; the youngest girl had been born before Dan left Williamson. Inez did not want to come to Utah until she heard her husband was satisfied with his new position as she remembered the sometimes peripatetic life Mam had led with the Captain.

Inez read Dan's stories about the beautiful Utah capital; the impressive Mormon temple, commenced in 1853 and completed forty years later and the walls of which are sixteen feet thick at the base; the remarkable Tabernacle in which the acoustics is so perfect the drop of a pin can be heard for 200 feet; Eagle Gate, once the entrance to Brigham Young's private estate; the Great Salt Lake, seven times as salty as the ocean, the largest inland body of water in the west, and the remains of prehistoric Lake Bonneville, which was 350 miles long, 145 miles wide, and as deep as 1,050 feet; the first university built west of the Missouri river, the University of Utah, founded in 1850, three years after the Latter-day Saints came to Salt Lake Valley, as the University of Deseret.

Dan told the remarkable story of the seagulls. This modern miracle came two years after Brigham Young, following directions laid out by Joseph Smith, Latter-day Saint prophet and leader who was killed in the midwest, had risen on his elbow in a wagon, and looking out over the Salt Lake Valley had said to his westward migrating followers the memorable, "This is the place." The Mormon colony, after the first hard winter, was threatened with starvation as crickets poured in from the east and began to fall upon the succulent grain. The settlers fought the invasion vainly and their rich fields were rapidly turning into barren acreage. As if guided by some supernatural force, great swarms of seagulls came in cloud-like formations and fell upon the gormandizing crickets. The seagulls stuffed their maws with the crickets, flew to the lakes and riverlets and disgorged. Subsequently the birds resumed their attacks again and again on the insects until every one of the pests was taken out of the fields. This unique rescue from starvation led the Utah pioneers to make the seagull a sacred bird in their state.

Dan wrote of the beauties of the Utah scenery; the snow-capped Wasatch Range, on the western slope of which is Salt Lake City; almost indescribable Bryce, flaming so brilliant under the noon-day sun it is often called "the canyon of fire"; Zion Canyon, where no Indian dared sleep in the shadow of the Temple of Sinawava, and in which rough hewn, queerly colored pillars and pyramids quicken the pulse of imaginative men; and the northern rim of the Grand Canyon reached after miles of travelling through the virgin trees of the Kaibab Forest.

Inez read in Dan's large bold-lettered handwriting how the Mormons had sponsored the arts, the dance, and the theatre and how Brigham Young had ordered rooms built in his meeting houses for dancing and theatricals so that the young people could be kept under the supervision of his leaders. This attitude led to the famous Salt Lake Theatre, in its time perhaps the finest playhouse in the United States, and where Maude Adams, a Salt Lake girl, made her debut.

And Dan made many comments on one subject, recalled to him by his dates at Virginia College and Hollins, as well as the summer trip he had made to Mountain Lake while at Virginia Agricultural and Mechanical College. He wrote about the Salt Lake City girls and one of his comments was "the girls here are a delight to the eye, beautifully formed and they know how to wear their clothes."

Inez was now certain Dan was satisfied at Salt Lake City. She wired him to meet her and the children at Denver!

CHAPTER XV

"*W*HERE the new town of Durango is to be or not to be, God and the Denver and Rio Grande only knows!" So wrote the editor of the Animas City *Daily Southwest* in 1880 when the Rio Grande was pushing its narrow gauge tracks into southwestern Colorado near the ancient cliff dwellings at Mesa Verde.

General Palmer's railroad builders were planning Durango so that the Rio Grande would have control of the new community and were by-passing nearby Animas City, then the most thriving town in that section of Colorado. The words of the perplexed journalist failed to halt the exodus from Animas City when Durango was built and today Animas City has a population of around 500 and Durango about 7,000.

Not always was the D. & R. G. as successful in its plans as at Durango. The Rio Grande battled with the Santa Fe then known in Colorado as "the banana line" because of its yellow coaches. The conflict between "the baby railroad" and "the banana line" reached tense moments with armed gangs upholding the alleged rights of each company. The most important battles ended in victory for the Santa Fe at Raton Pass and for the Denver and Rio Grande at Royal Gorge. Glory was aplenty in pioneer railroading for both companies.

Dan thought of this historic background as the Rio Grande's *Scenic Limited* rolled slowly through the narrow gorge of the Arkansas river rapids. For a thousand feet on each side of the tracks, the sheer rocks rose almost perpendicularly and dwarfed the D. & R. G. train until it resembled a toy one in a department store's Christmas window. Dan and his family sat in the open observation car and looked at the boiling water of the river alongside the roadbed. The youngsters were thrilled by the way the train snaked between the tall walls of rock.

The triumph of the railroad in putting tracks through the Royal Gorge was one of the real engineering victories of the men who built the trails for the Iron Horse. The Rio Grande tracks in 1875 had reached Cañon City from Pueblo, stopped, and the construction men sent their "hell on wheels" outfit elsewhere. Under the impression the Rio Grande was not going to tackle the job of extending its line deeper into middle Colorado, the citizens of Cañon City organized the Cañon City and San Juan railroad and made plans to build their own line to connect up with the Rio Grande.

At the same time the Santa Fe had its eyes on the Arkansas river route as it was realized such a rail line would control the traffic in that area of Colorado as well as service the rich mines in Leadville. From Pueblo rushed Santa Fe workers to the mouth of the Arkansas river canyon to start grading for tracks. When the A. T. & S. F. workmen reached their destination, they found the Rio Grande engineers already in action. Disturbed by the steps taken by the Cañon City residents, the D. & R. G. had quickly resumed its building program.

Nevertheless, Santa Fe men started to move in on the Arkansas river territory and the Rio Grande men grabbed their guns. So started one of the most celebrated "railroad wars" in American transportation history. Actually, it is doubtful if anyone was really killed in the conflicts, but fights were numerous and the tension was such that the likelihood of actual private warfare was ever present. As the rival workers continued to draw guns on each other, the battle went to the courts and, after a lengthy legal battle, the right of way was awarded to the Rio Grande after costs of the conflict had run around half a million dollars.

Feelings of the Santa Fe were assuaged by their important win over the Rio Grande in a similar situation at Raton Pass and this victory was partially responsible for General Palmer's failure to carry out his original plans to send the Rio Grande south of Colorado to the Mexican border at El Paso.

The D. & R. G. engineers were forced to suspend workmen from the top of the red granite cliffs to drill blasting holes in many parts of the gorge. Too, at one place, as it was impossible to put down any road bed in the narrow gorge, engineers suspended a bridge from the sides of the gorge using an inverted V support. Whereas with most other bridges water flows under at right angles, at Royal Gorge the water flows from end to end beneath the railroad bridge. After this unique bridge was completed, the railroad had to use special locomotives low enough to clear the supports. The conquering of the river gorge allowed the Rio Grande to build on through Colorado to the Utah boundary.

Inez was intrigued with the Rocky Mountain scenery so different from the multi-colored desert at Needles, the green mountains of Virginia and the coal-bearing lands of West Virginia. When the railroad had crossed the plains of the middle west and come into the mountain country at Denver, the three Cunningham girls were like the children in the fairy tales whose eyes got as wide as saucers.

When the visitors were told that Colorado has some 1,500 peaks rising 10,000 feet or more, it was difficult for them to picture the flat plain the land had been in prehistoric times ranging back as far as 500,000,000 B.C. The mighty peaks almost made the fact that Colorado has been partially submerged four or five times by the seas seem utter fantasy. Beautiful, colorful Denver, the state capital, belied the fact that 20,000 years ago savages roamed the site of Denver and, at the time of the birth of Christ, Colorado was occupied by the Basket Makers, a skilled people later fused with the vanished Cliff Dwellers. Even as gold brought on the rush of 1859 with its "Pike's Peak or Bust!" slogan, so the vision of gold lured the first white men into Colorado. It is said Coronado, in 1541, while searching for mythical Quivera and the Seven Cities of Cibola—the towns of gold, was the initial white man to view Colorado. Later Spain and France fought for domination in this territory which, with Jefferson's purchase of the Louisiana Territory from Napoleon, became a part of the United States. Denver itself was officially organized in 1858, three years before Colorado became a territory and eighteen years before it was admitted to the Union as a state. The cosmopolitan makeup of the people of early Colorado is attested to by the story of General James W. Denver, Kansas territory governor, for whom the city was named, although the namers were unaware Denver was no longer in office.

James Denver was born in Winchester, Virginia, in 1817, was a lawyer in Ohio, newspaper editor in the midwest, state official in California, commander of Kansas troops in the War Between the States, and, on his death, buried in Ohio!

As the train moved toward Salt Lake City, Dan told about the famous mountain peaks along the routes of the Rio Grande tracks; Mount Ouray, Arapahoe Mountain, Sangre De Christo, the collegiate peaks—Yale, Harvard, and Princeton, and "last the great mountain of the Holy Cross with its symbol of the old rugged cross made by nature, filling the chasms with pure white snow forming a perfect cross, forever reminding us of the man of Gallilee."

Peaks coned with eternal snow, tumbling mountain streams, forests which met the horizon, all flashed through the window of the Rio Grande train. Now and then the entranced children spotted a mountain goat atop a craig, herds of deer, or a huge bear watching the train go by and, as Dan said, "no doubt wondering what it is all about the same as you or I."

Dan told about the longest railroad bridge in the United States which runs across Great Salt Lake and is the nineteen-mile-long Lucin Cut-off carrying the tracks of the Southern Pacific and which led to the discontinuance of the northern route via Promontory Point. He spoke of Ibex, Colorado, where the Rio Grande tracks reach an elevation of 11,522 feet, the highest point touched by any standard railroad in the United States (the World War II built standard gauge of the C. & S. between Leadville and Climax is now highest); and of the long, straight track of the D. & R. G. running nearly 53 miles in Colorado from Villa Grove to Alamosa in the San Luis Valley and which, built in 1891, runs at an elevation of around 7,500 to 7,900 feet with rugged mountains on each side of the tracks.

Like all children—and grownups, too—Donna, Margaret and three-year-old Dorothy, liked to eat in the dining car. The colored waiter served mountain trout, caught fresh from the Colorado streams, and when Dan asked how the fish bite in the Colorado waters, the jovial waiter replied, "Boss Cunningham, them fish in Colorado bite so fast you has to hide behind a tree when you bait de hook!"

Colorado citizens are proud of their rivers well stocked with game fish and this has led to a colloquialism in which a native of the state, in expressing contempt for an individual, will say, "Why that fellow is a catfish in mountain or trout water."

After Inez and the children had gone to sleep in the Pullman, Dan, in the smoker, thought about the magnificent job the railroads were accomplishing in hauling passengers through what had been the wilds of Colorado and Utah. His thoughts expanded beyond the Rio Grande and the Denver and Salt Lake, yes, beyond the Santa Fe and the Southern Pacific, the Union Pacific and the Burlington; encompassed all the railroads of the nation whether it was a line running through the cotton fields of Dixie or the maple forests of New England. Big Dan took out his notebook and wrote:

"I never get into my Pullman berth at night that I don't visualize the men who keep the trains moving in safety. There is the locomotive engineer on the 'head end' with his hand on the throttle, guiding the engine through the darkness with gleaming headlights laving a glisten on the two ribbons of steel. He handles the brake valve to steady his train a little while rounding curves or going down grades. He and the fireman watch for the color of the block signals. Whoever sees the signal lights first calls out the message. If the lights are green, this indicates every thing is all right in the next block; if the lights are yellow, the engineer proceeds with caution and reduces his speed; if red, he stops the train. The fireman watches the water in the water glass, looks at the steam gauge, gets down and examines his fire; if the fire is not burning right, the fireman makes some adjustments in his stoker, sometimes regulating the stoker jets. All the time he is working in connection with the engineer keeping the right amount of water in the boiler, the maximum amount of steam as indicated by the steam gauge, watching so that the engine will not pop as this means a fuel waste.

"Knowing how these men are working and looking out for the safety of their passengers—or of their cargo if they are running a freight—I often wonder what kind of men they are, what are their thoughts, their joys, their homes and families? The train moves on while men, women and children sleep, not realizing the drama which is going on up at the 'head end.'

"If awake, the passengers can hear the exhaust of the Behemoth of the rails, feel the air brakes going on and then released, see through the curtains of the berth the gleam of the lantern carried by conductors or brakemen as they patrol the train. The smooth handling of the train reveals that all is well and the passengers fall asleep, secure in the statement, 'The safest place in the world is on a railroad train.'

"The headlights of the incoming train flash into view at a division terminal. Perhaps this is where an engine switch is to be made. The fireman and engineer on the outgoing crew check over the locomotive, start the stoker, try the injectors, commence the water pump. The hostler moves the locomotive out of the main track and backs it into position where it is tested for air. Meanwhile workmen have been examining the entire train, grooming and, where necessary, repairing any flaw. The new crew takes over and the trainmen compare their orders and see that their watches are together. The conductor gives the 'high ball.' Out starts the train for the next division terminal.

"Meantime the incoming locomotive which had been taken from the train, is in the enginehouse where it will be thoroughly conditioned for its next run. This procedure goes on twenty-four hours a day in hundreds of enginehouses and terminals over the nation. Men toil and sweat and worry so that the locomotives will make their runs in the most perfect condition possible.

"I wonder if people riding in trains ever think of the large army of men who work around the clock getting trains and engines ready to take them to their destinations. The movement of trains en route is watched by alert train dispatchers making meets, putting less important trains into sidings and, at the same time, trying to make meets which will not delay the trains. Then, if they do delay a train, the trainmen will swear at the dispatcher and say he could not make a meet between a thirsty Dutchman and a glass of beer!

"I have heard passengers complain because their train

BIG DAN

was ten minutes late; yet, after the train arrives, the identical passengers go to a hotel and sit up three hours waiting for bedtime. My sympathy goes out to the conductor and brakeman when a train is delayed as those passengers who complain show their displeasure by telling the trainmen what a rotten railroad it is and how they should be working for the Red Sea Line or some other railroad which is always on time!"

In the light of unreasonable complaints, railroad men have to develop their own philosophy to take care of the situation. Such a philosophy of making the best use of a bad spot is illustrated by the favorite railroad story of Edward A. West, general manager of the Rio Grande and vice-president of the Denver and Salt Lake. West, Canada-born and who, after graduation from Tufts and Massachusetts Institute of Technology, rose to be one of the best known street car municipal transportation executives and originator of the modern trolley coach, became a D. & R. G. W. executive in 1937.

According to Edward West's story, an applicant was being examined for the position of tower man. The trainmaster had the neophyte up in a wayside tower which controlled a passing track. He asked the young man what he would do if both switches were set for the main line and two trains were in sight approaching each other at sixty miles an hour. The fellow replied, "I would throw a lever and put one of the trains on the siding." The examiner said, "Yes, but suppose when you try to throw the lever the cable breaks. Then what?" The man answered, "I would run down and throw the switch by hand." The trainmaster said, "Suppose you found the switch locked?" To this the young applicant replied, "I would go to the section house, get a hammer and break the lock." But the examiner wasn't satisfied, "Let's say the section house was locked. Remember all the time these two trains are coming closer at sixty miles an hour. Now what would you do?" The man sighed, "Well, I'd get on the telephone and I'll call up my wife. I'd say, 'Honey, get the hell down here as fast as you can, cause there's going to be the damndest wreck you've ever seen!' "

Opportunities for wrecks—especially runaways—were greatly reduced on the main line of the Rio Grande in 1913-14

The Royal Gorge Conquered!   Photo credit: *Rio Grande*

One of the scenic wonders of American railroading is the Royal Gorge route.

when a new track was laid from Detour to Soldier Summit. Although the new track made the distance longer, the 4 per cent grade was cut to 2 per cent enabling one locomotive to do the work of two. The new track took a year to complete and cost $1,500,000. It paid for itself in six months.

When Inez settled down in Salt Lake she became attached to the city as had Dan. Too, Frank Wyman, one of the original Norfolk and Western "Three Musketeers" tired of the Tonopah and Goldfield railroad and came to Salt Lake. Needles days were discussed and Inez told how she found Salt Lake such a contrast to the desert town where rain had often assumed cloud burst proportions and water, sweeping everything before it, rushed down arroyos twenty or thirty feet deep. Dust storms had lasted for as long as three days and the sand would seep in around the crevices in the doors and windows and pile an inch deep on the floor of her home. Inez recalled how the hot winds off the Mojave had seared her Virginia peaches and cream complexion until her skin resembled leather.

Frank Wyman told of an investment he had made in a gold mine while working on the Nevada railroad, but until the mine paid off he wanted a place on the Rio Grande. So Dan made him foreman at Salt Lake City and later general foreman at Thistle, Utah. That pot of gold at the end of the Nevada rainbow did slide all the way over into Utah and the Belmont Mine made Frank a wealthy man. He left the Rio Grande, opened an automobile parts factory in Los Angeles and pulled in another treasure from the rainbow. After he had sold the factory he retired to a beautiful ranch near Riverside, California. So did the three machinists from Roanoke, who set out to win the west in 1900, find their ultimate fate: rich Frank Wyman on a ranch in California, John Van Lew, on a farm near his old railroad shops at Roanoke; and Dan Cunningham, in the shadows of the Wasatch at Salt Lake City.

Both Frank and Big Dan were amused by a request the Rio Grande received from the town council at Nephi, Utah. As Dan tells the story, he was requested to forward the message on to the head office at Denver. It seems the railroad had a

branch line on the Marysvale route which ran from Manti to
Nephi where the Rio Grande connected with the Union
Pacific. After entering the town limits of Nephi, the D. &
R. G. tracks crossed a number of streets before reaching the
depot. According to law, the engineer would blow a crossing
signal of two longs and two shorts before entering each crossing. This train was scheduled into Nephi at 4 o'clock in the
morning and the continual whistling of the locomotive awakened everybody in Nephi. As time passed, there were so many
babies born in Nephi the infant population created a problem.
The town considered the matter and decided to send the railroad a request to set up its schedule an hour so the train
wouldn't come in until 5 o'clock.

According to Dan, the understanding management of
the railroad granted the request.

Speaking of wide-awake people, Nephi did not have a
corner on them. Red Sullivan of the Salt Lake shop was wide-
awake enough to grasp an opportunity when he saw it.
"Got a West Virginia boy I want you to meet," Sullivan,
boilermaker apprentice, said to Dan one afternoon. "He was
born in Logan and used to work there in the mines as a boy,
but he really grew up in Salt Lake. He's been helping us at
the boiler shop and I think he's got a swell future as a prize
fighter. I've been coaching him for a fight with a fellow
named Flynn at Midvale, Utah."

Dan walked with Red over to meet the promising prize
fighter. Red came up to a dark-haired young man rippling
with muscle. Spoke Red, "Fellow, I want you to meet Dan
Cunningham, the shop superintendent here. After Jack Johnson dropped 'Gentleman Jim' Jeffries at Reno, Nevada, we
used to call Dan Cunningham, 'the White Hope.' But he's
more interested in fighting the Rio Grande's battles than
anything else. So I guess you'll have to be our champion, Jack
Dempsey."

So it was that Big Dan met the future World's Heavy-
weight Champion and one of the great prize fighters in all
the squared ring history. Jack Dempsey later moved to New
York, but he left a host of friends in Salt Lake City where he
bought a beautiful home for his mother.

After Dan had taken a good look at Red's protegé, he was certain Red had a find and Dan's hunch was that Logan's claim to fame would have additional support besides the fact that Thomas Dunn English, the author of *Ben Bolt*, was the town's first mayor.

Other men left the Salt Lake shop to become noted in their line. Dan saw the old drop pit where A. D. Williams, W. J. O'Neill and Walter Chrysler worked as machinists. A. D. Williams eventually became superintendent of motive power for the Southern Pacific at Sacramento, California; W. J. O'Neill became an official of the Rock Island, then chief mechanical officer for the Rio Grande, and is now superintendent of motive power for the Western Pacific. Walter Chrysler, who at the age of 33 was the superintendent of motive power for the Chicago Great Western, left railroading to become manager of the Pittsburgh works of the American Locomotive Company. Then he became interested in automobiles, helped build the once famed Maxwell and then made the Chrysler company one of the Big Three in the automotive industry along with Ford and General Motors.

W. J. O'Neill is a master *raconteur* in western railroading and he and Big Dan have spent many an hour swapping yarns of the iron highway.

O'Neill recounted how at El Reno, Nevada, the river rose until the water pump was under twenty feet of water. He dove to fix the pump, but found the task required an hour. So he had his men get pop bottles, blow their breath into them, cork them up and then, when he was under water, these bottles would be lowered to him on strings; and, when he felt the need of air, he would uncork a bottle, take a whiff of air, and so was able to get the pump repaired.

When O'Neill was foreman on the Southern Pacific at Minor, Nevada, a locomotive overturned, and, as frequently happens, the engineer's leg was caught in the wreck. The river beside the tracks was rising rapidly and threatened the trapped engineer. To save the engineer, O'Neill rushed to the tool car, obtained a hand saw, amputated the man's leg and dressed the wound. When the injured engineman reached the hospital, the chief surgeon commented, "Some doctor made a mighty fine job on this amputation. All I have to do is put the man to bed." O'Neill admitted he had performed the operation and that he was a railroad man, not a surgeon.

Bandits were one of O'Neill's favorite subjects and he would counter Dan's anecdotes of the West Virginia-Kentucky feuds with a recounting of his tilts with western badmen. At Chickasha, robbers had the town terrorized and the railroad's Special Agents department was unable to locate the desperados. O'Neill decided to take over, climbed a forty foot high pile of coal in the railroad yards so as to have a good observation point. While atop the coal heap, the fuel suddenly gave way under O'Neill and he tumbled down, crashed through wooden supports. As his fall broke the boards, O'Neill realized he was dropping into a room concealed in the coal pile and found himself confronted with eight armed men. Swinging from the timbers, O'Neill lunged out with his heavy boots and kicked down two men; then he knocked down two more with his fists and the others gave up and howled for mercy. O'Neill realized he had unearthed, or perhaps, "un-coaled," the gang of bandits. He lined them up and marched them to the sheriff's office. And so was solved the mystery of the gang hideout which turned up in the middle of the railroad yards.

One of O'Neill's really classic chronicles concerns the time a gang of robbers held up a train on which he was riding in the locomotive. He waited until the badmen were opposite the blowoff cocks. Then he opened up the cocks and let 'em have it. The jets of steam blew the scoundrels over into a field. O'Neill calmly cut down the bell cord and tied up his prizes. He then turned them over to the law. So once again the railroad triumphed.

Criminals have been known to strike back and O'Neill figured at one time he was a marked man. He had stepped off the train in a western frontier town and, carrying a heavy travelling bag in each hand, he started up the street to a hotel. Without warning he heard a shot. The grip in his right hand fell to the street. A second shot. The grip in his left hand fell. Bullets had cut the bags from the handles. But it wasn't O'Neill who was the target. Unsuspectingly he had walked into the cross-fire of two lead-slingers who were shooting it out.

O'Neill tells of the time in his travels when he was going through the railroad shop at Little Rock, Arkansas, and he ran into a man in the blacksmith shop haranguing the men to go out on strike. The agitator's words infuriated O'Neill and, grabbing the anvil right out from under the speaker, he threw it at him. The anvil missed its mark, went through a brick wall twenty feet away. Later O'Neill had the shopmen weigh the anvil. It sent the scale pointers to 750 pounds!

W. J. O'Neill would have come in handy at some of the wrecks Dan encountered. Because of the mountain terrain over which the D. & R. G. operated, Dan had his share of freight wrecks with which to contend. Loss of equipment was bad enough, but loss of life was far worse. (In recent years the Rio Grande has made a brilliant safety record. Actually, in the past twenty or so years, the D. & R. G. W. has had only one passenger fatality. And, in 1944, for example, the Rio Grande carried more than one and a half million passengers a total of 585 million miles. The same year the Rio Grande handled 18 million tons of freight, an average of 49,000 tons a day. This is more freight per day than was hauled the entire first year of the Rio Grande's operation.)

High water washed out a track and an oncoming locomotive was turned over into the river. The situation was similar to the wreck which O'Neill had told about. Trapped under his engine, the engineer was endangered by rising water and all his would-be rescuers could do was hold his head out of the water until the wrecker came. Dan had arrived at the scene of the wreck and cold sweat popped out on his face as he watched the water creeping up over the engineer. The rescuers had stretched the trapped man's neck as far as they could, but the water soon would cover his face.

Came the welcome whistle of the arriving wrecker. Wreckmaster Pat O'Donald shouted, "Boom right down with the light line" as the wrecker stopped opposite the overturned locomotive.

Dan held his breath. The wreckmaster was gambling in not putting any outriggers on the wrecker to steady it as such a delay most assuredly would doom the victim of the wreck. At the same time, if the damaged locomotive was on a teeter—and there was a fifty-fifty chance it wasn't—the wrecker engine would tip over because of the absence of the outriggers and plunge into the river itself. The wreckmaster would be disgraced as to tip his wrecker into the river would be as bad for him as losing a ship would be to a Sea Captain.

Pat O'Donald knew all this as he stood up to his neck in water and made a hitch on the tail bar with the light line hook. He signalled to hoist away. The cables strained and the big wrecker shuddered and leaned over like a man walking against a hard wind. The cables raised the locomotive a few inches, but not enough to free the engineer. The mammouth steam wrecker seemed to suck in new wind for its task and the engineer aboard it gave the cylinders a little more steam, and again the cables strained at their load. The "Big Hook"—as the wrecker is called—rocked again, but the cables held and the locomotive inched out of the water. Suddenly the engineer's crushed leg was released and the grasping hands of the rescue men pulled him clear. Everyone was cognizant of the fact another minute's delay would have cost the man's life. Yet, even now, the "Big Hook" might lose its precarious balance and topple over.

At the wreckmaster's orders, the wrecking crew, treading as lightly as if they were walking into a baby's nursery, pulled out the outriggers and secured the huge wrecker. At last there was little possibility of it turning over and for the first time everyone could breathe easily.

The wrecked engine was lowered back into the water so proper hitches could be made for rerailing the locomotive. Soon the wrecked engine was out of the water and in place on the temporary rails.

Bold Pat O'Donald had cast his dice with an Irish prayer and he had rolled a winning combination. He had saved a life, rerailed the wreck, and not tipped over the "Big Hook." But everyone at the scene was aware the wreckmaster had made a most difficult instant decision in not using his outriggers in the beginning. Had he judged the position of the locomotive wrong, an even worse disaster might easily have taken place.

The work of the fearless men who run the wreckers never has been really appreciated or understood by the travelling public. Paying tribute to these men, Dan said at a railroad club meeting:

"I think the men of the 'Big Hook' can be compared to our Coast Guard in ever being ready to risk their lives to save property and the life of their fellow men. Their motto easily could be that of the Coast Guard, *Semper Paratus* or 'Always Prepared.'

"Even when off duty and at home the wrecking crew men are prepared for a call as no one knows when the next wreck will occur. Then, when the call comes, and if they do not get their outfits out in short order, they will have to answer to 'the big boss.' When a call comes in to send a wrecker out, the roundhouse foreman tells the hostler what engine to take and, if no other locomotive is available, the wreckers do not hesitate to take the one which has been set out for the Limited.

"With the hostler setting the engine on to the wrecking outfit, an army of men is oiling, supplying, coaling, sanding, watering and otherwise conditioning the engine for its mercy run. The air is tested so that when the locomotive crew arrives the 'high ball' signal can send the 'Big Hook' on its way.

"As the wrecker leaves, the crew on it sits with solemn faces wondering if anyone has been hurt or killed and if engines, cars or both have been smashed up. The engineer gets all he can out of his locomotive as he knows every minute counts. Back in the cook car, the chef and his helper prepare food for the crew men as well as those in the wreck. No one is in any mood to eat until after the work at the wreck has been surveyed and, if immediate action is imperative, the 'Big Hook' put into service.

"After the wreck has been cleaned up the 'Big Hook' starts back to its base. The crew, now able to relax, gets up a card game and the men consume coffee by the pot. Yet, the men know, even as they play their penny-ante game, that at an unrevealed time, Chance will again uncover a Black Ace!"

264   BIG DAN

Freight wrecks and hobos are an allied subject in that
the wrecks dislodge the "boes" from their places in or under
the cars. Yet hobos are frequently not bad fellows and on
washouts and derailments the "boes" will pitch in and help
the wrecking crew. The hobo fraternity, while loosely knit
has a certain comradeship. Many a former boomer machinist, who has risen to an official position on a railroad, "rode
the rods" in his youthful days.

The "boes" have their own peculiarities. A few years
ago the name "J. B. King" began to appear on railroad freight
cars, enginehouses, turntables, bridges and other railroad
property. The hobos were doing a top job of advertising
"J. B. King." Dan called over a friendly hobo in the Salt Lake
yards and asked him why the "boes" were doing this. The
hobo did not know why such a name was selected, but the
hobos would bet each other on who could write the name the
fanciest. Later Dan saw a box car from the Soo Line—the
Minneapolis, St. Paul and Sault Ste. Marie—on which some
railroad hobo literary figure had written:

"J. B. King, you see his name on everything,
On box cars high and flat cars low,
You see his name wherever you go.
He may be poor or he may be rich,
But who in hell is the son of a bitch?"

The hobos have their troubles with railroad "bulls" or
detectives. "Boes" hate two things intensely—railroad detectives and tunnels. This aversion to tunnels, readily understood, aided the Rio Grande trainmen after the Moffat
Tunnel had been opened. The trainmen, no matter what was
the train's actual route, told the "boes" the train was headed
for "The Hole" and not for the Royal Gorge. Immediately
the hobos would desert the train and this saved the trainmen
the trouble of having to put them off.

A fireman brought a hobo over to Dan's office in the
Salt Lake shop and said he would make a good man for the
Rio Grande which, at the time, was short of firemen. The
fireman told how he had picked up the hobo to help shovel
down coal on a locomotive which was a hard steamer. Despite

the regular fireman's efforts, the engine failed to steam. The hobo asked for a try at the job and, using the coal scoop as a shield for his eyes, he opened the firebox and located a bank. Throwing the coal where needed, he let the bank burn out and, by his skillful firing, soon had the steam gauge rising. The curious regular fireman learned the hobo was a former "tallowpot" who had lost out in railroading because of repeated violations of Rule G which prohibited the use of liquor on the job; however the ex-fireman yearned to get back on a railroad.

Dan gave him the chance on his promise never to violate the liquor rule. The new fireman on the Rio Grande did his work well and, in time, became a road foreman of equipment on a western line. Dan said all this happened as the result of the fireman, who had picked up the hobo, having a heart, something which is characteristic of the great majority of American railroad men.

This "one for all and all for one" spirit might be demonstrated on the humorous side by the story of Big Dan and C. L. Edman, passenger coach foreman, and a Bishop in the Church of the Latter-day Saints.

Often Dan had to be around the Salt Lake passenger station when the tourist-packed trains arrived. Frequently passengers asked Dan to pose for a snapshot and drawing up to his full six feet four, Dan would put on his widest western smile as he stood in front of a Rio Grande passenger car. Almost always, when the tourists thanked Dan for posing, they said the picture would really be something to show back east.

Dan posed for so many pictures he began to wonder what was the magic attraction he held for the good looking women travelers and he chided Inez about his popularity with the visitors. Later, while at the passenger station, he noticed two girls, who had stepped off an incoming train, go up to Edman. The Mormon Bishop was working around one of the passenger cars. Quickly the girls left Edman, came over to Dan, asked him to pose for a snapshot.

After Dan had complied with the request, he walked over to his friend who had an amused look. "Look here, Ed,"

Dan spoke, "what's the idea of all these girls wanting my picture?"

The passenger coach foreman laughed, "Well, Big Dan, I guess you've finally caught up with me. You see, these tourists get off the train and come up to me as I'm working around the cars. The first thing they ask is where they can take a picture of an-honest-to-goodness Mormon. You look so big and prosperous all I have to do is point you out and say, 'Girls, there's a real one!' "

So in many an eastern tourist's photograph album, Baptist Big Dan is the black and white reproduction of a prosperous Utah Mormon.

But all of Dan's experiences in Salt Lake were not as amusing as that one. His efforts to improve the Salt Lake shop had met with considerable success, but the one Denver and Rio Grande officer who didn't like him could never be pleased and was a constant Abaddon to Dan. In the Salt Lake shop was a locomotive the Rio Grande had taken over when the Castle Valley railroad was purchased. The C. V. was a short line which had run up to the Hiawatha Coal Mines until the Utah railroad had built as far as Hiawatha.

The engine was badly designed with a wide boiler and a cab so narrow the engineer had to get out on the gangway to reverse his locomotive. In an accident in the yards, this engine had been sideswiped and the cab torn off. Dan figured the accident might be turned to good use by having the locomotive rebuilt with a wider cab. He laid his plans before the master mechanic at a time when the Denver official was visiting the shop and was in the master mechanic's office.

Dan had finished explaining the work necessary when the Denver man spoke up roughly, "Dan Cunningham, you are either a damn ignorant farmer or else you just talk like a damn ignorant farmer. It would have been a happy day for the Rio Grande if we had left you buried in that little coal mining town on the Norfolk and Western!"

Big Dan knew his plans for building the cab were well executed and he tried to explain further the setup. But the official heaped more abuse on him apparently trying to make him feel as bad as possible over his suggestion.

Taking the undeserved tongue-lashing as long as he could, Dan flared, "Mister, you aren't talking to me!"

The visiting official answered, "You damned Virginia idiot, who am I talking to?"

"To my successor," answered Dan quietly He turned and walked out of the office.

Dan headed for the car yards to let his temper cool. He knew what a good job he was doing at Salt Lake. He knew the work was comparing favorably to the engines being turned out by the mechanically superior Rio Grande shop at Burnham, Colorado. Coming in as an outsider, he had won the respect of his men, and, in turn, he had taken a delight in the way the shop had improved. Mormons and non-Mormons, railroad people and non-railroad people, Dan could count his friends by the hundreds in the Utah capital. Yet the arrogant attitude of this one Denver official was more than Dan could endure. Essentially a man with a heart as big as Great Salt Lake, Dan could not fathom the indefensible attitude with which the official persecuted him.

While in the yards, Dan noticed the most beautiful piece of mahogany wood he had ever seen. Lying in the July sunlight it had evidently been purchased for repair work on the interior of a private car. Dan called over Edman, then one of the Rio Grande's cabinet makers.

"Get some of the boys, wrap that big mahogany board in burlap, put it in a box and bury the box near the shed," Dan instructed. Edman looked as if the boss had suddenly been touched with light-headedness.

Dan explained. "This is my last order at the Salt Lake shop. I've resigned from the Rio Grande. But someday I'm coming back to Salt Lake and the D. & R. G. and, when I do, my first order will be for you and the boys to dig up that box and you can make me as pretty a desk as a railroad official has ever seen."

As he ate his dinner at home, Dan's stomach was a tumble of nerves. Inez had taken the news of his resignation calmly and commented that she and the girls were ready to "hit the pike" with him. But in his heart, Dan knew his wife and children did not want to leave the west and he also realized trying to land a position as good as shop superintendent on another western railroad would not be easy. Dan had no desire to leave Utah or Colorado.

The telephone rang. Listlessly Dan answered it. "Denver calling," said the phone operator. Dan's listlessness left him. He hugged the receiver closer to his ear, heard, "Dan Cunningham, this is W. E. Morse, the vice-president and general manager of the Denver and Salt Lake railroad. W. W. Lemen has just recommended you for the place as superintendent of motive power on our railroad. We can offer you twice as much salary as the Rio Grande is paying you at Salt Lake."

The suddenness of the D. & S. L. offer left Dan without words. His silence was misinterpreted by Morse who said, "Can't blame you for hesitating. Why don't you come on to Denver and look over the railroad?"

By now the spell was broken and Dan replied, "Mr. Morse, I don't want to see the Denver and Salt Lake on those terms. I'll have plenty of time to look at your railroad when I work for it. I'm accepting your offer!"

Dan had a friend, Joe Nelson, president of the Salt Lake and Garfield Western, a short railroad which ran to Saltair Beach. One year after Nelson had made a quarter of a million dollars on his railroad, he remarked to Dan, "Brother Cunningham, the arms of the prophet were around me!"

And so, on the very day Big Dan resigned from the Rio Grande, he accepted the unexpected offer from the Denver and Salt Lake with its more important position, its larger salary, and the opportunity to continue railroading in the Rocky Mountain area.

Truly Big Dan felt, as had his friend Nelson, that "the arms of the prophet were around me!"

CHAPTER XVI

Dream of Rocky Mountain railroad builders for years had been a short route from Denver to Salt Lake City, but the Continental Divide was a gargantuan rock barrier unconquered. The Chicago, Burlington and Quincy actually had started such a route and had by-passed mighty James Peak west of Denver. An old tunnel at Yankee Doodle Lake is evidence showing where the Burlington abandoned the proposed rail line as it was thought too expensive and also the many miles of 4 per cent grade would be too difficult to operate.

The Denver and Rio Grande route to Salt Lake was through the Royal Gorge. George Fitch, the noted author of the *Siwash* stories, once said, "When you want to go from Denver to Salt Lake, you first run 100 miles away from where you are going, then you go through and over and under the Rockies. You run so close to the scenery only one coat of varnish can be put on the cars and if there is more than one fat man on the train the engineer and fireman get paid time and a half. The tourists ride to Salt Lake on one side of the train, then buy a ticket back and ride on the other side so they will not miss anything. And don't forget when you get to Salt Lake, if you want to cross the streets, always call a taxi as the streets are too wide to walk across unless you want to stop and fish or take a swim as streams of water run down both sides of the street."

The Moffat Tunnel and the Dotsero Cutoff have changed part of the statement made by George Fitch. One can now go from Denver to Salt Lake in sixteen hours and thirty minutes. The rest of the statements made by Fitch still stand, especially those about the scenery on the railroad.

Now the Rio Grande has the slogan, "Thru the Rockies —Not Around Them."

The D. & R. G. W. offers travellers their choice of the Moffat or Royal Gorge routes. Many other railroads connect with the North-South line of the Rio Grande. The Union Pacific, Colorado and Southern, Chicago, Burlington and Quincy, all enter Denver. The Chicago, Rock Island and

Pacific comes into Colorado Springs from the east, and the
Atcheson, Topeka and Santa Fe and Missouri Pacific connect
at Pueblo where the Royal Gorge route actually commences.
At the bottom of the Rio Grande standard gauge Colorado
tracks at Trinidad, the D. & R. G. W. connects with the Santa
Fe and the Colorado and Southern.

Around the turn of the century, one man looked at the
mighty Rockies barring the railroad short cut from Denver
to Salt Lake and planned a railroad which would span the
distance. This man was bulldog David H. Moffat, who had
amassed a fortune in mines around Leadville, Cripple Creek
and Colorado Springs. He knew how Colorado transportation
had progressed from the days of the Rocky Mountain "can-
ary"—the burro, the Spanish *Caretta*, the Red River cart,
the prairie schooner, and the widely heralded stages of the
Leavenworth and Pike's Peak Express, the Butterfield Overland Dispatch, and later, Wells Fargo.

Too, David Moffat knew how General Palmer's Rio
Grande railroad had vanquished mountain ranges, as he was
president of the D. & R. G. for many years in the 80's.

David Moffat felt that he could top even Palmer's railroad building. He called in the best railroad engineering
brains and, in 1902, backed by local financing, commenced
construction on the Denver, Pacific and Northwestern railroad, later renamed the Denver and Salt Lake railroad and
which is frequently known affectionately as the Moffat railroad.

Three railroad surveys had been made for David Moffat.
One was for a six mile tunnel bored through James Peak; the
second planned a three and a half mile tunnel constructed
higher up on the peak; and the third tentative plan was for a
high altitude railroad over Corona Pass.

Moffat wanted to bore the big tunnel through James
Peak, but his engineers persuaded him to build over Corona
Pass by saying that if the long tunnel were attempted first, the
railroad, which was to open up the rich coal fields in Routt
county, would be delayed. Too, by building over the pass,
materials and railroad equipment could be pushed ahead along
with the construction and a comparatively fast job of track

laying accomplished. Then, argued the engineers, after the railroad was in operation, the tunnel project would be commenced.

The engineers' contentions were not without a modicum of logic. But they neglected to take in account the area around Timberline which demanded a 4 per cent grade and which was in the most critical part of the Rockies as far as snow and high winds were concerned.

So the railroad was built to Tolland—there are now 28 tunnels on this part of the Denver and Salt Lake railway—and then over Corona Pass and on to Craig in the northwest part of Colorado. From Craig the railroad could be expanded almost due west to Salt Lake City.

But before the rairoad could progress even to Craig and construction could begin on the huge tunnel, two things burst: one was David Moffat's finances; the other was his heart. He put $11,000,000 of his own money into the Denver and Salt Lake and, in 1911, died virtually broke in New York while seeking additional financing.

And the Denver and Salt Lake was still scaling the high mountains when Dan took over his position as superintendent of motive power on the railroad.

Dan found out the severe weather conditions under which the Denver and Salt Lake operated as soon as winter set in. He rode out of Tabernash—named for a Ute chief who was killed in 1879—where, at the 8,337 feet altitude, the railroad had yards, an enginehouse and a telegraph office, and the first terminal out of Denver. The freight, pulled by three engines, was trying to make the snowsheds at Corona, the top of the Continental Divide.

By midnight a terrific blizzard had hit the train and Engineer Lee Fuller worked Number 121 to full stroke. Snowdrifts slowed up the progress and, as the headlight was soon covered with snow, the engine proceeded in both complete darkness and the fifty below zero storm. Dan knew the rotary plow was somewhere ahead in the darkness. What worried him was how far ahead.

Anxiously Dan said to the engineer, "Lee, do you know where we are?"

Lee Fuller opened the cab window and tried to look out. The cold was so intense it froze his eyes shut and it took some moments before he could open them. Then he said, "I'm sorry, but I don't know where we are."

With visions of running into the snowplow, Dan fired the same question at Pat Breen, the Irish fireman. Pat didn't worry about a little matter such as the rotary being ahead of them. "Sure, Mr. Cunningham," Pat answered, "I know. We are right along here on the D. & S. L. tracks." Pat laughed heartily at his own joke.

Despite the storm, the train reached the protection of the Corona snowsheds and Engineer Sweeney, who was running a helper engine, came up to Dan and explained he had lost the right bottom guide on his low pressure engine cylinder (Mallet engines have high and low pressure cylinders). Dan investigated and found the guide missing, but the piston was not bent and the engine was in the clear so it could be disconnected and blocked.

Dan grasped Sweeney by the hand and spoke, "If you had discovered the lost guide before we reached Corona, you would have stopped to prevent damage to your locomotive. This blizzard will last for a couple of days and we'd have been snowed in for possibly a week. So for losing a part of your engine and not knowing about it until we reached Corona, I'm going to give you sixty credit marks."

Sweeney's eyes got as wide as the snowdrifts. This was perhaps the only time in the history of any railroad where an engineer received commendation for an error!

Shortly after this, a main bearing burned out on one of the large rotaries and the essential plow was tied up at Corona until a new back-end brass could be sent from Utah Junction. The only engine available for the mission was a light locomotive. This small engine set out for Corona. Some hours later a half frozen engineer stumbled into Corona dragging behind him a sack containing the back-end brass. After the man had warmed up and was able to speak, Dan learned what had happened. The light engine had bucked the storm to within two miles of the Corona sheds where it stalled. Leaving the fireman in charge of the engine, the engineer put the brass in

a sack and started out on foot for Corona. At times the gale
was so ferocious he was forced to crawl on his hands and knees
to make progress. The two mile journey took him over four
hours and he was more dead than alive when Corona was
reached. Soon the new back-end brass was put on the rotary
and it plowed down the tracks to open up the way for the
stalled locomotive.

The snowsheds at Corona stretched some three miles and
in the middle was a Wye or "Y" (a track arrangement used for
turning an engine around in the absence of a turntable), a
telegraph station, eating house and bunk rooms and quarters
for the six families who lived and worked in the sheds. All
trains going through had to be inspected before they were
allowed to descend the 4 per cent mountain grade. Special
retainers were applied to cars from prairie railroads, as these
did not have brakes suitable to the steep descent. When these
cars reached the bottom of the mountain, the special retainers
were disconnected and returned to Corona.

A few weeks later, Dan and W. E. Morse were at Tabernash trying to break a traffic blockade caused by a storm
ranging over the entire length of the Moffat railroad. The
temperature was 60 below. The country around Tabernash
—as that around Minturn on the Rio Grande railroad—re-
tained evidences of the Glacial Age. By digging down fifteen
or twenty feet one can find ice left there during the glacial
periods. Dan and Morse would get up at the first sign of dawn
so as to have as much working time as possible.

First two of the Mallets pushed out the snowplow to
open up drifts which had accumulated on the tracks during
the night. Then trains were run as frequently as possible
behind the rotary before additional snow piled on the tracks.

The task confronting the Moffat can be visualized when
one recalls that one engine on a midwestern railroad can pull
one hundred to one hundred and fifty cars. On the Denver
and Salt Lake a consolidated engine with forty-one thousand
pounds tractive effort and two Mallets with sixty-four
thousand pounds tractive effort were required to pull twelve
to sixteen cars of coal. Dependent on the amount of power
available at Tabernash, the engines and cars would be sent

out in fleets of five or six trains at a time. So to get sixty or seventy cars to the top of Mt. Corona took all of fifteen engines.

As one engine would dump scores of cars from the mid-western coal fields, a bottleneck could occur very easily in the Tabernash yards. An unusual feature at Tabernash was the enginehouse. Instead of the customary roundhouse, this was a square house and had no turntable. The tracks were laid on twenty foot centers and parallel to each other outside the enginehouse.

One night after Dan and Bill Morse had worked from sunup to relieve the congestion in the yards, they were sitting in the *Marcia*, the general manager's private car named for David Moffat's daughter. Clarence, the colored waiter, was replenishing the coffee cups when the telegraph operator handed Morse a message. After the general manager had read it, he passed it on to Dan without any comment. Dan read:

"Mallet engine 202 on its side at Sulphur Springs Section House. Mallet hit a rock in the canyon, derailing the pony truck and engine ran one mile with truck on the ties and when opposite section house turned over and stuck its stack in window of section house where Japanese foreman's wife was sleeping. Please advise."

Dan thought perhaps he might advise the Japanese woman to sleep a bit further from the tracks if she didn't want an engine to make a rowdy entrance into her bedroom; however, he wrote out a wire advising that the steam wrecking derrick was at Tolland rerailing one of the rotaries which had run off the end of the Wye and was twenty feet down the bank; however, the derrick should be ordered to Sulphur Springs to rerail the Mallet.

Taking a sip of coffee, Dan remarked it wasn't enough to have the rotary derailed, but now a Mallet had to turn over. Dan had a great deal of admiration for the fearless men who ran the big rotary snowplows. Sometimes an avalanche would roll down the mountain and bury the men alive or the terrific slide would overturn the plow and engine and dash it off the tracks and over the side of a steep mountain. Men without nerves manned the rotaries which kept traffic open through the canyon-like snowdrifts.

After a few minutes the telegrapher brought in another message. This wire stated there were six freight cars off in Bogans' shed completely snowed in and the drifts had knocked down the shed. Bogans' shed was between Tolland and Sulphur Springs so this meant the derrick wrecker could not reach the derailed Mallet.

Dan and Morse conferred a moment and then sent instructions to get the Bridge outfit from Phippsburg on a special and have them transferred at Sulphur Springs; go on to Bogans', clear out the snow and the freight cars so the wrecker could make it through to Sulphur Springs.

"That ought to be our share of complications for the night, Dan," spoke Morse just a bit wearily as they prepared to go over the next day's operations at Tabernash. The two officials knew they could count on the Bridge and Building outfit to do its assignment.

Perhaps half an hour later, the telegrapher walked in a bit hesitantly and said, "You've heard from the B. & B. boys."

What this message contained was the news the large trestle at Toponas had burned up and the roundhouse at Phippsburg had been totally destroyed by fire. The Bridge and Building outfit, which was next to the roundhouse, was completely burned.

With this news changing plans, instructions were rushed to the B. & B. group at Utah Junction to take over the task of seeing to it the wrecker got to Sulphur Springs.

On the heels of the message about the fires at Phippsburg and Toponas, arrived a wire stating that Train No. 2—engine and cars—was covered in snow and stalled at Arena. The train couldn't be allowed to turn into an elongated ice box and the speediest remedy would be the rotary plow of the Colorado and Southern railroad at Denver. The request to borrow the rotary brought a reply from the C. & S. they were mighty sorry, but their plow had been sent north to clean out their own lines near Cheyenne, Wyoming. The only thing Dan and Morse could do was wire instructions to Denver to hurry every available man to No. 2 and dig it out with shovels.

About this time the two D. & S. L. officials were certain nothing else in the way of bad news could come to them concerning their railroad when another message was brought to them. The telegrapher shook his head and said not a word as he handed over the paper. This communication read:

"Snow slide at Loop caught one of the Moffat Mallets and it is now one half mile from the track down the side of a mountain. Also the timber in tunnel 17 is on fire and the rocks have come loose and are completely blocking the bore."

At this point, General Manager Morse turned to Dan with a wry smile and said, "Dan, it's about time for you to tell us a story."

"Well," Dan started, "I'll tell you about a mountain freight back on one of the southern railroads. The freight was coming down a grade when it lost its air, making the air brakes useless. The engineer blew for hand brakes. The conductor and the rear brakeman commenced setting the hand brakes as fast as they could for the speed of the train was gaining at every turn of the brake wheel. The conductor looked up and saw a rookie brakeman sitting on a brake wheel calmly looking at the scenery as the train whizzed along. The conductor shouted, 'Damn it, get the hell off your butt and start setting brakes!' The rookie brakeman waved an assuring hand and kept his seat. Finally the train was stopped and the rookie came up to the conductor and said, 'you know we get paid by the mile and the fastest and farther this train went the more miles we would have covered. If you damned fools hadn't been so hept on setting those hand brakes, I'd have been ahead $3.65!' "

Morse had a good laugh at this story. The tangled mess was cleared up after several days; that is, all except the Mallet down the mountain. It was too far gone.

Although one had to possess an excellent sense of humor, if the harassing conditions of Rocky Mountain railroading were to be tempered, the experiences were often on a most serious side. For example, there was the time Dan had to investigate the wreck of a Mallet in which a number of men were killed. The practice on the Moffat, or any other railroad subject to heavy snow, is to keep water in the tank by shoveling snow into the cistern. The heater melts the snow and the water is put in the boiler by either pump or injector. In this case, the Mallet had stalled between Corona and Tabernash and section men shoveled snow on top of the tender while other men shoveled it into the tank manhole.

While this went on outside, the fireman and engineer were inside the tank moving the snow ahead in order that the manhole would not become clogged.

Without any advance warning, a snowslide hit the engine with such force it plunged the locomotive and tender down the mountain. After twenty or so revolutions, the tender came to a stop and the engineer and fireman crawled out with only slight injuries. When the slide had hit, the men had grabbed on to the braces in the tank and held on as the tender tumbled down the grade. Dan thinks this is perhaps the first time railroad enginemen saved their lives because they were inside the locomotive tank or tender.

The Mallet was so far from the tracks, it had to be cut up into sections for salvage. And who were the men killed in the accident? They were the men shoveling the snow!

The biggest battle fought by the Denver and Salt Lake was not the war of competition with other railroads for business. It was the battle against the elements. Such a sample skirmish is so described by Big Dan:

"The cold in the Rocky Mountains froze the marrow in your bones and the snow, blinding and freezing your eyes shut with its wraith-like whirling and its continual blowing and ghost-like drifting, reminded one of an inferno of the departing spirits conjured up by the Vikings. The cold and snow and wind tore at your very soul.

"Sometimes, when I rode in a freight caboose, the snow would be so deep only about six inches of the telegraph poles were visible over the white bank. Above Timberline the entire world looked like the frozen wastes of some far planet. Under such conditions, a train I was riding went through the gorge of snow churned out by the rotary preceding the locomotive. All at once the brakes went into an emergency and, looking from the caboose, I saw car after car jumping up and piling into the rear of the locomotive.

"I put on my winter coat and boots, crawled through the cupola window and stepped onto the snow which was level with the caboose top. A 60 mile gale ripped at the crewmen, who linked hands together to keep themselves from being blown away. The air was so rarified at the over 11,000 feet altitude our lungs seemed empty and we struggled for enough air to keep going. All the time the wind and the snow fought us as if they hated the steel tracks scarring the mountainside. Finally by crawling and working our way forward, we reached the derailed cars, which were all piled up crosswise like a mass of jack-straws.

"The smoke from the engine poured a feather-like blackness across the sanctuary of the Winter Gods. Soon the engine, the wrecked cars and the part of the train remaining on the track were blanketed by the snowfall. Unable to get to the derailed cars with the rotary, we took our telegraph set, carried for possible use in such exigency, tapped the telegraph wire, and sent the chief dispatcher news of our trouble. And, naturally, a request for help.

"This meant a rotary had to be sent us from Tabernash and it was to stop and pick up all section men along the way. Too, all the D. & S. L. trains had to be held at Corona, as if they had been allowed to proceed down the mountain, they never could have backed up the heavy grade and, in turn, would have been snow bound.

"After the rotary had come to our rescue and plowed up to the engine, we had to send it back to turn at Irvins Wye as it was headed up the mountain against us and it would have been snowed in itself. One car at a time the section men shoveled out by hand and, with large chains they rerailed the cars which were not smashed up so badly. After this, the remainder of the train was dug out. Eventually we had the train in shape to move on to Tabernash where the big rotary rejoined us and cleared the track so we could finish our run.

"Once again traffic was resumed and the freight and passenger trains could make their way over the mountains. Slowly the trains crawled up the grade, twisting and turning around curves, bucking drifting snow, the heavy explosive exhaust showing the locomotives were being worked all the way to the corner, giving the valves full travel, admitting all the steam to the cylinders they would take. The pounding of the big Westinghouse air pump could be heard, ready to set air at any time it was needed. The weary watchers at Corona could see for miles down each side of the mountain. They eagerly watched trains pull the grade bringing them their food, fuel and supplies and best of all black and grimy—but human—faces.

"Yet ever the snow and gale and ice marshalled forces for another blow although the courage of the men of the Moffat, from lowliest track workers to the officials, had struck them down for the moment."

Dan thinks the funniest story of railroads fighting snow storms is the one told him by the late E. L. Brown, who was president of the Denver and Rio Grande. A snow storm and blizzard blocked one of the Great Northern railroad lines where Brown was division superintendent. Brown sent his rotaries out and, deciding he needed additional help, went to a Sioux Indian reservation. There he rounded up two hundred braves and with their chief guiding them brought them to a deep cut filled with snow and sand.

The Sioux leader looked at the mass of snow and inquired, "What you wantum to do, Mr. Brown?"

The division superintendent waved toward the mass of braves he had supplied with shovels and spoke, "Have your people shovel out the snow, Chief."

The Indian chief turned to his people, raised his arms and said loudly, "White man damn fool. Try to do now what sun do by and by. Go back!" The Indians dropped their shovels and, with the chief in front, marched back to their reservation.

The Sioux chief was, of course, correct in his conclusion about the sun even though the time element meant nothing to him. But sometimes the Colorado sun hindered the operations of the Denver and Salt Lake. After a bad storm, the sun would thaw the ice which, in turn, lost its hold on the mountainsides and sheets thumped down on the railroad tracks. Often a sudden drop in temperature froze solid the mass of ice and water. This sheet of ice made it virtually impossible to get trains started on a grade.

At passenger stations the Moffat trains would freeze to the tracks before engine switches could be made. The oil waste in the journal boxes froze and this meant another engine had to be sent to the rear of the train to bump it loose. Meanwhile the waste in the lubrication boxes would freeze causing the wheels of the cars to slide and, before a passenger train could pull out of the station, steam had to be sent from the engine throughout the length of the train, otherwise it soon froze up.

One wintery day with the temperature around 45 below, Dan watched a hostler run a steamed up Mallet out of the enginehouse at Tabernash to connect it with an awaiting train. Shortly after the engine got into the open, it derailed on the heavy ice which was as hard as granite. The locomotive's momentum carried it across the ice to the track where the train was standing. The Mallet hit the track in a slow slide and all the wheels of the engine and tender settled exactly on the track. The startled hostler climbed from the Mallet to find it was rerailed satisfactorily and all he had to do was back the Mallet up and couple it on to the train. The whole action had taken less than two minutes. Such a method of moving a mighty Mallet from one track to another is not recommended by Big Dan!

Not long after Dan witnessed the remarkable chance by which the Mallet retracked itself, he saw a locomotive hit the rear of a freight, demolish the caboose, and rear itself into an empty coal car. So loaded, the locomotive was moved to the shop to be repaired. It was as if the engine were trying partially to rectify its bad behavior in smashing into the freight.

One of the oddities of the Moffat railroad was a glacier underneath the tracks near Ptarmagan's Point. In the winter the trains ran over the solid glacier without difficulty; however, in the summertime, trackmen had to heave the rails back into line every day as a result of the accelerated glacial movement.

Action on the Moffat when Big Dan was superintendent of motive power. Top—
Digging out a snowed in train at Rollins Pass, Colorado.
Bottom—Roaring across the top of the west, a D. & S. L. train approaches Tim-
berline.

Photo credit: *Denver and Salt Lake*

DAVID H. MOFFAT

Early president of the D. & R. G., builder of the mountain conquering Denver and Salt Lake, affectionately known to railroad
men as "the Moffat." Photo credit: *Denver and Salt Lake*

Designed by Big Dan, Lima built these Mikado type locomotives for the Denver
and Salt Lake in 1917. Photo credit: *Denver and Salt Lake*

Dan had a reason to remember Ptarmagan's Point. Here it is:

"I was detailed," said Dan, "by Morse to accompany a bunch of Boston bankers over the line to show them the railroad. We hoped our guests would put up enough money to build the Moffat on west of Craig as this was as far as our lines had been constructed. Our business car was attached to the rear of a passenger train leaving Denver. We got along very nicely until the train ran into a blizzard which snowed us in at Ptarmagan's Point. Well, we weren't stuck for a matter of a day or so. We were stuck for almost ten days with this bunch of Boston bankers whose time was worth a thousand dollars an hour. We ran out of heat, food, and everything else but gloom. The New England bankers were sitting around wrapped up in blankets like Ute Indians and doubtless feeling like the Pilgrim fathers when blizzards hit their colonies.

"To get a respite from the sight, I walked back to the kitchen and as I got there I heard one of the imported cooks tell Clarence, 'If I had all de money dem white folks has, Clarence, I'd buy dis part of the land and give it back to de Injuns.'

"After the train had been dug out by section hands and the train crew, we continued our interrupted journey west. When the train approached State Bridge, we could see Mt. Massive all covered with snow. One of the bankers asked, 'Mr. Cunningham, what mountain is that?' Feeling that perhaps the bankers arctic spirits were thawing out, I answered in my most cordial manner, 'Why, sir, that is Mt. Massive, the highest point in all Colorado.' I smiled as if my words had created a beatifying atmosphere on the easterners. The banker soon proved my error as he said to his fellow financiers, 'Why in all mighty Hell, didn't David Moffat build his railroad across that also?'

"I realized the money was off and the bankers would just as soon finance a railroad through Tibet as one on top of the Rockies and, at the next telegraph station, I threw off a message advising the Denver Moffat office the deal was dead. I had always heard about the coolness of some bankers, but I think on that trip I had more 'cold bankers' than ever were brought together in one bunch!"

So it is Dan has recollections of Ptarmagan's Point.

The Denver and Salt Lake, of course, wasn't the only railroad having trouble keeping its trains on schedule. This story is told about a train moving slowly from the Deep South to Washington, D. C. A Southern senator, who said he had an appointment with President Woodrow Wilson and Secretary of the Treasury Carter Glass, twisted his windsor tie and rapped on the Pullman floor with his cane as he protested to the conductor that the train's snail's pace would cause him to miss these important engagements. The conductor listened to the miniature filabuster and, at its conclusion, remarked, "Mah deah senutah, you have no reason to complain about the way this train is handled. Did you notice that train we passed which was standing on a siding? You did, suh? Good, senutah. Do you know that side-tracked train is loaded with Georgia soldiers on their way from Atlanta to reinforce General Robert E. Lee's Confederate lines at Gettysburg!"

Another amusing run-late story Dan remembers was told by Dora May Priester, former west coast newspaper columnist, and later financial writer for the California Bank, at a Pacific Railway Club meeting in Los Angeles. Said the speaker:

"It is debatable as to which group of people boast the loudest and longest, railroaders or Texans. Having crossed Texas on nearly every line that runs through it, at times I have thought its boosters had something as far as size went as no matter where you start there is no change in scenery for three days.

"However, another angle was brought to my attention recently when an enthusiastic ex-officio member of the Chamber of Commerce, giving an illustration of the size of the United States to a visiting delegate from Australia at the recent Conference for International Security, said impressively, 'You can board a train in the state of Texas at dawn and twenty-four hours later you will still be in Texas.'

" 'Yes,' said the man from Down Under with feeling, 'we've got trains like that in Australia, too.' "

Although Dan had returned his party of bankers to Denver from Craig without incident and the train had come into Denver on the nose, he didn't have similar luck later when he left Craig on Passenger Train No. 2. The train left Craig at 3:30 a.m. and pulled into Denver at its scheduled time of 8:10 p.m.—two weeks later!

A blizzard had swept down across the barren peaks above Timberline and stalled the train; and, the blizzard continued with such duration, the rotaries could not dig the train out. The wind had a clean sweep from the top of Mt. Corona and the snow drifted as high as forty feet. Section men dug the snow from the front of the rotary so the plow could throw it aside.

Fortunately the train stalled near a siding where full coal cars had been placed in anticipation of such an emergency. Plenty of heat was available to keep the train warm. Yet the railroad had somehow neglected the food problem and, to keep the passengers and trainmen from starving, rushed in supplies by men on skis and snowshoes. Outside of the extreme delay, there were no real hardships suffered by the passengers.

In wintertime, a small portion of the Moffat would run through tunnels made of snow. The drifts sometimes piled so high the rotary plowed a tunnel through them. The snow, drifting and piling on top, would harden and make tunnels usable until warm weather came. The sight of trains running along under the snow was one of the unusual scenes offered by western railroading.

Although it seemed as if the winter calendar was so elastic it would stretch out forever, summer did come to Colorado and with it came the beauty of snow capped mountains and the profusion of wildflowers kaleidoscopic against the mountainsides. At Corona enthralled tourists picked flowers from the snow banks left from winter and little realized the struggle the D. & S. L. had gone through to keep its lines open during the long winter. Above the timberline, dwarf oak, reindeer berries, waxlike flowers, grew out of the patches of snow. Colorado's state flower, the Columbine, grew in luxurious profusion on the mountainsides and intermingled with Indian paint brush and delicate blue flowers. As Dan put it, "This natural beautiful bouquet was as if God wanted to compensate the people of this land for the awful hardships they had to endure during the cold months of the winter."

And in the Colorado summer, there was one man especially who remembered the rigor of the storm and a stranger named Dan Cunningham. Late in the winter Dan had walked into the railroad station at Craig. Huddled around the small stove were a man, his wife, two small children and the family dog.

"Waiting for the train, folks?" inquired Dan.

"Nope, just waiting for spring," answered the man a bit hopelessly. Dan knew the man was a "Zulu"—the term used by railroad people for immigrant farmers who moved their horses, cows, farm and household goods in a box car to some unsettled country.

The man edged away from the fire and, noting the friendly interest on Dan's part continued speaking, "Came in from the midwest with my family. Have some land just west of here and we staked out in a tent 'cause I figgered winter was about over. That storm yesterday destroyed my tent so I came on down to the station with the wife and kids. It's warm here. Spent nearly all our money getting west, but as soon as the snow's over we can get on our feet again. Kinda hard to find a place to stay, mister. Say, mister, if you want to buy my land, I'll strike it back to the midwest."

Dan looked out the station windows and saw an empty box car which had been set off its wheels and at one time had been used by an extra gang. He glanced toward the family hugging close to the stove and then walked over to them. "Don't worry, folks," Dan assured them, "I'm Dan Cunningham, the superintendent of motive power on the Moffat railroad, and I'll get you a place to live."

Taking the man by the arm, Dan led him out of the station to the deserted box car. "Not exactly a Colorado mansion," Dan said lightly, "but the Moffat's letting you have it rent free, fellow, until you can get back on your feet and work your land. All I ask is for you to remember it's railroad property." With these words Dan pitched in and helped the man clean up the box car and build a fire in the stove.

After the family, happy over its good fortune, was quartered in the box car, Dan caught a train out of Craig and forgot all about the incident as, several months later, when he returned to Craig the family was gone. About two years afterwards Dan was sitting in the lobby of the Brown Palace Hotel in Denver when a man came up to him and asked if he were Dan Cunningham, the superintendent of motive power on the Moffat. Dan replied he was, but he was now assistant superintendent of motive power on the Denver and Rio Grande. There was something familiar about the questioner yet Dan couldn't place him. So the man identified himself. He was the Zulu Dan had aided at Craig.

As the former immigrant looked as prosperous as a railroad president, Dan asked him what had happened and the man told his story. He and his family had lived in the box car until warm weather had set in. Then they moved to the land, cleared the sage brush and plowed up the soil and conditioned it for a crop of corn, wheat and alfalfa. Four months later oil was located on his land and one of the big companies leased it. The family moved to Denver and bought a real Colorado mansion and lived on the oil royalties. The grateful man explained to Dan none of this could have happened to him if Dan hadn't been kind enough to let them use the old box car at Craig. Without a place of shelter, they would not have had the courage to last out the winter. Too, if Dan had bought the land, the first use made of the money would have been train tickets home and a box for the dog in an express car. As Dan ate the finest steak in Denver that night as guest of the man he had befriended, he thought of the words James Thomson had written nearly two hundred years before, "A lucky chance, that oft decides the fate of mighty monarchs."

With the summer months passing, the D. & S. L. had to prepare for the early snows. In the fall workmen dragged coal down the mountain at Corona to the pump house in which was a small boiler and pump. Attached to the pump house were the living quarters for the pumpman and his wife. This had to be stocked with provisions to last through the entire winter. After the first snow the pump house was holed in for months. The only means of communication to Corona was the water pipe line which ran from the boiler through the telegraph office. Using the Morse code, the pumper could tap out messages to the operator by striking the pipe with a hammer. This method of communication was not one which led to lengthy chats between the two men. The pumpman and his wife lived, in the words of Charles Dickens, "secret and self-contained and solitary as an oyster." Few Moffat workers envied the pumpman his lonely job.

Like the Santa Fe at Needles, the Norfolk and Western at Portsmouth and Williamson, the Moffat had its characters who interested Dan. The most colorful of these employees was Mike Canavan, an Irish section foreman handling track gangs. The Irish had helped build the earlier railroads in the east even as the Chinese had laid the tracks coming east from the Pacific. One day Dan and Bill Morse took Mike along with them on a track and roadbed inspection. The general manager turned to Mike and asked, "Mike, whatever became of all the good old time Irish section men?" Mike took his pipe from between his lips, answered, "Mr. Morse, the Irish built the railroads and now they are down in Washington running them!"

Among Mike's classic statements was his one that although all other railroads went through four seasons, the Denver and Salt Lake had only three seasons, namely, high water, snow, and then falling rocks!

Mike was a foreman with imagination. Dan received a report from a roundhouse foreman that a railroad spur track had been built from the main line to the Colorado river. No one in the Denver office had authorized such a track and Dan went out to find who was the builder. This didn't take him long. It seems Mike had discovered a large sand bar in the Colorado and had put in the spur track, placed a Clam Shell on the sand bar, and loaded enough sand in coal cars to last all winter. This eliminated the necessity of hauling in engine sand by truck and teams. Actually, it was a smart move, but Mike had done it on his own initiative without asking company permission. Railroad policy required the Moffat officials to put Mike on the carpet for not getting the head office's permission. When the general manager had concluded his chastisement, Mike put in his defense, "Sure, Mr. Morse, I built the track without getting orders. But, bigorra, I used only company men and materials and it didn't cost anybody a penny." Mike, of course, was not fired as his action had saved the railroad time and money, and he returned to his work.

For a long time the Denver and Salt Lake was able to obtain only white spruce ties which were laid on dirt ballast. These ties were so brittle that after some usage they would break. One day Dan asked Mike how his track was and Mike answered, "Why, Mr. Cunningham, we have a very pious railroad here. Even the ties are pointing Heavenward!" When the white spruce ties broke, they would part in the middle and the ends outside the rails would stick up.

In time the Denver and Salt Lake railroad put in an excellent roadbed with volcanic ash ballast, heavy rails, creosoted fir ties double spiked with tie plates; and, to Mike, the railroad had lost its religion. Before the new tracks were installed, Morse asked Mike what the Moffat needed most. Mike looked at the snow covered tracks, quipped solemnly, "Ties and friends."

These three words told the history of the pioneering Denver and Salt Lake as it drove its Iron Horses across the top of Colorado.

Mike was inspecting track when he ran into an old chow right from Ireland who said, "Good morning, Mr. Canavan, and be ye from County Mayo and where is Tim O'Flarity who worked for the Moffat and the Rio Grande?" Mike replied, "Never mind O'Flarity, get the rocks off the tracks!" The old chow slowly filled his pipe, peered at Mike and said, "God rest poor old O'Flarity's soul. He is dead now."

When necessity demanded it, Mike had a way of getting enginemen and trainmen to help drive spikes and line rails after a derailment. With his flow of Blarney, Mike always managed to get the two groups into a contest to see which could do the most track work.

Once, though, the joke was on Mike Canavan. He was

continually praising Irish "bacon"—he called anything from a hog "bacon"—and told his friends on the Moffat they didn't know what bacon really tasted like until they had eaten some of his meat cured in Old Erin. Dan suggested to Mike perhaps some of it could be shipped to Denver. In accordance with the suggestion, Mike wrote to his father in Ireland to send over some real Irish bacon. After several months the shipment from Ireland arrived in Denver and Mike invited Dan, Bill Morse and other D. & S. L. people to his home for a real feast. When the guests arrived, Mike hadn't uncrated the shipment as he wanted everyone to witness the ceremonies.

So with most of the mechanical officials of the Moffat looking on, Mike broke open the crates and took out the real Irish bacon. To everyone's surprise—including Mike Canavan —the labels on the meat read "Packed by Swift and Co., Omaha, Nebraska, U. S. A."

Mike took the disappointment well and ordered the Swift hams cut up for the feast and, to make certain the authentic Irish atmosphere would not be missing from the menu, he started off the festivities with real Irish whiskey right from the Emerald Isle.

Dan advised Mike not to feel badly about being foxed on the real Irish bacon and he related the story of Pat Breen, an Irish engineer on the D. & S. L.

"All master mechanics," commenced Dan, "realize how hard it is to place responsibility when someone flattens the driving wheels of a locomotive. Everybody passes the buck until the master mechanic is ready to give up in disgust. Well, at Tabernash somebody put four inch flat spots on Mallet 200. I tried in vain to fix the responsibility and had given up hope of ever finding out. A few days later, I was on an inspection trip at one of the roundhouses in the First Division and at night stayed at a fireman's house. My room was a spare one which had been partitioned off with very thin board and any noise in the next room carried right through the partition. Awakened in the night by loud talking, I recognized Pat Breen's Irish brogue as he talked to the landlady who was showing him to the room. In the middle of the conversation, Pat said, 'I hear the old man is visiting from Denver. I'd bet Dan Cunningham would give his right arm to know I flattened the drivers on the 200.' With this evidence of an unintentional self-confession, I rolled over in bed, rapped on the wall and rendered my verdict, 'Pat, sixty days suspension!'

"Pat came into my office in Denver later and told me how his blood had boiled when he heard my voice coming through the wall and what a resultant ribbing he received from other engineers who had found out he talked not only out of turn, but right through the partition."

Between the ham and the Irish whiskey, Bill Morse told a story of an Irish section foreman who carried an old brake beam in his hand so that when a derailment occurred, he could drop the brake beam in the middle of the track as evidence the brake beam coming down had caused the derailment. When cars pile up, brake beams are torn up and scattered around. On one occasion, the section foreman made a mistake and dropped his brake beam on the wrong end of the derailment. When taken to task for this effort to deceive, he laughed it off saying, "Sure and it must have fallen off another train going the other way!"

One afternoon, a young man walked into Dan's office at Denver. The caller was Dan's brother, Frank, who as assistant general manager of the Standard Stoker Company, had left Erie, Pennsylvania, to test the original Standard Stoker on the Denver and Rio Grande railroad. Dan was greatly amused by this story his brother told:

"We were making the initial trip up the mountain to Tennessee Pass and, as I was a stranger, the fireman was very courteous, showing me the scenery and telling about different incidents that happened along that section of the Rio Grande railroad. He was so interested in my comfort that he forgot to notice the operation of the stoker. I was watching the engineer and I could see he was shutting off the injector and putting it on after the engine picked up a little steam and at every interval he would look at his watch as we had only a few minutes to clear the main line for the passenger train following. In other words, the engineer was swapping steam for water.

"It finally got to the point where we had about a hundred

pounds of steam and no water. The fireman then noticed we were moving very slowly and he jumped from the seat box to the deck of the locomotive. At that point he looked at the water glass and the engine had commenced to foam which showed about two inches of suds in the water glass. Then he did the wrong thing. He grabbed the engineer, who was already furious, and shaking him he said, 'My God, Bill, what's that in the water glass?' The angry engineer replied, 'That's ice you damned son-of-a-bitch, get down and hook her!'

"The fireman did this and we cleared the main line by one minute for the passenger train."

Frank wanted to know how Dan was coming along with his D. & S. L. position and Dan laughed. "Well, Frank," he said, "I'm very much like the hod carrier who wrote his brother in Ireland to come to America as all he had to do was carry brick up to the top of a fifteen story building and there was a man who did all the work."

Actually Dan was "helping the man on the roof" too. The Moffat railroad had its share of the war effort. After President Woodrow Wilson had suggested a "peace without victory" to the European belligerents in January, 1917, the United States had broken diplomatic relations with Germany the first week in February, and April found us at war with the Central Powers. In May the Conscription Bill had been signed by President Wilson and on July 3 the first American expeditionary force arrived in France.

In October, just about the time the British had finished capturing the Turkish Mesopotamian army led by Ahmed Bey, the American army was preparing to fire its first shot, and a French firing squad was training its rifle sights on Mata Hari, Dutch dancer and spy, Dan received an urgent message from the Denver and Rio Grande. The mechanical officer, who had created the acrimonious condition with Dan, had died suddenly, and President Brown and Vice President and General Manager James Russell had named Dan's friend W. W. Lemen as superintendent of motive power. Now the Rio Grande wanted Big Dan back on the D. & R. G. as assistant superintendent of motive power with headquarters at Salt Lake City.

The altitude-defying Denver and Salt Lake had won Dan's deep respect, yet he knew the Rio Grande offer at Salt Lake City called for but one answer. He accepted the position.

As to David Moffat's dream, the big tunnel was commenced in 1922 and financed by the state of Colorado. Cost was estimated at about $6,800,000 and four years were allotted for the task of boring through the northern shoulder of James Peak.

But even as the engineers had been wrong about the practicability of operating a railroad over Corona Pass, so they misjudged the interior of the mountain. Workmen soon ran into masses of muddy shale which necessitated the timbering of every foot in that condition. When the tunnel was completed in 1927, costs had soared to $18,000,000.

But even at this high cost, the Moffat Tunnel was a remarkable accomplishment. It is six miles six hundred feet in length and reaches an altitude of 9,257 feet above sea level. The bore shortens the rail distance between Denver and Salt Lake via the Rio Grande by 173 miles. At the time it was built, the tunnel was the longest railway tunnel in the United States, but, in 1929, the Great Northern railroad opened nearly eight-mile-long Cascade Tunnel in Washington.

The Moffat Tunnel, linked with the opening of the Rio Grande's Dotsero Cutoff for the first time put Denver directly on a main transcontinental route. And the brave little Denver and Salt Lake continues to operate to its rails end at Craig.

In the words of George William Curtis, disbelievers had said that David Moffat had "dreamed a dream that could not be."

From deep in the interior of James Peak, comes the answer to those skeptics. It is echoed and re-echoed by the roaring trains of the Rio Grande!

CHAPTER XVII

*B*IG DAN patted the object standing before him with all the affection of a horse opera movie star fondling his horse. He walked around and around looking it over with the approving eyes of a Kentucky colonel inspecting his entry in the derby. Then Dan sat down. He glowed with a satisfaction equal to that of Satan in Milton's *Paradise Lost*:

> "High on a throne of royal state, which far
> Outshone the wealth of Ormus and of Ind,
> Or where the gorgeous East with richest hand
> Showers on her kings barbaric pearl and gold,
> Satan exalted sat. . . ."

Yes, Mephistopheles in all his glory never could have felt better than did Big Dan Cunningham as he sat down in his new office as assistant superintendent of motive power for the Rio Grande at Salt Lake City. For there in front of him was a brand new desk of polished mahogany, hand built by cabinet maker Edman, who had supervised digging up the plank from its hiding place near the yard shed.

Dan Cunningham had kept his vow. He had returned to the Rio Grande, to Salt Lake, and to a beautiful mahogany desk!

As Little Buttercup sings in Act II of *H. M. S. Pinafore*, "things are seldom what they seem," so Dan's magnificent desk did not mean he had a "desk job." Not with the rush of Rio Grande trains carrying war supplies and troops through the heart of the Rockies. He put in eighteen to twenty hours a day fighting the problem of keeping engines and cars rolling, wiring ahead for supplies and riding troop trains.

Americans, Australians, Maoris, all came by the way of Salt Lake City. Dan's Mormon friend, O. B. Evans, met the Maoris from New Zealand at the train and delighted them when he talked in their native tongue.

With Dan at work almost every minute, news came from Washington he was to receive a commission as captain in the Railroad Engineers and to report to San Francisco. On the Salt Lake Division, Superintendent Racy, Assistant Master Mechanic James, and Road Foreman McGinnis had received their commissions and left the Rio Grande.

E. L. Brown, president of the Rio Grande, said flatly Dan could not be released to the army as his work was essential to the railroad's operation. Brown protested to General Richard Henry Aishton, who had risen from axman in the engineering corps, Chicago and Northwestern railroad, to president of that line, and who became regional director of the United States Railroad Administration for the Northwestern region. The protest of the Rio Grande president was allowed and Dan remained a civilian fighting on the home front with his theme song to the railroad's engineers *Johnny Get Your Run!*

The action of the Federal government in taking over the railroads instead of aiding the railroad men worked a hardship in many instances. In the language of the railroaders it was "one hell of a mess." Here was the old story of men, who knew nothing of a particular railroad's problems, trying to tell that line how it should be run. Some of the men so assigned were not capable and the situation could have been summed up by Quintilian when he wrote in his *Institutiones Oratoriæ* "Those who wish to appear wise among fools, among the wise seem foolish."

At Dom-le-Mesnil, France, on the morning of November 11, 1918, three French soldiers, Beaufils, Durocq, Seyler, died under German fire at 10.59 a.m. These men were the final Allied soldiers officially reported as killed in France in World War I. One minute after their deaths, the bugles sounded "Cease Firing."

World War I was over.

Historians and diplomats and journalists wrote of the glory of the Youth who had died so that vandal powers no longer could menace the small nations and a new freedom was born for the enlightened world and never again would the lights go out in Europe.

With the war's conclusion, the American railroads were taxed to their capacity delivering the Doughboys to their homes. Big Dan rode over the Union Pacific with Director General of the Railroads William G. McAdoo. This was shortly after McAdoo had issued a circular requesting the public to stay off the trains in order that the railroads could handle the returning veterans.

Spoke Dan to McAdoo: "Mr. McAdoo, if you pardon me, I think you used the wrong psychology on the public. What you should have done was to send everybody in the United States an annual pass on the railroads. Because it was free, no one would have wanted to go anywhere!"

Time was also changed by the government and one colored porter on the Rio Grande said to Dan, "Boss, seems as like the Rio Grande missed something in not getting Mistah Woodrow Wilson to work for us. Why that President Wilson is a greater man than Joshua. Why Joshua only made the sun stand still. President Wilson, he not only made the sun stand still, but he took the railroads away from the white folks and gave them to his son-in-law!"

Part of Dan's work was visiting all the shops and roundhouses on the Rio Grande. At Leadville, Colorado, he was inspecting the enginehouse and at the sand house he ran into an old Irishman. Recalling his Irish friends on the Moffat, Dan walked up and said, "What is your name and what do you do?"

The chow puffed away at his clay pipe for a few moments. Then he wiped his pipe on his red undershirt and said, "My name is Pat Murphy and I dry the sand for the locomotives. Now what is your name and what do you do?"

"I'm Dan Cunningham and I'm the new assistant superintendent of motive power on the Rio Grande."

Pat filled his pipe, lit it with a live coal from the fire in the sand stove, looked right past Dan and gazed at Mt. Massive. Finally he spoke, "Well, son, you have a darned good job and see that you take care of it."

Dan felt himself dismissed and he walked away "knowing that as far as Pat Murphy was concerned, he owned the railroad and I was just so much surplus baggage doing very little to keep the wheels moving."

A few years after the war the Rio Grande expanded its

power and built new enginehouses. In 1921 the railroad purchased thirty Mountain type 4-8-2 and ten Mallet 2-8-8-2 engines. President Brown resigned and J. H. Young succeeded him. Under Young's direction new identical shops were built at Salt Lake and Burnham, Colorado, and, for the first time on the Rio Grande, Dan had really modern top shops under his direction. Dan was quite proud of his new 18 stall roundhouse with room inside for all the locomotives. Fine shops were also built at Grand Junction, Salida, Pueblo and Alamosa.

With the Rio Grande all fussed up like a girl making her debut at a Junior League dance, came trouble. June, 1922, the shopmen of the nation's railroads walked out on strike.

The Rio Grande shopmen lined up, turned in their locker keys with the words, "Goodbye, Boss, we'll be back in a few weeks." Most of the men had not wished to strike as the Rio Grande and the shopmen had completed a mutually satisfactory contract. But the Grand Lodge had pulled them out on the surmise that if all the shopmen walked out, the strike bound railroads would have no men to draw upon for labor.

Dan felt the union made a mistake in not ordering out the men on a few lines, thereby allowing the men at work to support the strikers and their families.

As the railway shop employees left the premises, Salt Lake newspaper reporters gathered around Dan and asked on what terms the strike would be settled. Dan replied, "Whoever wins the victory will dictate the terms of peace!" This remark was quoted by the press throughout the nation.

Most of the foremen had stayed in and, later in the day, they went into a huddle in the corner of the old corrugated iron roundhouse. Soon Dan saw them running from the place almost panic-stricken. "We've been bombed!" one of the foremen shouted to Dan. Actually what had happened was that Bill Sullivan, erecting shop foreman, as a joke had thrown a big rock on the iron roof. But some of the foremen were so frightened they never returned to the shop.

Dan knew train operations must continue despite the strike. With Jim Thayer, superintendent of shops, aiding him, Dan had the men who weren't on strike clean the cars out of the coach shop, set up two large cooking ranges and two hundred iron cots with mattresses and blankets. Cooks, waiters and guards were hired. From Fort Douglas, an army officer sent Dan a German Luger revolver and a supply of shells. Dan sent back a note of thanks; locked the revolver in his desk where it was to stay for the duration of the trouble. The Salt Lake shop was ready to stand the seige of the strikers.

Soon strikers from foreign railroads drifted into the Salt Lake shops and asked for work. These men needed money to support their families. At first the local strikers were not worried and from the top of the Fourth Street viaduct, which ran over the middle of the shop, they shouted to Dan, "Boss, how are you coming along with your scabs?"

As days passed into weeks and the strikers saw newly painted and conditioned locomotives move out of the shops, violence broke out. Strikers stoned the so-called scabs. Dan felt sorry for the strikers, yet he had to maintain order. When the Salt Lake Police department was unable to furnish protection, Dan turned to the army. At Fort Douglas, Dan found many young men, sons of army officers, vacationing from college. These men readily accepted an offer to work in the shops. In a few days a striker injured a young worker from the fort. Immediately the army rushed down soldiers and General Mc-Alexander, known as "The Rock of the Marne," said, "I'll make this damned place fit for an American to work!" The military set up machine guns and from then on there was no violence on the part of strikers around the shop.

Dan was never molested. He walked among the strikers and chatted with them. His only protection was his set of shop keys. Several times he had food passed out to the men as he could not stand the idea of their families going hungry. Night and day Dan was on the shop premises and never did he lose the respect of either the strikers or the non-strikers.

Finally the labor dispute ended. The railroads, having won, dictated the terms of peace. Dan passed out the locker keys and the men returned to work.

The strike was not without its humorous moments. The Rio Grande had hired a few negroes. While the strike was on, Dan told them never to go off the shop grounds, but one

"Teakettle" narrow gauge locomotives pull one of the first passenger trains over Veta Pass for the "baby railroad" in the early 70's.

Photo credit: *Rio Grande*

A Rio Grande narrow gauge stock train moves up Marshall Pass.

Photo credit: *Rio Grande*

Power in the mountains. Five engines pull a passenger train up Soldier Summit before the grade was cut from 4 per cent to 2 per cent. This picture was made around 1911.

Photo credit: *Rio Grande*

Moffat's railroad carries on. A 3600 class engine in action on the Denver and Salt Lake.

Photo credit: *Denver and Salt Lake*

darkie slipped out and went up town. Coming back he was molested by a group of pickets. When he arrived back at the shop he told Dan, "I know, suh, I was wrong, but I got lonesome. I was tending to my own business when I run into a bunch of them thar pickups. One of 'em made a pass at me with a club. I reached into my pocket for my social instrument. If it had not got hung on my pants whar they was tore, if the pickups had not run when they seen what I had in my hand, it would have taken a doctor foah days to have sewed 'em up!"

This story of the colored worker and the "pickups" recalls to Dan's mind James Lenard, so black a piece of coal would have made a white mark on him, and for many years office janitor at the shops.

One evening Dan returned to his office quite late. Dan's office was next to that of the late Jack Snyder, road foreman of equipment, whose death had taken place only a few days previously. As Dan entered his office he found James cleaning it.

"James, how late do you work?" Dan asked.

The negro answered, "You know I have to keep the Big Boss' office spick and span."

"Never mind that stuff," Dan replied, "but I want to warn you about working late at night. The other night I came in on a train, came to my office to sign some letters that had to go out in the morning. Now I was sitting right here at my desk, James, when I heard the bells on the Cathedral sound the hour of midnight. That's the time when the graves open up and the dead wander around.   All at once Jack Snyder's office lighted up and there at his desk I saw Jack Snyder all dressed in white. I said, 'Jack, what do you want?' and the white figure turned to me and said, 'Mr. Cunningham, I can never rest in my grave until I find a certain letter.' Then quickly the lights went out and Jack's ghost disappeared before he could find the letter. Now, James, Mr. Snyder was a mighty fine man and, if you are around the office at midnight and Mr. Snyder speaks to you, I want you to answer him very polite."

James Lenard's arms trembled all the way down to where

they reached his knees, and he spoke shakily, "No, Boss, he might speak to whar I wuz, but he won't speak to me. If I see him first, it will take a gang o' the carpenters a mighty long time to stop up the walls whar I went fru!"

Never again did James Lenard take so long to get his work done that he stayed at the offices until after dark!

Sometime after this, Lenard came into the Rio Grande offices bandaged up as if he were an Egyptian mummy. Dan asked the janitor if he had been in a wreck.

"No, Boss," responded the janitor, "I just jined the Masons."

"What happened to you, James?"

"Well, Boss, I jined the Flower of the Night Lodge made up of cullid folks. They gave me two words, one of which I was never to write on pain of death. They set me down at a desk. Then the members of the lodge got into an argument about the gals wearing their dresses shorter and what this might do to us men. I was taking it all in and kinda got my mind off the word I was not to write. About this time a lodge brother said, 'Now, James, how would you write this word?' Not thinking, I wrote out the forbidden word. The lodge brother looked at it and said slowly, 'Ah, James, too bad.' "

Dan shook his head in sympathy. "Surely, James, they did not hurt you."

James looked over his bandages, answered, "Just enough, Boss. Just enough to put me almost in my grave!"

Shortly after the strike was settled, President Young resigned from the Rio Grande and T. H. Beacom from the Rock Island came in as president and W. J. O'Neill returned to the D. & R. G. W. from the Rock Island as chief mechanical officer. W. W. Lemen, Dan's friend dating back to Williamson, left railroading to go to Los Angeles and enter business for himself.

In 1924, the Rio Grande's management again changed and Samuel J. Pyeatt became president. Pyeatt, who was born at Prairie Grove, Arkansas, had entered railroading in 1894 as a clerk on the C. C. & St. L., progressed with the St. Louis, Iron Mountain and Southern, the Pere Marquette, the St. Louis-San Francisco, until, in 1918, he was president of the

Gulf Coast Lines and, during World War I, had been federal manager for many of the southwest railroads. It was during Pyeatt's early administration that the famous Dotsero Cutoff, linking Denver and Salt Lake via the Moffat Tunnel, was built.

In 1935, Wilson McCarthy and Henry Swan became Trustees of the Rio Grande. Denver-born, Princeton graduate Henry Swan had been prominent in Colorado banking circles, and since 1923, had been vice-president of the U. S. National Bank. Wilson McCarthy, born in American Fork, Utah, graduate of Osgood Hall in Canada and Columbia University, had become well known in his public career in Salt Lake embracing such positions as district judge, state senator, and western director of the R. F. C. In December, 1934, he became president of the Denver and Salt Lake railway and a year later was made co-trustee of the Rio Grande along with Henry Swan.

With the coming of O'Neill to the Rio Grande, the position of assistant superintendent of motive power was abolished and Big Dan was made master mechanic at Salt Lake in charge of that Division.

About this time, Dan had a visitor in his office—a tall, heavy set man in his late thirties—who introduced himself as William H. Sagstetter, president of the Salt Lake Iron and Steel Company. The visitor wanted the Rio Grande to roll some steel boiler sheets for him as his plant did not have the facilities for such work. Dan was pleased to fill the request and showed Sagstetter around the shop.

"Know anything about railroad shops?" queried Dan.

"A little bit, Mr. Cunningham," the visitor answered. "I used to be a machinist."

Dan's interest heightened. "I was a machinist myself for the Santa Fe and the Norfolk and Western. What roads were you on?"

The visitor chuckled, "Quite a few of them. Started out in my hometown of Wabash, Indiana, as an apprentice on the Wabash. Then I was a machinist with the Texas and Pacific, Guatemala Central, Costa Rica railroad, Panama railroad, Pennsylvania, the Cleveland, Cincinnati, Chicago and St. Louis, the Los Angeles and Salt Lake, and the Southern Pacific. Yes, I was a much travelled boomer. In 1907 I became general foreman and shop superintendent for the Cannanea, Rio, Yaque and Pacific railroad at Emppalme, Sonora, Mexico, and in 1910 I left there to become master mechanic for the Kansas City Southern, first at Shreveport, Louisiana, and then at Pittsburg, Kansas. I left Pittsburg, where I was president of the Pittsburg Boiler and Machine Company, to come to Salt Lake in 1922."

Dan felt any explanation of the operation of the Rio Grande shop was quite unnecessary. Soon he and Bill Sagstetter became good friends. Big Dan little knew that in 1937, after Sagstetter had been assistant superintendent of motive power for the Wabash, he was to return to the Rocky Mountains as chief mechanical officer for the Rio Grande and assistant to the president for the Denver and Salt Lake. Under his direction the Rio Grande, among other accomplishments, has developed one of the most outstanding research laboratories in the national railroad field. Aggressive A. E. Perlman is chief engineer of the Rio Grande.

Dan's office at Salt Lake was a mecca for unusual visitors. Around 1928, for example, Charles Sexton came in from Palisades, Nevada. Sexton ran the Eureka Nevada railroad and was a brother of the late John Sexton of the Eureka Nevada, colorful individualist in western railroading who, like Charles, had kept his railroad running against mounting odds.

A fire had destroyed the Eureka Nevada roundhouse at Palisades and burned up practically all of the railroad's equipment. Charles Sexton wanted the Salt Lake shop to rebuild one of his burned narrow gauge locomotives—brought over on a Western Pacific flatcar—and Dan soon had permission from the sympathetic Rio Grande officials at Denver to aid Sexton and his fire-ravaged railroad.

While this permission was being granted, Sexton told Dan the story of the picturesque Eureka Nevada as well as yarns of such railroads as the Virginia and Truckee, the Nevada Central, the Ruby Hill, the Battle Mountain and Lewis, the Carson and Colorado, the Austin City railway and other bonanza country iron pikes.

Charles Sexton was practically the entire management of the railroad which he ran with the aid of four brothers left over from the days when the Eureka Nevada was the Eureka and Palisades. The E. N. trains were operated under a windup telephone communications system. The conductor would hop from his train, call in by a wayside phone, get his orders to proceed to the next telephone station, or else to wait until his brother's train had cleared the track.

In its prime, Eureka, Nevada, was noted for lead; both the lead dug from the ground and the lead spewed around its streets by the six shooters of the "reach for your hip" frontier mining men. Eureka in its boom days needed only William S. Hart, Tom Mix and a movie camera.

The business headache at Eureka was the high cost of ore transportation from there to Palisades which was ninety miles away and on the Central Pacific. Wagon freighters charged twenty dollars a ton for the trip, and from Palisades the ore had to be shipped to Salt Lake City for final refining. With this situation in mind, the mining interests planned a railroad.

After several preliminary efforts had failed to materialize, construction on the Eureka and Palisades railroad was started in December, 1873, backed by a strange pair, Darius O. Mills, president of the Bank of California and W. L. Pritchard, known from Salt Lake west as "Nick of the Woods." Pritchard was a product of the 1849 days when he had commenced freighting with one team and had multiplied his business until he had hundreds of wagons and several thousand horses.

From the Central Pacific came Chinese laborers to build the E. & P. and in October, 1875, after the freight wagon king had withdrawn his support, the completed railroad was toasted from huge kegs of beer. The Eureka and Palisades had cost $1,500,000 to build, but in a year it had paid for itself! Ore filled the cars on the narrow gauge line and thrilled Indians rode atop the box cars on passes given them so as to keep the redmen's good will.

But the once flourishing mines slackened and in 1900 the E. & P. went into receivership and, in 1910, floods damaged the railroad so badly complete operation was halted for two years. Then, backed by Boston capital, the E. & P. became the Eureka Nevada railroad and from a California narrow gauge, the Colusa and Lake, came colorful, fighting John Sexton to manage the revamped line.

Nothing awed John Sexton, not even the mighty Southern Pacific with which he sometimes crossed swords. At one place where the S. P. tracks crossed his, Sexton had a gate built and every Southern Pacific train had to stop while the conductor unlocked the gate so that the S. P. trains could proceed. Too, Sexton demanded that the S. P. men close the gate and lock it after them or else the gate key would be placed in the Eureka Nevada station and this meant a hike to the station by the Southern Pacific men.

John Sexton's most publicized bit of rugged individualism came not long after World War I. The United States government owed the Eureka Nevada for the mail contract but "red tape" held up the check. Sexton's railroad was short on money and the need for this check was acute. But Washington gave little heed to the requests which came in on the letterhead of a tiny railroad way out in Nevada.

One day the Southern Pacific's famous *Overland Limited* pulled into Palisades. On the Eureka Nevada tracks sat a train to which was attached a lemon hued car on which was lettered in brilliant red "This Car For Dogs and Japs." The startled passengers on this and other trains coming through Palisades soon spread the story of the Eureka Nevada's "special car." Government men rushed out to Sexton to protest and tell him such an incident might precipitate a war. John Sexton patiently explained the government had the wrong attitude as this car was an extraordinary concession he had made to Japs and to dogs; however, if the government were displeased there was the matter of a little check from Washington.

Not long afterwards the car disappeared from the E. N. tracks. And John Sexton looked contentedly at his bank book and the deposit of a United States government check for the mail contract. A few years later John Sexton died and Charles Sexton took over the railroad's management.

Despite Charles Sexton's capable efforts to carry on the business, after spasmodic prosperity the Eureka Nevada was discontinued in 1938. By then its only train was a not too modern gasoline motor car. So passed another small railroad which had written its history in the brave new world of the west. History had moved too fast and there was no place for the Eureka Nevada as the pages turned.

Dan heard other stories of western railroading from such men as his friend Frank Haymond, now vice-president and general manager of the Bingham and Garfield railroad, owned by the Utah Copper Company. Haymond was a conductor on the early Rio Grande Western.

When General Palmer built the Rio Grande Western, the tracks were laid on dirt ballast which meant the trains raised more dust than a herd of bison on the plains. Colonel Dodge, who was associated with General Palmer in the building of the Denver and Rio Grande and the Rio Grande Western, was the subject of hay fever. Because of this engineers dreaded to see Dodge's private car come on the R. G. W. tracks. To keep the dust out of his car, Colonel Dodge would have it run in front of the locomotive. Consequently, the engineer and fireman were almost smothered by the dust.

Haymond would tell of the early railroad war between the D. & R. G. and the R. G. W. When engines from Denver reached the Colorado line, Rio Grande Western men would hi-jack them and, in turn, when locomotives came from Utah to the Colorado boundary, the Denver and Rio Grande men would seize them. Each railroad contended for the support of the trainmen and sometimes when a train reached the boundary, the engineer would order his fireman to pull out the pin and the crew and locomotive would desert to the rival railroad.

This conflict between the two railroads made co-operation in freight and passenger traffic difficult and the lines wisely decided to get together and this co-ordination became closer until the two merged. Any fights between the

Colorado and Utah divisions from then on were simply "family spats."

It cannot be denied there was some rivalry between Utah and Colorado interests. Frank Haymond's Bingham and Garfield as well as the Utah railway came about as a result of inter-state disagreements.

Colonel D. C. Jacklin, who developed the Utah Copper Company, wanted the management of the D. & R. G. to build a short line running along the mountains from the mines to the smelters thereby avoiding the long drop to Welby and then on to the smelters. The Rio Grande had built the Welby branch line from the main tracks at Midvale. This branch had a 4 per cent grade and the ore trains came down the mountain to Welby and then to the smelters at Magna and Arthur.

Jacklin's request was refused by the Denver officials of that time and the Utah Copper Company built its own Bingham and Garfield railroad.

The Utah railway might be called the railroad which was built by a picture! Around 1915, A. B. Apperson, general superintendent of the Utah lines of the Rio Grande, clashed with H. U. Mudge, short time president of the D. & R. G., who had come from the Rock Island. Apperson had risen from switchman on the Union Pacific at Cheyenne and was highly popular. As a result of the conflict, Apperson resigned, went to New York City where he showed a picture to financial interests active in the Utah Fuel Company. In this photograph five Rio Grande engines were pulling a nine car passenger train up the 4 per cent grade from Tucker to Soldier Summit. Using the passenger train as an example, Apperson related the difficulties the Rio Grande encountered in hauling coal mined by Utah Fuel into Salt Lake City. As a result, the Utah Fuel Company built the Utah Coal Route, now known as the Utah railway, and the D. & R. G. lost the revenue from hundreds of cars of coal. Victor E. Chasles, the French author and editor, once wrote "The sure way to miss success is to miss the opportunity." The Bingham and Garfield and the Utah railway came about because opportunities were not wasted.

And speaking of opportunities, the Rio Grande had a

With its unique glare-shield a heavy Rio Grande locomotive thunders through Glenwood Canyon.

A Norfolk and Western coal train passing the Palisades along New River, Virginia, as the N. & W. serves a mighty expanse of black diamonds.
                                                    Photo credit: *Norfolk and Western*

During World War II, such giants of the rails as this sped troops and materiel through the Rocky Mountains.
                                                    Photo credit: *Rio Grande*

roundhouse foreman who took every opportunity to tell how active he was in signing requisitions, time cards and such. Dan and W. J. O'Neill sent in a requisition by one of the shop boys for this foreman to sign. Back it came with the man's signature. The requisition called for twenty feet of hemp rope to hang the roundhouse foreman. The foreman had signed his own death warrant! Later the same foreman signed a time card made out to George Washington and Abraham Lincoln for shoveling snow off the top of the roundhouse.

One winter afternoon Dan and O'Neill stood under the viaduct in a foot of snow and ten below weather. Trouble had piled on the Salt Lake Shop. Out of three boilers in the stationary plant, two of them had headers broken; there was an engine off the track on the cinder pit and the turn table was inoperative as there was no air to run the motor. There were three overdue passenger engines in the roundhouse trying to get steam enough up to go out on the road. The powerhouse had only thirty pounds of steam and the smoke stacks laid down a barrage which poured out over the city. Dan and O'Neill were watching this smoke, when a man walked up and said, "I'm Smoke Inspector Beck and who has charge of this plant?"

Big Dan answered, "Inspector Beck, I'm in charge."

The inspector replied, "Mr. Cunningham, don't you know I could put you in jail for making all this smoke!"

Dan laughed and ran over his troubles at the shop to Beck. Then he said, "Mr. Beck, bring on your jail. That's where I'd like to be right now!"

Beck saw the situation and retreated into the smoke.

Like all railroad men, Dan had a deep affection for locomotives whether they were puffing switchers or mighty mountain types. Dan recalls when engineers had regular locomotives and treated their engines as if they were members of the family. On this subject Dan once wrote:

"My brother, Frank, who is a railway supply man, and who has designed, built and run locomotives for the past thirty-five years, says that a locomotive has a mind and a soul all its own. They have their moods and are as temperamental as a Prima Donna. I know one engineer who, when his engine would not steam, would get out on the ground and throw rocks at his engine and then he would hurl cuss words which would make a mule skinner turn green with envy at his poor old locomotive which was puffing and blowing as she tried to get hot enough to pull the train. He would call the engine an 'Old Bitch' but, after the steam was up and the train moving, the engineer would change his mood, pet his locomotive and call her 'Good Old Betsy.' And the locomotive seemed to respond to the petting. I have never been able to figure out how a locomotive will respond to the petting, caressing or the damning of their engineers, but I know they do."

Big Dan's brother, Frank, who helped develop the Franklin locomotive booster, later was with Graham-White Sander and Prime Manufacturing Company, poured out his feelings about locomotives to a reporter on the Indianapolis *News*. Quoting the Indiana newspaper:

"Frank Cunningham is a specialist in locomotive diseases and from the Santa Fe to the Soo, wherever the rails of steam railroad lines spread their way, Cunningham is known as 'the engine doctor.' In fact, veteran engineers, who know what it is to coax and cajole and pet a fractious iron horse when the wind is blowing the wrong way, invariably allude to the specialist as Doctor Cunningham.

" 'I've been tinkering with locomotives since I was eighteen years old,' said Frank Cunningham, 'and I've become pretty well acquainted with their aches and pains. Engines do have such things, you know; in fact, I've seen them when I thought it was the toothache. I'm convinced that a railroad engine is the next thing to human.

" 'I trust the ladies will pardon me, but after years of patient experience with the whims, the moods, the changes, the spells, and I might say the hysterics of the modern locomotive, I am of the opinion she might be compared to a woman. Both are magnificent, alluring, uncertain and interesting.

" 'It is the law of the railroad that an engine is of the feminine gender. I have never heard of a locomotive called Doc or Sam or Bill, but I have known scores of engineers to adopt the name of Katie or Mary for their locomotives and I

know one engineer on a southern line who refers to his locomotive as Irene. An engine can be as fickle, faithless and dis-
loyal as one of those Kipling vampires. When she wants to
go and is in good humor—and she is most of the time—our
new modern locomotives are one of the wonders of the age.' "

Gustav Kamptner, locomotive designer for the Rio
Grande, Austrian born and who often has said, "Big Dan
made an American of me," wrote in "The Battle Cry of the
Modern Locomotive" published in the *Locomotive Engineers
Journal*:

"Whenever we pass through our railroad yards or
through one of our roundhouses we see quite a number of
locomotives standing around. Without steam in the boiler,
without fire in the firebox, they impress one as being a mass
of cold steel—a complicated assemblage of boiler, frames,
rods, wheels, pipes—a conglomeration of metal.

"One is impressed with their immensity, weight, strength
of structure—yet they are cold and dead! But the picture
changes entirely when there is a fire in the firebox and the
steam is up.... She inhales and exhales. She stretches and moves
her mighty limbs. Her motions are mighty, majestic—and
beautiful.

"As the jockey, during the last lap of a championship
race, urges his steed, whispering to her to give her utmost—
to bring glory and riches to him; as the ancient mariner, alone
on the deck of his sailing brig—stark to the waist—holding
the steering wheel with his iron grip, while heavy swell buffets
his ship from side to side, so that the mast nearly touches the
waves; through a night when heaven and earth crash in a
monstrous deluge—with a curse or a prayer upon his lips that
the mast will come up once more to steady his ship—so does
the engineer whisper to the very soul of that monster engine.

"There must be no derailing of the engine truck when
she is pounding and rocking over the rails. There must be no
breaking of a spring-hanger at the front of the trailer truck
equalizer, which would let down the front end of the equalizer to ram against the rail ties and derail the engine. There
must be no breaking of a side-rod, which would pound

through the cab, killing the engineer and throwing the engine into the ditch.

". . .With a sigh of immense relief the huge steel monster comes to a stop. . .She has been kicked around, punched and tormented beyond endurance. For miles and miles; for hours and hours she struggled in travail. Yet she is still together—but immensely tired. You hear a groan and sometimes she shivers. She may be hurt internally. Who knows?

"The hostler takes her slowly to the roundhouse for a rest. There she is examined. Her intestines and 'limbs' are inspected. She will be cleaned inside and outside. After a good rest—well conditioned and prepared—with fire again in her bowels and steam pressure up to 285 pounds—life again pulsating through her mighty body—she is again ready to do battle, to become a living monster—a *human beast of burden*.

"We work on her. We laugh at her. Sometimes we swear at her. But we do love her—because—with us, not yet and never will be dead the romance of railroading."

While Dan was on the Moffat he designed an engine for the railroad which was built by Lima. About the same time the Rio Grande bought their first 1400 or Santa Fe type locomotive. At the time it was the largest freight engine in the world and the sight of it inspired a railroad poet to letter on the sides of the tank, "They built you for a battleship, but they didn't have any guns, so they sold you to the Rio Grande to pull ten thousand tons."

One of Dan's favorite locomotive yarns was written by Mark Hager, correspondent for the *Norfolk and Western* magazine at the Williamson shops. Hager is a well known spinner of railroad tales and some of them have appeared in the national magazines. Wrote Mark Hager:

"One night back in the year 1915, when Hostler Mose Francis took engine 589 down to the coal wharf for coal and water to get her ready for No. 3, he noticed two men walking up Pond Creek track in the vicinity of the Pond Creek Bridge, and the two men were singing, and the song was *My Old Kentucky Home* and it sounded good in the still moonlight.

"After Hostler Francis got the engine coaled and watered, he left her there and went back to the roundhouse, and in about an hour he went back to take her to the passenger station. When he got there he called up the roundhouse and said the engine wasn't there, that he couldn't find her anywhere. Roundhouse foreman Dase and several shopmen joined in the search for the engine. It was unusual to lose a live engine. They went round and round and, in their bewilderment, they even looked in the willow bushes over by the river, and it reminded me of when I had to hunt the cows in the woods late of evenings, and how the cows got to know by the setting sun about what time of the evening they would be come after, and they didn't want to be disturbed. They'd lie down and chew their cuds and get as still as a mouse, but all you had to do was sit down on a log for a few minutes, and soon one would forget she had a bell on and take a swipe at the flies. But now, of course, in hunting for the engine they had to remember that an engine doesn't have to swipe at flies. That's one of the main differences between cows and engines. You never heard of flies bothering an engine, so they couldn't depend on her shaking her head and rattling the bell. But still, engines do make a lot of noise. A live engine just won't keep quiet. They groan, growl, wheeze, sneeze, hiss and fret, and are generally rather ill-natured and impatient.

"And while they were searching for the engine, the roundhouse telephone rang, and it was the agent at Stone, Kentucky, and he wanted to know why a passenger engine was being backed up the creek at that time of night and said a man was blowing the whistle and giving it 'the lonesome moans' as if the man at the throttle was the spirit of Casey Jones.

"The first thought was that some reckless, rambling Romeo of the rails had eloped with her in the moonlight. Roundhouse foreman Dase, Hostler Mose Francis, and a couple of the other shopmen jumped on the 1022 and struck out up the creek after the 589. At Toler, Kentucky, they met her coming home from her spin. With presence of mind, Francis reversed the 1022 hoping to run fast enough back down the creek to cushion the inevitable shock, although he knew he couldn't hope to outrun her. But the other shopmen on the 1022 felt a bit flighty and, preferring the air with the night birds, bailed out. The companion of the 589 must have also felt some misgivings and jumped, deserting his lady of the rails for the shadows of the Kentucky hills, for there wasn't a soul on the 589 when she overtook the 1022, embraced her fondly, and gave her a long, loud, ardent kiss there in the Kentucky moonlight, and while the damage was slight, she was too weak to go on her run that night.

"I don't remember whatever became of the man who ran the 589 up the creek that night, but it turned out that one of the fellows singing *My Old Kentucky Home* was an old man who had been away for a long, long time, and he'd missed the Pond evening train, and couldn't get home that night; the second fellow came up and joined him in the song, and the old man told him how his folks had no doubt listened for the whistle and met the train. And they sang some more, and cried a little, and the second fellow got the engine, and blew the whistle, and took him home to the head of Pond Creek, and was returning with the engine when he was met by the 1022."

Samuel Johnson wrote, "If a man doesn't make new acquaintances as he passes through life, he will find himself left alone." So it was the returning traveller found in his singing companion a new friend capable of running a lonely locomotive and thereby, instead of being left alone, rode on a "private locomotive" to his old Kentucky home.

CHAPTER XVIII

*E*VER since the tin-types began to gallop and the infant moving picture industry made *The Great Train Robbery,* tales of the Iron Horse have come to life in the shadow world of the silver screen. From the days when Pearl White and Ruth Roland were tied to the tracks by villains, who didn't realize they could have made more progress with the beautiful heroines if they had resorted to stereopticon slides of the Boer war and a horsehair sofa, photoplays of the railroads have proved full fare tickets at the box office.

A medium-height, slim young man stood in Dan's office at the Rio Grande shops. "Mr. Cunningham," he said, "I want three railroad engines of the 1876 period."

Dan laughed. "The Rio Grande has lots of things, but I think, sir, your request could be filled better by the Smithsonian Institution."

A smile widened the young man's face and he said affably, "I'm Jack Morris from Hollywood. James Cruze is going to make a film called *The Night Flyer* starring William Boyd and Jobyna Ralston. We want to shoot the film down at Thistle and use Denver and Rio Grande Western equipment. My job is being the technical director. Your job, if you want it, will be to antedate all railroad equipment used in the movie to the 1876 period."

And so Dan took over the task of turning back part of the Rio Grande to the days when General Palmer was smashing his railroad across the Rockies. The shops built balloon stacks over the straight ones on the oldest locomotives in the shop, removed electric headlights, air pumps and hoses, and put in a long nosed cow-catcher with a Johnson bar in place of an automatic coupler. Picturesque oil headlights took their place on the front of the locomotives and cord wood was piled in the tender.

For the use of the Hollywood unit, a special train was made up of ten Pullmans, club car and work car with an electric engine in it for furnishing lights. Five full train and engine crews were dispatched to the aid of the Cruze people.

Six weeks were consumed in the filming around Thistle and Dan spent much of his time helping on the railroad angle. While at Thistle he met a girl who looked familiar to him, said hello, and discovered she was Ann Little, script girl, who had played with Wallace Reid in the famous *Whispering Smith* railroad movies.

The Night Flyer told the story of the rivalry of a locomotive engineer and a fireman (William Boyd) for the hand of a pretty hasher (Jobyna Ralston) at the railroad beanery at Medicine Hat. The unsentimental master mechanic had ordered the faithful Old 99 engine dismantled. But Boyd had a fondness for the veteran locomotive and hid it in some cottonwood trees behind the roundhouse. Shortly after this the railroad on which Boyd worked competed with a rival line for the mail contract. When Boyd's engineer got drunk and wrecked the locomotive assigned to the important mail run, Boyd brought out the Old 99 from the cottonwoods and went on to win the contract—and the girl.

While helping with the photoplay, Dan learned some of the tricks of moviedom. For the wreck scene, the engine was run half way across a stream at Thistle. Then the camera was stopped and the engine reversed. Railroad track men cut a rail and spiked it so the engine would plunge into ten feet of water. The locomotive started out again, the speed was increased, and the crew dropped off. After the empty locomotive had crashed into the dammed up water, Bill Boyd and the villain got under it and Bill came out looking as if he had made a split-second escape.

The heroic Old 99 had a cab built out of quarter inch board put together in sections. The cab, smoke stack, and sand box were fixed so they could be pulled loose by a man concealed in the tender.

Dan watched from the station at Thistle as Bill Boyd pulled Old 99 in just five seconds before the mail contract time had elapsed. Everything had fallen off the locomotive except Boyd and the throttle. So the mail contract was won and Old 99 had emerged from her hiding place for her final glory run.

In appreciation of the Rio Grande's co-operation, James

"Let her roll, let her roll, Mr. Engineer!" Santa Fe Diesel equipped freight
nears Needles, California.
                                                    Photo credit: *Santa Fe*

It's not always fair weather on the Rio Grande!   Photo credit: *Rio Grande*

Inset—FRANK H. CUNNINGHAM.   Photo credit: *Prime*

When the Rio Grande was organized in 1870, an average of 30 passengers weekly rocked between Denver and Colorado Springs by six-horse stage. It was the only means of transportation besides horseback. In its first full year of operation in 1872, the Rio Grande carried an average of 484 passengers weekly between the two towns. Other pictures show type of equipment in use in 1883, and an artist's conception of the new streamliners with "vista domes" placed in service in 1946 between Chicago and San Francisco over the Rio Grande and connecting lines of the Burlington and Western Pacific.

Photo credit: *Rio Grande*

Cruze let the Rio Grande lease *The Night Flyer* for a week's showing in Salt Lake City as a benefit of the Rio Grande Shop Relief Society. The railroad technical angle had been correct and this would have pleased the Smithsonian. The photoplay itself was excellent and this pleased the Rocky Mountain railroad people who came to Salt Lake to view the film. About the only unhappy people were those at Thistle. They missed their checks received for "extra" work!

But the movie audience isn't the only one which has seen Big Dan's handicraft on engines. With W. W. Lemen, Dan invented Mallet locomotive riding pads which eliminated the use of studs in the boiler and with it stud-leakage. This device has been used on many railroads.

Then, around 1937, Clem Schramm, post commander of the American Legion at Salt Lake and Dan's son-in-law, asked Dan to build an engine for the local chapter, 230, of the 40 and 8.

"Dan," said Schramm, "We want an engine 35 feet long with pony trucks, steel boiler and cab, sand box, electric headlights, pilot guides, crossheads, rods, sanders and piston valve cylinders. We want the prettiest engine ever seen by anybody and give it the zip of the old *Cannon-ball Express.*"

"What'll you do with this engine?" queried Dan.

"We'll exhibit it at the American Legion convention in Los Angeles. Here's a chance to make an engine, which will out do Hollywood, to be used in parades."

Dan immediately contacted his many friends in the railroad equipment business and from over the nation came gift parts for the highway travelling locomotive. From the Utah Copper Company came a thousand dollars worth of burnished copper to cover the entire engine and tender. The Silver King Mining Company sent enough silver to trim the engine with the Rio Grande and American Legion emblems and letter "Utah, the Silver and Copper State. The Center of Scenic America."

The sight of the magnificent copper engine with smoke pouring from its stack, is well known to Legionaires everywhere as the Salt Lake engine has been sent to conventions over the country. From civic affairs in Utah at such towns as St. George, Cedar City, Provo and Price to huge Legion gatherings in Chicago and New York and numerous other large cities, the Rio Grande-built engine carried the fame of its home.

Today *The Copper Engine* is only a memory as, in 1944, it was destroyed in a Rio Grande coach shop fire at Salt Lake City.

Oddly enough, Big Dan had played a leading part in the reorganization and modernization of the Salt Lake Fire Department. From the time Dan and John Van Lew had fought blazes with the Roanoke Volunteer Firemen, Dan had secretly yearned to be a Fire Chief. Early in 1941 Mayor Ab Jenkins asked Dan to come to his office. When Dan arrived he found assembled Fire Chief Levere M. Hansen, the City Commissioners, and the press. As the cameras clicked, Mayor Jenkins pinned a solid gold badge on Dan. From then on Dan has been the honorary Fire Chief of Salt Lake.

And just in case some of the Utahns missed the spectacle of the gleaming badge, the new fire truck and aerial ladder, with a water tower attachment extending 100 feet which can be elevated in thirty seconds by one man, was named the *Big Dan*. This combination truck—at the time the largest in the country—had been especially constructed for Salt Lake by the American-La France Foamite Company. *Big Dan* proved so successful New York City soon afterwards ordered five similar ones. Former Mayor LaGuardia may not have missed many fires in Gotham, yet The Little Flower did miss an excellent publicity opportunity when he didn't name one of his giant New York fire trucks the *Big Dan*.

Nevertheless, Dan's many friends in the Rocky Mountain area weren't satisfied with merely a gold badge and a fire truck in his honor. Mother has her day and Father his. There is a Guy Fawkes Day and All Saints Day; Army Day and Navy Day and Columbus Day; St. Valentine has a day and so does St. Nicholas. There is, of course, Dog Day and Groundhog Day.

June 11, 1941, was a day unique among all days as this was Dan Cunningham Day in Salt Lake City. Commented the Salt Lake *Tribune* in an editorial on Dan, "He is big of body, brain and heart."

This celebration was the result of a proclamation by Mayor Ab Jenkins, which read:

"WHEREAS, on Wednesday, June 11, 1941, Salt Lake City will have the opportunity to view the first D. & R. G. W. Diesel-electric engine and

"WHEREAS, railroad engines of this type are being placed in service in Salt Lake to conform with the new smoke abatement Program, and

"WHEREAS, Mr. D. G. Cunningham, Master Mechanic of the D. & R. G. W. Railroad has rendered valuable service far beyond the ordinary call of duty in furthering the Smoke Abatement Program, and further in cooperation with the Salt Lake Fire Department in its modernization program and,

"WHEREAS, the citizens of Salt Lake City owe D. G. Cunningham a sincere tribute for his unselfish work in helping build a better Fire Department for Salt Lake City and in assisting with other matters of civic betterment,

"NOW, THEREFORE, I, Ab Jenkins, Mayor of Salt Lake City, do hereby proclaim and set aside Wednesday, June 11, 1941, as 'DAN CUNNINGHAM DAY,' in order that the citizens of Salt Lake City may have an opportunity to honor suitably a man whose service has been nobly and freely given with no expectation of reward except of the knowledge of a good task well done."

The fame of Dan Cunningham Day spread throughout the railroad world. This day was a topic of conversation with such men as A. C. Shields, president of the Pittsburgh and Shawmut railroad in Pennsylvania and Larry Richardson, official of the Boston and Maine. Another person who read of it with interest was Dr. George Baskervill, chief surgeon of the Columbus and Greenville railway in Mississippi. Baskervill had been a classmate of Dan's at Blacksburg.

So had the name of Big Dan followed the iron pike.

Dan Cunningham took his honors in stride and his friends recalled a speech he had made at the Rio Grande shops when a veteran employee was retired with the usual ceremonies. Toward the end of an eloquent speech of tribute, Dan noticed his audience was almost in tears. So, changing his pace, Dan grasped the hand of his former employee, said loudly, "Sir, I have one last wish for you. I hope you live to be a hundred years old and I'll be a pall-bearer at your funeral!"

This closing comment made Utah platform history.

And, speaking of history, the early development of the Denver and Rio Grande had been brought into wide prominence in 1929-1930 when bronze tablets in honor of General Palmer, donated by his friend and associate, George Foster Peabody, were unveiled at the Union Depot, Denver; Union Depot, Salt Lake City; Colonia Railway Station, Mexico City; Colorado College and Hampton Institute in Virginia. Big Dan had participated in the unveiling ceremony at Salt Lake. Shortly after Dan Cunningham Day, Salt Lake City received another reminder of Rio Grande history when the first D. & R. G. engine which entered Salt Lake was placed in the Aviary grounds in Liberty Park. This Aviary land had been given the city by Russel Lord Tracy, Utah philanthropist and chairman of the Board of Directors of the Tracy Loan and Trust Company.

After the ceremony, which had been in charge of Big Dan, Russel Tracy revealed the fact he had ridden in the cab of the old engine, the 223, in April, 1885, on an assignment from the Mansfield, Ohio, *Daily News*. Born in Mansfield in 1860, Tracy had attended Oberlin College and come west shortly afterwards.

The writeup said:

"Cheyenne, Wyoming Ter., April 29, 1885.—Leaving Ogden today, I started for Denver. It is beautiful country, with flowers in full bloom, apple and peach trees in blossom and clover several inches high. Apparently within a few yards a background of mountains perfectly white with snow. Now all is warm; windows open and the fragrance from the fields speak in no mistaken terms of summer. A few hours later we are slowly but surely climbing the mountains. The windows one after another are closed; the green fields and blooming trees are all below us; the people on the platform come in; the porter builds a fire, and now snow and ice form the bed over which we ride.

"What a change in one afternoon. Having heard of the beautiful scenery we pass through on the morrow, I retire early. Am on the platform at 5 a.m., but oh, *what a country!*

"As I lean over the steps and look ahead I wonder where I will go. 'Could I but be on the engine,' is my thought, but I have already learned it is positively forbidden; nevertheless I will try. As scenery grows more and more fascinating I am more impatient to reach the next station and try to get on the engine. It is here, and hurriedly I run to the engineer and explain my wish but he finally says: 'It is against the rules.' Reaching in my pocket I draw forth two dollars but in reply he again says 'it is against the rules, I cannot let you ride.' A third and fourth dollar is brought out and still he has the same reply. I examine my pocketbook. A fifth dollar appears. I will offer it and stop at a cheap hotel in Denver. 'Tis done, but in reply I hear the same words—'But it is against the rules.' My hopes fall and I replace the money in my pocket as I step abroad the moving train. The newsboy with his cigars makes his usual trip. He has passed a hundred times before without my noticing them. I stop him with the words, 'Fill my outside pocket with your very best cigars.' The next station is reached and again I hasten forward to the engineer.

"As the train starts I step aboard the engine with the remark: 'You won't kick a man off will you?' He looks at me saying: 'You know it is against the rules' (but as he sees the cigars he adds) 'to kick a man off,' and gives me a seat in the fore part of the engine. The scenery, grand before, increases in grandeur and magnificence from this better lookout, and with one near to explain every point of interest. On we dash through the black canyon of the Gunnison. The fierce river is at our right, and the perpendicular cliffs on our left rise, one, two and even three thousand feet above our heads. The canyon is dark and so deep that the rays of the sun never fall within. It is narrow and scarcely room for even the river which for centuries has held the only claim of passage through it. Now the train dashes on with the river, each determined to have the right of way. But where is the opening and how will we go out? The train follows every point of the compass and still no nearer sunlight than before. The engine and rear car actually appear to be playing 'I spy,' so sharp and varied are the curves, that one is seldom out of sight of the other. We emerge from the canyon and gradually climb the mountain.

"Extra engines are put on, the grade being 212 feet to the mile. Slowly we ascend until near the summit we reach Marshall Pass, 10,500 feet; *the highest point* with one exception reached by any railroad in the world. The view is magnificent in the extreme. A few moments before the whole world seemed above us but now all seems below us. Nothing now but the limit of sight to restrict our view. We see the track away in the valley like a silver thread 'carelessly dropped down.' Here we see the headwaters of rivers which flow into the Atlantic and those of the Pacific. The train creeps cautiously along the edge of the precipice where the road bed is so narrow that two feet means two thousand, and eternity. We begin the descent. Our engine leaves the others and starts on its downward course alone. For an hour I am carried away with the wonder and beauty before me.

"The engineer calls my attention to a city, Salida, which is ten miles distant. 'Take out your watch and see if we can make it in ten minutes.' My feet, which have been out of the window resting on the boiler, are drawn in. I close the window, and what a ride it is! You can ride on a broad-gauge with cars behind you to steady the engine, one mile per minute and think possibly you are safe; but put yourself on a narrow-gauge road and go a mile per minute and you will think your days are numbered. I was shaking so that I could not tell whether my hand held a watch or a pocket book. My hat was jolted off and occupied a position in midair fully half of the time. Both my hands were now holding desperately to the seat, in vain trying to keep my body at least within two inches of it and still I was going like a trip hammer. I wanted to speak and tell the engineer not to jump the track for sake of showing how fast he could go; but I dare not speak. Had I once opened my mouth my tongue would have been severed into a dozen pieces. Oh, why did I not stay on the regular train instead of getting an engine, number 223, already behind time and which must reach the crossing by a certain minute. But we reach Salida in safety and I assure you I will know what engine I get on another time."

On the subject of unusual rides on trains, Dan believes the funniest experience he ever had was back on the Denver and Salt Lake when he was superintendent of motive power. In telling this story, which involves a railroad supplyman, Dan prefaces it with:

"I have always wanted to pay tribute to those good fellows, the so-called 'peddlers.' These wonderful fellows breeze into your office with a warm handshake, a new story and some excellent ideas they've picked up on some other railroad. Often the information they pass along helps overcome an apparently insurmountable problem that has worried you for a long time. These supplymen are walking *Information Please* experts and they bring the news and events of railroad land from the Delaware, Lackawanna and Western to the Nickel Plate, the Clinchfield, the San Diego and Arizona Eastern, and the Panhandle and Santa Fe.

"They put on their overalls, go into the shop and show a mechanic how to make some gadget work and quite frequently it is another company's device. Normally once a year we meet the peddlers at the mecca of all the hopes and joys of railroad men and their families—Atlantic City. At the railway conventions there the supply companies have on exhibition all the very latest machines, tools, locomotives, cars, and a multitude of educational displays. The conventions have their social side, too. Pushed by a negro porter you ride up and down the famous Board Walk and, as you pass some fellow railroader who knew you years ago, he will hail you with something like this, 'Pretty soft, Big Dan! I can remember you eating corn beef and cabbage out of a tin pail. And say, Dan, remember the first time you ever saw a man with socks on and you wanted to know if his shoes were so big he had to wear washers on his feet!'

"When I would get back to my home office enriched in knowledge, I would try to repay the supplymen's hospitality the best I knew how as I realized they also had to produce for their companies to make their bread and butter."

And so comes up the classic story of Big Dan and Johnny

Mourne, representing the Locomotive Superheater Company.

Tabernash, Colorado, had been engulfed by a blizzard for days and the bottom had fallen out of the mercury as the reading plunged past 60 below zero. Dan was swathed in so many clothes General Manager Morse told him if he fell down the wrecker would be required to pick him up.

Johnny Mourne, who had been making a service call on the Moffat, sided up to Dan and said, 'I've got to be in Chicago in several days. If I can make it to State Bridge, I can snowshoe it over to Wolcott and catch the Rio Grande at Denver."

Dan shook his head, "Sorry, Johnny, we can't take you anywhere. Haven't moved a wheel in five days. We're snowed in. Anyway, you'd never make that twenty miles on snowshoes in a ninety mile an hour gale."

"But," countered Johnny, "If I don't get to Chicago on time for an important meeting I'll be fired!"

All Dan could offer his friend was sympathy.

Several hours later Dan was sitting in the lobby of a Tabernash hotel when a call boy handed him a message from the head office reading: "Call out two Mallets, train crew and rotary and plow out the line from Tabernash and tie up at Denver. Get going as soon as possible!"

Dan sent the call boy to get Mourne. When his friend, shrouded in gloom, arrived Dan questioned, "Johnny, how bad do you want to get to Denver?"

Mourne answered slowly, "I will give you my right arm to get me there."

As Dan listened to these dramatic words he shook his head as if in meditation; then he spoke deliberately to the call boy, "Jimmy, this is Mr. Mourne and I have to get him to Denver right away. I want you to call two large Mallets, caboose, train crew and rotary and crew as quickly as possible and tell the train crew to put in lots of chow as I have a guest with me."

Johnny Mourne was speechless. Finally he stammered, "Dan, you mean to tell me you are calling all that big power and a rotary just to get me to Denver?"

Dan patted the supplyman on the shoulder. "Johnny,

JUDGE WILSON McCARTHY
Photo credit: *Rio Grande*

HENRY SWAN
Photo credit: *Rio Grande*

W. H. SAGSTETTER
Photo credit: *Rio Grande*

W. B. HALL
Photo credit: *Rio Grande*

H. S. WALL
Santa Fe

R. G. HENLEY
Norfolk and Western

L. C. SPRAGUE
Minneapolis and St. Louis

FRANK HAYMOND
Bingham and Garfield

J. D. LOFTIS
Atlantic Coast Line

JULIAN BAMBERGER
Bamberger

you are my friend and there is nothing I would not do for you. Now I think the smart thing for you to do is to stock up the caboose so the crew can eat as well as we when we are going over the Divide."

With tears of gratitude in his eyes, Johnny almost cleaned out a grocery store and a butcher shop and, when the train hit the snow, Johnny helped the brakeman prepare dinner. Big, thick steaks were smothered in onions and a Mulligan was cooked in a large kettle. The Mulligan consisted of tomatoes, corn, macaroni, beans, canned oysters, potatoes, ham hocks and onions. Grateful Johnny had spared nothing as far as food was concerned.

From his seat in the cupola, Dan could see the snow being thrown out by the rotary and by the exhaust of the locomotive he knew the engine crew had the reverse gear down in the corner and they were getting all they could out of the power. A few of the trainmen at a time came back to eat and later— gorged on steak and Mulligan—soon had the rotary pushing aside the snow in best possible time. All during this period, Johnny was cooking and talking to himself. He would shake his head and say, "I can't understand it. All this just to get me—a poor supplyman—to Denver!"

That night the conductor fixed a bed so Dan and Johnny could sleep in "the crummy" and occasionally Dan would be awakened by the noise of the exhaust of the engine and the purr of the rotary told him all was progressing satisfactorily.

With the coming of daylight, Johnny was up helping the brakeman prepare breakfast. No sooner were the ham, eggs and hot cakes piled high than the ravenous crewmen melted the food stack away about as thoroughly as the rotary was cutting down the snow.

Around 10 o'clock that morning the snow-clearing train pulled up at Utah Junction, the terminal at Denver, and a light engine took the outfit into Denver. After the engine pulled to a stop, Dan thanked the entire train, engine and rotary crews for their speed in bucking the snow. Johnny, had dollar cigars been available, would have passed smokes out by the box. Dan left the still flabbergasted supplyman at the Brown Palace hotel.

And the odd thing is that up until the time Johnny Mourne reads this story he will still think Big Dan ran the special rotary from Tabernash to Denver just in order to get him there in time to make his meeting in Chicago!

But the adventures of Big Dan and Johnny Mourne are not confined to this snow-special episode. One incident recalls the words of George MacDonald in *At the Back of the North Wind*:

"Where did you come from baby dear?
Out of the everywhere into the here."

As with the private snow train, the setting was again the Denver and Salt Lake. Dan sat on the head end watching the rotary inching its way through snow piled over a score of feet high on the tracks. Outside the creeping train, wind and snow mingled in a severe storm. Dan's attention to the elements was interrupted by Johnny's sudden appearance from the observation car.

"Dan," exclaimed Johnny, "there's a woman on the train!"

"Sure enough," answered Dan, "and it's about time you discovered her as she is the only other passenger."

"Not for long, Dan. She's about to have a baby!"

It seems the high altitude made it difficult for expectant mothers to carry their babies and the Moffat was in the clouds at James Peak when Johnny fortunately discovered the plight of the female passenger. He and Dan rushed back to the observation car and found the woman was much further along than either of them had anticipated. There was no alternative to assisting in the birth.

After what appeared to the men as hours, Dan found himself holding a nine pound baby boy who was greased in olive oil from the dining car and wrapped in Pullman blankets. Instinctively Dan began singing to the baby, "Rockaby, baby, on the tree top. . . ."

Johnny didn't think this was the time for song and he said, "Dan, you damned brute, the baby doesn't know that song. We better take care of his mother."

Dan got a cot from the baggage car and he and Johnny strapped the woman's feet down and elevated the cot so that the foot section was some 45 degrees higher. This stopped the flow of blood and perhaps saved the woman's life.

The next day the Denver *Post* played up a front page story on how the actions of Big Dan and Johnny Mourne had saved the lives of a mother and her baby caught on a slow moving train in a snow storm. Dan often wonders if the Moffat baby grew up to be a railroad man and so followed the trail of glistening rails.

Quite naturally, Big Dan's position with the Rio Grande led him into contact with prominent men outside the industry. Among his friends in the political circle were George Dern, Simon Bamberger, Reed Smoot and Ab Jenkins. Governor of Utah, Dern later was Secretary of War under President Franklin D. Roosevelt and Dan recalls that friends of the late Cabinet member at his funeral filled the Mormon Tabernacle, although Dern was not a member of the Latter-day Saints Church. Late Governor Bamberger, who was president of the Bamberger Electric railroad, always called on Dan when he wanted advice on labor matters. Julian Bamberger has carried on his father's work with the Bamberger line which accomplished miracles of transportation for the Ogden Arsenal during World War II. When Reed Smoot was United States senator, he and Dan had many conferences and the great Utahn held Dan's affectionate respect. Ab Jenkins, former mayor of Salt Lake City and a close personal friend of Big Dan's, first won fame with his racing car *The Mormon Meteor,* renowned in sports circles.

While George Dern was governor, he and Dan were together on many occasions. Once the two of them went together when Dern filled a speaking engagement at the State Penitentiary. Warden Davis introduced the governor and, as a politically-minded person would say before a packed house, Dern commenced his speech with, "Gentlemen, I am certainly pleased to see so many of you here tonight!"

At these words, a convict in the rear of the hall shouted, "Governor, just sign a piece of paper for me and I won't be here long!"

Some months afterwards, Dan and Governor Dern were invited out to the prison to witness a baseball game between the Penitentiary team and the Rio Grande squad. Although the railroaders were the visitors, the inmates rooted for them and when the umpire—a lifer—made a bad decision against the Rio Grande, one convict spectator shouted "No wonder you're locked up here, you damned burglar!"

The rather unusual character of the opposing teams led to amusing comments from the stands. An argument between the Rio Grande captain and the umpire was interrupted by a spectator shouting, "Play ball!" Up from a nearby seat sprang a fellow prisoner who yelled, "Shut up, you s.o.b., you ain't going nowhere."

Given a choice, Dan prefers college football to prison baseball. Ever an ardent follower of the pigskin parade, Dan found the colorful Utes of the University of Utah to his liking. As often as possible, he watched Coach Ike Armstrong —a Drake University graduate—mold a Utah team which was often the powerhouse of the Rocky Mountain Conference and which ranged the country in intersectional tilts from Northwestern to Southern California.

Men from the Ute squad have fulfilled Dan's belief in the character building qualities of gridiron conflict. Some of these former Utah players have been Frank Christensen, All-American back, now a Salt Lake businessman; Pete Dow, chief of the Utah Highway Patrol; Lt. Commander Sid Kramer, U. S. Navy; General Sanders, youthful Army leader; and "Feets" Tedesco, Commissioner of Parks for Salt Lake City.

Two of Ike Armstrong's former players went down on the *Lexington* and later, when rescued, told how they had recalled Ike's words that a game wasn't over until the timekeeper fired his gun. This recollection of campus days kept their courage up the hours they struggled in the water.

On his 70th birthday anniversary, Big Dan had to summon his courage. Invited to what he supposed was a War Bond Drive program, the railroad executive found he was appearing at a surprise birthday gathering arranged by the Rio Grande shopmen for the "Old Man." It was as difficult for him to keep back tears as, when a child, he thought the Captain was leaving Pelham at The Big House.

PRESIDENT HEBER J. GRANT, of the Church of Jesus Christ of Latter-day Saints, and BIG DAN.

Photo credit: *Deseret News*

Famous American Legion engine built by the Rio Grande Salt Lake shops under the supervision of Bug Dan.

Spoke E. E. Monson, representing Governor Maw, "A beautiful tribute to one of Utah's finest and most cooperative citizens." Said R. K. Bradford, executive assistant to the Trustees of the Rio Grande, "This is the finest thing that has ever been done for the finest man I have ever known."

As the shop force presented Dan with birthday gifts, the Army Air Base band played *Hail to the Chief*.

At this time 1917-18 scenes were being repeated in Salt Lake City as troop trains moved through Rio Grande territory which was important as a railroad link between the midwest and the Pacific coast. The huge military bases in Utah and Colorado strained the capacity of the rail lines with men and material, but never to the breaking point.

Although Dan has no sons, the record of his ancestors, who have been in every war this nation has fought since Revolutionary days, remained unbroken. His daughter, Dorothy, a graduate of Rowland Hall and the University of Utah, was a sergeant in the United States Marine Corps Women's Reserve.

In January, 1943, Big Dan retired. Up from his sick bed rose Dan's beloved friend, President Heber J. Grant of the Church of the Latter-day Saints, to attend a retirement party given by railroad and Utah officials for the Rio Grande mechanical executive. "Big Dan Cunningham," commented the railroad's *Green Light* "is the highlight of railroading in the Salt Lake division's history of the Rio Grande."

Excluding the time spent as superintendent of motive power on the Moffat, for some thirty years Big Dan had been an official of the Denver and Rio Grande Western. He had held his position in Salt Lake longer than all other Salt Lake master mechanics combined!

Naturally Big Dan has missed the regular contacts with his railroad friends such as Frank Thayer, who for many years was his chief clerk; W. B. Hall, Rio Grande purchasing agent, who started his career as a messenger boy in Salt Lake; J. D. Loftis, who left the D. & R. G. W. to become general superintendent of motive power for the Atlantic Coast Line; and L. F. Wilson, the Rio Grande assistant manager, who never swears, but who can say "dog-gone!" in such a manner it gets results. He missed his men in the shops, the machinists and the foremen, the car builders and the boilermakers, the hostlers and the engine crewmen.

Big Dan recalled his friend genial W. H. Sagstetter, the chief mechanical officer of the Rio Grande, and chuckled at the recollection of the time Bill Sagstetter dropped a twenty dollar bill in the collection plate at St. Patrick's back of the shops much to the amazement of Monsignor Giovannoni ("Father Joe"). The good father later queried Dan about "your rich friend from Denver."

And, in a similar vein, Dan thought of the time he, Sagstetter, Billy Hall and Curt Green, of Baldwin Locomotive Works, had lunch in a small restaurant at Alamosa, Colorado. This is the site of the Rio Grande narrow gauge shops. Curt had paid the moderate check with a hundred dollar bill expecting the waitress to register some surprise. But hundred dollar bills weren't as exciting to the small cafe as a twenty dollar bill was at St. Patrick's.

The waitress said not one word.

Still ever paramount in Dan's mind is the amazing task the American railroads have performed in building the nation through the communities they serve. As he once wrote:

"The spirit of the officers and men of the railroads is one of helpfulness. The railroads send out experts to lecture on soil conservation, establish farm laboratories, take interest in County Fairs and encourage the 4-H and Future Farmers clubs. The rail lines establish scholarships at colleges and furnish employment for boys and girls working their way through school. The railroads ever seek to improve their performance and their personal service. This has won for them the confidence and affection of the communities they serve."

And when Big Dan is with a group of retired railroad men such as at the famed Old Timers Club in Los Angeles or who gather in the parks at Long Beach, California, to banter the merits of the Southern Pacific, the Rio Grande, the Santa Fe, or the Katy, he can speak knowingly of the progress made by his railroad.

Under the present management the Rio Grande has had new heavy rail, reballasting over the entire system, grade and curve revisions and a Central Train Control (C. T. C.) network which is the largest in the United States. To free Denver and Salt Lake from smoke, the railroad equipped the yards with Diesel switch power.

All wayside depots were replaced by modern stations; flood lights and radio communication were installed in the larger yards. Shop equipment was modernized and new power purchased. Crack mountain engines from the Norfolk and Western changed their dress from that of the South to Rocky Mountain attire and went to work for the Rio Grande.

It was like a breath of air from the Shenandoah Valley when Dan saw these behemoths arrive on the Rio Grande from the Roanoke, Virginia, shops. They were like finding a picture of ones first love. He had visions of Williamson and Portsmouth; of the Captain sitting at The Big House in Bedford county and, bathed by the shifting shadows of the Virginia afternoon, saying to his boys:

"We have to build for the future. . . . so that a new South will grow and prosper and the nation will not be made up of loosely bound sections, but be a country held together by bonds of iron. That, sons, is what the railroads can do."

And Dan thought of Billy Mahone and his dreams of a railroad empire brought to life by the great Norfolk and Western; of the pioneers of the Santa Fe, who freed the commerce of the southwest from the bondage of the wagon-train; of courageous General Palmer, who conquered the mighty peaks of the Rockies to throw his Rio Grande tracks across the top of the world; and daring David Moffat, who literally gave his life so that his Denver and Salt Lake line might live.

As one Confederate general said of his troops, "Angels could have done no more!"

. . . . Big Dan hopes that somewhere beyond rails end the Captain in his gray uniform with its gold buttons sits astride Pelham, listens to the distant roar of the rushing trains of America's railroads and knows that his sons have played their roles in the drama of the nation's High Iron.

THE END

BIBLIOGRAPHY

Alexander, E. P., *Iron Horses*, 1941, W. W. Norton and Company, New York City.

Blake, Nelson Morehouse, *William Mahone of Virginia*, 1935, Garrett & Massie, Richmond, Va.

Bradley, Glenn Danford, *The Story of the Santa Fe*, 1920, R. G. Badger, Boston, Mass.

Cunningham, Frank, *The Saga of Herbert S. Wall*, 1943, Mechanical Department Committee, Coast Lines, Atcheson, Topeka and Santa Fe Railway, Los Angeles, Calif.

Cunningham, Frank, *Sky Master—The Story of Donald Douglas*, 1943, Dorrance and Company, Philadephia, Pa.

Freeman, Douglas Southall, *Lee's Lieutenants*, Vol. I, 1942; Vol. II, 1943; Vol. III, 1944; Charles Scribner's Sons, New York City.

Haupt, Herman, *Reminiscences of General Herman Haupt*, 1901, Wright and Joys Company, Milwaukee, Wis.

Henry, Ralph Selph, *The Story of the Confederacy*, 1931, The Bobbs-Merrill Company, Indianapolis—New York City. Grosset & Dunlap, New York City.

Henry, Ralph Selph, *First With the Most Forrest*, 1944, The Bobbs-Merrill Company, Indianapolis—New York City.

Hill, Dean, *Football Thru the Years*, 1940, Gridiron Publishing Company, New York City.

Hinckley, Bryant S., *Daniel Hanmer Wells and Events of His Time*, 1942, The Deseret News Press, Salt Lake City, Utah.

Hungerford, Edward, *Daniel Willard Rides the Line*, 1938, G. T. Putnam's Sons, New York City.

Jones, Virgil Carrington, *Ranger Mosby*, 1944, University of North Carolina Press, Chapel Hill, N. C.

Kneiss, Gilbert H. *Bonanza Railroads*, 1941, Stanford University Press, Stanford, Calif.

Lee, Captain Robert E., *Recollections and Letters of Robert E. Lee*, 1904, Doubleday-Page & Company; 1926, Garden City Publishing Company, Garden City, N. Y.

Leslie's, Frank, *Illustrated History of the Civil War*, 1894, Mrs. Frank Leslie, Publisher, New York City.

Macartney, Clarence Edward, *Little Mac—the Life of General George B. McClellan*, 1940, Dorrance and Company, Philadelpia, Pa.

Ramsdell, Charles W., *Behind the Lines in the Southern Confederacy*, 1944, Louisiana State University Press, Baton Rouge, La.

Simpkins, Francis B. and Patton, James W., *The Women of the Confederacy*, 1936, Garrett & Massie, Richmond, Va.

Swiggett, Howard, *The Rebel Raider*, 1934, The Bobbs-Merrill Company, Indianapolis—New York City.

Thompson, Slason, *Short History of American Railroads,* 1925, D. Appleton and Company, New York City—London.

Tracy, Russel Lord, *Some Experiences of Russel Lord Tracy,* 1941, privately printed, Salt Lake City, Utah.

Wiley, Bell Irvin, *The Life of Johnny Reb,* 1943, The Bobbs-Merrill Company, Indianapolis—New York City.

Battles and Commanders of the Civil War (edited by Marcus F. W. Wright), 1906, E. F. Stanley, Washington, D. C.

The Bugle, 1895, 1896, Virginia Agricultural and Mechanical College (Virginia Polytechnic Institute), Blacksburg, Va.

The Photographic History of the Civil War (Francis Trevelyan Miller, Editor-in-chief), 10 volumes, 1911, The Review of Reviews Company, New York City.

Who's Who in Railroading, 1940, Simmons-Boardman Publishing Corporation, New York City.

William Jackson Palmer, privately printed by George Foster Peabody, 1931, Saratoga Springs, N. Y.

American Guide Series: *Virginia,* 1940, Oxford University Press, New York City; *Ohio,* 1940, Oxford; *West Virginia,* 1941, Oxford; *Wyoming,* 1941, Oxford; *Utah,* 1941, Hastings House, New York City; *New Mexico,* 1940, Hastings House; *Colorado,* 1941, Hastings House; *Texas,* 1941, Hastings House; *Nevada,* 1940, Binfords and Mort, Portland, Oregon.

Newspapers: Virginia; The Roanoke *Times,* The Roanoke *World News,* The Richmond *Times-Dispatch,* The Richmond *News-Leader,* The Lexington *Gazette,* The *Rockbridge County News,* The Lynchburg *Advance.* Colorado; The *Rocky Mountain News,* The Denver *Post.* Utah; The *Deseret News,* The Salt Lake *Telegram,* The Salt Lake *Tribune.*

Magazines: The Denver and Rio Grande Western *The Green Light,* The *Norfolk and Western Magazine,* The Southern Pacific *Bulletin,* The *Santa Fe Magazine, Railroad Stories, Trains, Railway Age, Locomotive Engineers Journal, The Improvement Era, Ghost Town News.*

ABOUT THE AUTHOR

"Frank Cunningham possesses a rabid curiosity for all that goes on. In other words he wants to know what makes the world go 'round." So wrote John Oliver, Richmond, Va., *News-Leader*, in reviewing the author's book *Sky Master*.

This desire has carried Mr. Cunningham and his typewriter into many settings. In fact, his first checks came from an editor while the author was still a student at Senn High School, Chicago. He has analyzed such diverse subjects as the political setup of Central America for *Scribner's-Commentator*, Arabian aviation activities for *Flying* and collegiate ice hockey for *Ski*. His pen-portraits of newsworthy names and events have appeared in over thirty different national magazines and have won him the commendation of the New York *Post*. Magazines have also published his fiction.

But this author's by-line has not been confined to the magazine field. He was a *United Press* correspondent for three years, did news-features for the Washington *Herald*, was a special writer for *Transradio Press* and *Universal Service* and had a syndicated column on Hollywood. He has written numerous feature articles for the Richmond *Times-Dispatch* and the Philadelpia *Inquirer*.

His radio adventure fantasies—recalling the chronicles of Sir H. Rider Haggard—have been on the air from networks in the United States and Canada to Australia and New Zealand. Also he has sold to the motion picture studios and has been by-lined on military releases when he was with the 40th Division Press Relations, G-2, A. U. S.

Now living in Santa Monica, Calif., Frank Cunningham was born in Roanoke, Va., in 1911, was graduated from Washington and Lee University, 1932, where he was a member of Delta Upsilon, Sigma Delta Chi and Pi Delta Epsilon.

Termed by the Baltimore *Sun* "one of the country's better known aviation writers," Frank Cunningham won national honors with *Sky Master,* a biography of Donald Douglas, airplane builder. A Book-of-the-Month Club recommendation, *Sky Master* received the Manuscripters Club Award as "the most outstanding book of 1944."

In *Big Dan,* Frank Cunningham turns his attention to a field he has known since childhood, the romantic land of High Iron, American railroading. The author's family has been prominent in railroad and railroad equipment circles since the days after the War Between the States when his paternal grandfather helped build the Shenandoah Valley railroad.

Besides his writing, Frank Cunningham has appeared on the radio as a commentator with his own program.

The one thing he admits he has never done publicly is to sing—*The Wreck of the Old 97!*

INDEX

A

Academy of Music, 117.
Adams, Mrs. R. B., 149.
Adams, Maude, 247.
Aishton, Richard Henry, 295.
Ainsworth, Frank, 230.
Allan, John and Frances, 135.
Alabama, The Captain moves to, 94.
Alamosa, Colo., 338.
Albuquerque, N. M., 165-167.
Alleghany Institute, 144-46.
Alleghany Portage, 43.
Allen, Horatio, 51.
Alexandria and Loudon, 63.
Alexander, E. P., 76.
Anderson, Edward, 125.
Anderson, Robert, 76.
Apperson, A. B., 308.
Appomattox Railroad, 82.
Armstrong, Ike J., 110, 334.
Ashby, Turner, 36.
Atcheson, Topeka and Santa Fe, 20, 161, 163.
  166, 169, 170, 245, 248-50, 270, 339.
Atlanta, Ga., 58, 70, 71, 72.
Atlantic City, N. J., 327.
Atlantic Coast Line, 219.
Atlantic, Mississippi and Ohio Railroad, 77, 82, 86.
Austin, Stephen E., 92.

B

Bass, Sam, 92.
Baldwin, Matthais W., 53.
Ballenger, Otto J., 176.
Ball, William A., 235.
Baltimore and Ohio, 53, 55, 60, 69, 71, 72,
  82, 86, 183.
Bamberger Electric, 333.
Bamberger, Julian, 333.
Bamberger, Simon, 333.
Barr, J. M., 179.
Baskervill, Dr. George, 323.
Beacom, T. H., 302.
Beauregard, Peirre Gustave Toutant, 66, 71, 76.
Beck, Inspector, 311.
Bedford county, 21, 22, 25, 38, 47, 78.
Beless, James T., 242.
Bennett, W. J., 222.
"Best Friend of Charleston," 52.
Big House, the, 21, 23, 26, 36, 38, 47, 49, 53,
  70, 75, 78, 79, 90.
Bible, Dana Xenophon, 110.
Bierman, Bernard William, 110.
Bingham and Garfield, 307-08.
Blanchard, Jean Pierre, 50.
Blacksburg, Va., 105.
Bonanza country railroads, 304.
Boston and Maine, 20.
Boston-Troy, 46.
Boswell, Louise, 189.
Boyd, Belle, 136.
Bradford, R. K., 337.
Bragg, Braxton, 76.
Brazil, Confederates in, 77.
Breen, Pat, 272, 290.
Bridgton and Harrison, 236.
Brigham Young University, 99.
Brown, E. L., 230, 279, 295, 297.
Buckner, Simon Bolivar, 56.

Buckner, Simon Boliver, Jr., 125.
Buchanan, President, 56.
Buell, ordered to advance, 67.
Buffalo Bayou, Brazon and Colorado Railroad, 92.
Buford, Harry T., 136.
Bunker Hill Monument, 51.
Burnham, Colo., 162, 297.
Burnham, Luther, 242.
Burrus, Julian Ashby, 112, 117.
Burnside, Ambrose Everett, 56, 77.
Bryant's, Dan, minstrel show, 39.
Byrant, Gridley, 51.
Byrd, William, 155.

C

Camden and Amboy, 51.
Camp, Walter, 110.
Canby, E. R. S., 74.
Canavan, Mike, 288.
Cannanea, Rio, Yaque and Pacific, 304.
Canon City, Colo., 249.
"Cannon-ball Express," 321.
Carey, James T. 54;
Carroll, Charles, 53.
Cascade Tunnel, 291.
Castle Valley Railroad, 266.
Central of Georgia, 20.
Central Pacific, 58, 92, 203, 240, 305.
Cervera, Admiral, 153.
Chapin, Chester W., 43.
Chasles, Victor E., 308.
Charlestown and Hamburg Railroad, 51, 53, 81.
Chesapeake and Ohio Railway, 81.
Chesterfield Railroad, 102.
Cheyenne, Wyo., 159-61, 164, 275.
Chicago, Burlington and Quincy, 160, 269.
Chicago Great Western, 259.
Chicago, Indianapolis and Louisville Railroad, 222.
Chicago and Northwestern, 160, 295.
Chicago, Rock Island and Pacific, 269.
Christensen, Frank, 334.
Chrysler, Walter, 259.
Cincinnati, Portsmouth and Virginia Railroad, 191.
City Point Railroad, 82.
Clark, Sarah, 38.
Clarke, Clarence H., 87.
Clothier, Isaac H., 233.
Coal, carried by the N. and W., 102.
Coal, discovered in Virginia, 101.
Coast Guard, 263.
Colorado and Southern, 160, 178, 251, 269, 275.
Colonial parsons, 49.
Colorado College, 239.
Colorado Springs, 239, 270.
Confederate railroad raids, 60-69, 183.
Confederate Torpedo Boats, 73.
Conference for International Security, 284.
Connecticut and Passumpsic River, 219.
Cooke, Jay and Company, 87.
"Copper Engine," 321-22.
Cornith, Miss., 66.
Corona, Colo., 271-73, 279, 285, 287.
Coronado, 250.
Cowan, Fred, 222.
Craig, Colo., 271, 283, 286, 287.
Crockett, David, 92.
Crouse, John, 41.
Crozet, Benoit Claude, 127, 140.
Cruze, James, 317, 318.

Cunningham, Dan, United States Marshal, 208.
Cunningham, Daniel Goode, about to be lynched, 19; born, 21; hears folk tales, 32; learns of cavalry exploits, 35; visits Lynchburg, 38; learns of General Haupt, 39; goes to country school, 48; Captain tells him of War Between States railroad fighting, 55-74; moves to Roanoke, 19; attends school, 87; at San Marcos, Texas, 90-93; becomes machinist apprentice, 95; builds Rio Grande whistle, 99; attends V. A. M. C. (V.P.I.), 104; shoots tree from gun, 112; vacations Mountain Lake, 119; makes football varsity, 121; with National Guard, 128; visits Elizabeth Van Lew, 137; at Smithfield, 133; works for N. & W., 141; entertains snake, 142; plays football for Alleghany, 144; marries Inez, 151; goes west, works for Union Pacific, 161, Rio Grande 162, Santa Fe at Albuquerque, 165; at Needles, 168; experiences with Indians, 172-76; hauls locomotive over mountains, 182; hires railroad cowboy, 184; saves Roosevelt special, 185-89; becomes general foreman at Portsmouth, 190; with N. & W. at Williamson, 202-221; improves water supply, 205; learns of and meets Devil Anse Hatfield, 208-12; runs for legislature, 214; made D. & R. G. Supt. of Shops, 221; learns Rio Grande background, 233; contacts Mormons, 239; begins friendship with Heber J. Grant, 242; writes on railroads, 252, 311, 338; with Jack Dempsey, 258; at wreck, 261; mistaken for Mormon leader, 265; is supt. motive power on Moffat, 268; fights storms, 271; carries Boston bankers, 283; aids Zulu, 286; returns to Rio Grande as asst. supt. of motive power, 294; handles shop during strike, 297; becomes master mechanic, 303; works on movie, 317; builds "Copper Engine", 321; named Honorary Fire Chief, 322; day set aside in his honor, 322; handles historic ceremony, 324; orders out "snow special," 328; delivers baby on D. & S. L., 332; with Governor Dern, 333; given surprise party, 334; retires, 337; visions railroad pioneers, 339.
Cunningham, Donna, 215, 246, 251.
Cunningham, Dorothy, 246, 251, 337.
Cunningham, Frank Henry, 90, 93, 155, 196, 199, 215, 291, 311.
Cunningham, George Lodiwick, 21, 22, 23, 42, 55, 60, 65, 68, 71, 72, 75, 79, 86, 94.
Cunningham, George William, 21, 87, 90, 103, 151.
Cunningham, Margaret, 174, 246, 251.
Cunningham, Otho Thomas, 21, 90, 94, 103.
Cunningham, Susan, 21, 94.
Cumberland Valley Railroad, 164.
Curtis, George William, 293.
Curtiss, Glenn, 116.
Custer, George, 69.

D

Dakota and Great Southern Railroad, 46.
Danforth, Jack, 117.
Dashiell, T. E., 126.
Davis, Jefferson, 59, 60, 70, 92, 137, 154.
Debs, Eugene V., 151.
Delk, Captain, 131.
Dempsey, Jack, 258.
Denver, James W., 250.
Denver and Cheyenne Railroad, 235.
Denver, Colo., 162, 245, 250, 269, 328, 331, 339.
Denver, Pacific and Northwestern Railroad, 270.
Denver and Rio Grande Western, 20, 99, 156, 162, 181, 220, 223, 224, 230-33, 235, 242, 245, 248, 251, 257, 258, 261, 270, 291, 292-93, 294, 300, 307, 317, 324, 339.

Denver and Salt Lake (Moffat Railroad), 20, 149, 225, 268, 270-91, 314, 328, 332, 339.
Dern, George, 333.
"DeWitt Clinton," 53.
Dickens, Charles, 288.
Dime novels, 89.
Doarnberger, John, 98.
Dodd, William Edward, 117.
Dodge, Colonel, 307.
Dodge, Granville M., 77, 159, 164.
Dotsero Cutoff, 269, 293, 303.
Dow, Pete, 334.
Durango, Colo., 248.
Duryea, C. A., 144.

E

Early, Bishop John, 41.
Early, Jubal, 69, 164.
Edman, C. L., 265.
Edison, Thomas, 143.
Eley, Bertie, 151, 175, 176.
Eley, Inez, 103, 118, 131, 133, 149, 151, 246, 257.
Ellet, Mr., 96.
Elliot, Washington L., 66.
Ellis, William Webb, 108.
Enright, J. F. 220.
Eureka and Palisades Railroad, 305.
Eureka Nevada, 304.
Eusey, Fred, 181.
Evans, O. B., 240.
Evans, John Henry, 242.
Ewing, Thomas, 56.

F

Farragut, "Oak Heart," 67.
Fink, Henry J., 141.
Fitch, George, 269.
Fillmore, Millard, 60.
Flint, Senator, 57, 58.
Fluhr, George, 169, 180.
Football, Inter-collegiate Assn. formed, 108; early history, 108.
Fort Sumter, 53.
Forrest, Nathan Bedford, 67, 76, 150.
Fuller, E. G., 96.
Fuller, Lee, 271.
Francisco, Peter, 140.
Frazier, Ralph, 118.
Fredericksburg and Valley Plank Road, 85;
Frisco Lines, 156.
Future Farmers, 338.

G

Garfield, James A., 47.
Gallipolis, Ohio, 193.
Garnett, General, 55.
Georgia Central, 72.
Gillett, Len D., 218.
Gillis, H. A., 141.
Gillespie, John, 243.
Girard, Stephen, 50.
Glass, Carter, 284.
Glass, Corbin, 144.
Goodman, Thomas W., 95.
Granite Railway Company, 51.
Grant, Heber J., 242, 335.
Grant, Heber J., 242, 337.
Grant, Ulysses S., 47, 56, 68, 69, 74, 76, 137.
Great Northern, 56, 279, 293.
Green, Curt, 338.
Greenwood, Frank, 20.
Gregg, William, 85.
Gummere, William S., 108.
Gunnison, Colo., 231.

H

Hager, Mark, 314.
Hail, W. B., 337, 338.
Halleck, Henry, 66, 77.
Hampton, Lieutenant General Wade, 36.
Hansen, Levere M., 322
Harris, Joel Chandler, 34.
Hatfield, Devil Anse, 208.
Haupt, General Herman, 41, 42, 43, 50, 64.
Havil, Fred, 169.
Hawk, Chief Black, 152.
Hayes, Rutherford B., 47.
Haymond, Frank, 307.
Helper, Utah, 222.
Henfry, Benjamin, 134.
Henley, Russel, 100, 220.
Henry, Patrick, 47, 155.
Hiawatha Coal Mines, 266.
Hippy, Fred, 144.
Ho Marka Ma Sava, 186.
Hood, General, 70, 71.
Holliday, Cyrus K., 166.
Hollins College, 116.
Hook, John, 47.
Hooker, Joe, 46, 77.
Hoosac Tunnel, 43, 45, 46.
Houston, Sam, 92.
Houston and Texas Central, 92.
Huber, Gus, 181

I

Ibex, Colo., 251.
Ingles, J. Lewis, 121.
Illinois Central, 56, 57, 58.
Iron Man, 32, 33.

J

Jacklin, D. C., 308.
Jackson, Stonewall, 44, 64, 125, 127, 136, 183.
Jamerson, George H., 125.
James River and Kanawha Canal, 38.
James, William Lewis, 123.
Jefferson, Thomas, 41, 121, 134, 155, 219.
Jenks, William J., 53, 54, 206.
Jenkins, Ab, 322, 333.
Jones, A. C., 121, 122.
"John Bull," 51.
Johnston, Albert Sidney, 66, 74.
Johnston, Joseph E., 76, 154.
Johnson, General Superintendent, 207.
Johnson, L. E., 221.
Johnson, Samuel, 316.
Junkin, George, 125.

K

Kamptner, Gustav, 313.
Kansas Pacific Railroad, 234.
Kearney, Alexander, 204, 215.
Kimball, Frederick J., 101, 157.
"King, J. B.", 264.
Kramer, Sid, 334.

L

Lampton, F. W., 195.
Latter-day Saints, (See Mormons).
Lawler, Jimmy, 169.
Lawrence, Ruby Grayson, 216.
Leadville, Colo., 296.
Lee, Fitzhugh, 36, 153, 155.
Lee. Robert E., 63, 64. 65, 74, 124, 154, 284.

Leftwich, Colonel Augustine, 38.
Lemen, W. W., 216, 220, 229, 268, 302.
Lenard, James, 301.
Lewis, Andrew, 200.
Lewis, W. H., 144, 148, 162.
Lincoln, Abraham, 41, 44, 59, 63, 69, 70, 71.
Little, Ann, 318.
Little Rock, Ark., 261.
Loftis, J. D., 337.
Louisa Railroad, 81.
Louisville and Nashville, 20, 67.
Louisiana Purchase, 250.
Louisiana State University, 58.
Lyman, Francis M., 243.
Lynch, Charles, 38.
Lynch, John, 38.
Lynchburg, Va., 26, 38-41, 55, 59, 80.

M

Maceo, Antonio, 150.
Macon and Western Railroad, 71.
Maher, Nicholas D., 54.
Mahone, William, 73, 77, 82, 85, 86, 87, 167, 191, 233, 241, 339.
Manassas Gap Railroad, 44, 63, 71.
Manning, Master Mechanic, 161.
Marlowe, Julia, 190.
Marshall, George, 125.
Marshall, John, 140.
Marshall Pass, 231, 232, 326.
Martin, Luke, 160.
Martinsburg, West Va., 183.
Massie, J. A., 110.
Maury, Matthew Fontaine, 154.
Meade, George, 45, 56.
Mecklenburg Declaration, 22.
Medlock, Walt, 156.
Menelik, King, 150.
Miller, E. J., 52.
Mills, Darius O., 305.
Mills, Robert, 154.
Mingo county, 199.
Minor, Nev., 259.
Minneapolis and St. Louis Railroad, 222.
Missouri Pacific, 270.
Mobile and Montgomery Railroad, 78.
Moffat, David H., 270, 339.
Moffat Railroad (see Denver and Salt Lake).
Moffat Tunnel, 269-71, 291, 303.
Mohawk and Hudson Railroad, 53.
Moore, Thomas, 134.
Monon, 20.
Monroe, President, 154.
Monson, E. E., 337.
Monson Railroad, 236.
Morgan, John H., 67, 68.
Mormons, 220, 239, 242, 246-47, 266, 267.
"Mormon Meteor," 333.
Morris, Jack, 317.
Morse, W. E., 268, 273.
Mosby, John S., 71, 72.
Mountain Lake, Va., 119.
Mourne, Johnny, 328.
Mudge, H. U., 308.
Mumford, Colonel Thomas T., 35.
Murphy, Pat, 296.
Mustgrove, Steve, 80.

Mc.

McAdoo, William G., 296.
McAlexander, General, 298.
McBryde, Dr. J. M., 105, 110, 112, 113, 119.
McCallum, D. C., 46.
McCarthy, Wilson, 303.

McClellan, George, 55, 56, 58, 60, 63, 65, 71, 77.
McDonald, George, 332.
McIntyre, Oscar Odd, 193.
McKinley, William, 47.
McLaughlin, Annie, 92.
McNamara, W. V., 208.

N

Nace, Uncle, 29, 30, 49, 79.
Narrow gauge fever, 235.
Nashville and Chattanooga Railroad, 44, 67.
National Railway of Mexico, 239.
Needles, Arthur C., 54, 146.
Needles, Calif., 168, 257.
Nelson, Joe, 268.
Nephi, Utah, 257-58.
New Mexico University, 166.
New Orleans, Jackson and Mississippi Railroad, 76.
New York Central, 53.
New York, New Haven and Hartford, 20, 51.
Nichols, H. E., 95.
Norfolk and Petersburg Railroad, 82, 85, 86.
Norfolk, Va., 85, 128.
Norfolk and Western Shop, 18, 95, 141.
Norfolk and Western Railway, 17, 19, 20, 54, 79,
    81 87, 94, 101, 126, 141, 157-58, 179,
    187, 191-92, 314, 339.
Norristown and Valley, 42.
North Carolina University, 125.
Northern Pacific, 47, 56, 160.
Nye, Henry, 219.

O

Ochee, 173, 175.
O'Donald, Pat, 261.
O'Farrell, Charles T., 117.
O'Flarity, Tim, 289.
Ogden, Utah, 236, 240, 241, 324.
Ohio and Mississippi Railroad, 60.
"Old Gabriel," 99, 100.
"Old Gabriel's Colt," 100.
"Old Ironsides," 53.
O'Neill, W. J., 259, 302, 311.
Orange and Alexandria Railroad, 44, 63, 64, 82, 85.
"Orukter Amphibolos," 50.
Owen, Robert L., 86.
Owens, E. T., 224.

P

Pacific Coast, initial railroads, 57.
Palisades, Nev., 304.
Palmer, J. I., 106.
Palmer, William Jackson, 233, 239, 324, 339.
Partington, Sally, 136.
Patton, George, 125.
Patten, James, 105.
Peake, Frank, 121.
Pelham, Major John, 32.
Pemberton, burned railroad shops, 68.
Pendleton, Brigadier General W. N., 31.
Pennsylvania College, 42, 45.
Pennsylvania Railroad, 42, 234.
Penewha, 173.
Perlman, A. E., 304.
Petengill, Charlie, 194, 200.
Petersburg Railway Company, 81.
Petersburg, Va., 72, 73, 142.
Philadelphia, Germantown and Norristown Rail-
    road, 53.
Philadelphia and Reading, 53.
Philadelphia, Wilmington and Baltimore Railroad,
    60.
Phoebus, Harrison, 152.

Pleasanton, Alfred, 77.
Plutonian Euterpean Academy, 115.
Pocahontas, Va., 128.
Poe, Edgar Allen, 121, 135, 140, 152.
Pope, General, 56, 64.
Potomac, 63.
Portsmouth and Roanoke, 81.
Portsmouth, Ohio, 190, 339.
Price, Sterling, 77.
Priddy, Lawrence, 134.
Priester, Dora May, 284.
Pritchard, W. L., 305.
Promontory Point, Utah, 203, 240.
Provo, Utah, 229.
Ptarmagan's Point, Colo., 280, 283.
Pullman, George M., 165.
Purdue University Laboratory, 233.
Pueblo, Colo, 249.
Pyeatt, Samuel J., 302.

R

Raines, Clyde, 204.
Railroad grades, 222.
Railroad hobos, 264.
Railroad motion pictures, 317.
Railroads, beginning in United States, 50-53.
Railroads, importance in War Between States, 42,
    55, 58, 60.
Railroads, necessary to South's rebirth, 71.
Railroads, War Between States leaders turn to, 75.
Randolph, John, 154.
Randall, James Ryder, 32, 65.
Randolph Macon Women's College, 126-27.
Ray, Charles, 182.
Records, Jack, 169, 177, 180.
Richmond, Fredericksburg and Potomac Railroad,
    44, 81.
Richmond and Danville Railroad, 46, 76.
Richmond and York River, 63.
Rice, Grantland, 121.
Richardson, Larry, 323.
Richmond and Petersburg, 81.
Rio Grande Western, 236, 239, 240, 241, 245,
    307.
Roanoke College, 144.
Roanoke, final return to, 94.
Roanoke Fire Department, 101, 111.
Roanoke Light Infantry, 17-19.
Roanoke Machine Works, 81, 95.
Roanoke Shops, 18, 98.
Roanoke Shops, 98.
Roanoke, Va., 80, 168, 189, 213, 246, 257, 339.
Robinson, A. A., 167.
Rodes, Robert Emmett, 76.
Roosevelt, Franklin D., 333.
Rose, Thomas E., 137.
Roosevelt, Theodore, 185.
Royal Gorge, 245, 248-50.
Russell, D. A., 164.
Russell, James, 292.
Rutland Railroad, 20.

S

Sabra, Grandma, 79.
Sacramento Valley Railroad, 57, 58.
Sagstetter, William H., 303, 338.
Salida, Colo., 326.
Salt Lake and Garfield Western, 268.
Salt Lake City, Utah, 99-101, 113, 146, 220, 224,
    236, 240, 241, 245, 246-47, 269, 294, 321,
    322.
Sanders, General, 334.
Sanderson, R. P., 163, 180.
Santa Fe, N. M., 244.
San Marcos, The Captain moves to, 90.
San Pedro, Los Angeles and Salt Lake, 241.

Santa Fe., N. M., 244.
Saunders, John Henry, 90.
Saunders, Susan Sabra, 21.
Schley, Commodore, 153.
Schramm, Clem, 321.
Scioto Valley Railroad, 157, 190.
Seaboard Railway, 81.
Searchlight, Nev., 182.
Selma, Marion and Memphis Railroad, 76.
Sexton, Charles, 304.
Sexton, John, 304, 306.
Shanks, David C., 114.
Sharp, Thomas, 183.
Shenandoah Valley Railroad, 78, 80, 157.
Sherman, William Tecumseh, 36, 56, 57, 58, 68, 70, 71, 72, 76.
Shepherd, Dr. T. B., 151.
Shields, A. C., 323.
Shields, James, 77.
Sheridan, Phil, 66, 71, 74, 164.
Shipp, Scott, 105.
Siallis, Sam, 218.
Sibley, Henry Hopkins, 165.
Sisnaros, Evangelin, 153.
Smith, Dr., 126.
Smith, Jesse W., 245.
Smith, Joseph, 246.
Smith, Kirby S., 74.
Smith, Lot, 245.
Smith, Robert H., 54.
Smith, W. S., 68.
Smoot, George H., 85.
Smoot, Reed, 333.
Snyder, Jack, 301.
Solms-Braunfels, Prince Carl Zu, 92.
South Carolina Railroad, 51, 52.
South Side, 63, 82, 86.
Southern, 20, 42, 52, 222.
Southern Pacific, 20, 58, 251, 259, 306, 339.
Sprague, Lucien C., 222.
St. George, Utah, 240.
Stagg, Amos Alonzo, 109.
Stanard, Jane Craig, 140.
Stanton, Edwin M., 43.
Stevens, John, 50.
Stevens, Robert, 51.
Stevenson, General, 72.
Stone, Ky., 315.
"Stourbridge Lion," 51.
Streator, Bob, 144.
Strong, William B., 167.
Stuart, Jeb, 36, 64, 65, 183.
Sullivan, Bill, 297.
Sullivan, Red, 258.
Swan, Henry, 303.
Sweeney, Engineer, 272.
Sweet Briar College, 116.
Sydney, Sir Phillip, 151.

T

Tabernash, Colo., 271, 273, 274, 290, 328.
Tapp, W. J., 181.
Taylor, Saunders, 121.
Tedesco, "Feets," 334.
Tennessee Pass, Colo., 291.
Terra Haute and Cincinnati Railroad, 77.
Texas, early railroads, 92.
Texas Pacific, 77, 92.
"Three Little Confederates," 47.
Thayer, Frank, 337.
Thayer, Jim, 297.
Thistle, Utah, 257, 317-18.
Toland, General, 136.
Todd, Mallory, 132.
"Tom Thumb," 52.
Tompkins, Sally L., 136.

Thomas, George H., 234.
Thomson, James, 287.
Thomson, J. Edgar, 234.
Tonopah and Goldfield, 189, 257.
Turchin, Colonel, 60.
Turner, Joe, 144.
Tusculum College, 68.
Tracy, Russel, 324.
Trimble, Isaac Ridgeway, 76.
Trinidad, Colo., 270.
Tyler, Daniel, 77, 154.
Tynes, Mary Elizabeth, 136.
Tynes, Samuel, 136.

U

Uintah Railway, 222-23.
Union Pacific, 77, 96, 159, 160, 203, 240, 269.
United States Military Railroads, 42, 43, 44, 45, 46, 68, 70.
Utah Central, 240.
Utah and Northern, 160.
Utah Railway, 265, 308.
Utah scenery, 247.
Utah State Penitentiary, 334.
Utah University, 99, 265, 308.

V

Valdez, Don Francisco Cuervo y, 165.
Van Lew, Elizabeth, 135, 137, 140, 165, 234.
Van Lew, Helen, 180.
Van Lew, John, 101, 103, 135, 161, 165, 180, 189, 257.
Valentine, Edward V., 154.
Valesques, Loreta Janeta, 136.
Vaughn, Operator, 220.
Vermont Central, 219.
Violet, Aunt, 34, 49, 79.
Virginia Agricultural and Mechanical College, 105.
Virginia College, 116, 118.
"Virginia" and "Monitor," 234.
Virginia, earliest railroads, 81-82, 102.
Virginia mansions, 132.
Virginia Military Institute, 85, 125, 127, 128, 145, 147, 148, 219.
Virginia Polytechnic Institute, 125, 127, 128, 141, 144, 146, 147, 148, 214.
Virginian Railroad, 200.
Virginia and Tennessee Railroad, 38, 63, 81, 82, 86.
Virginia, University of, 121.

W

Wabash, 20.
Wall, Herbert S., 178.
Wallace, Lew, 166.
Warner, Glenn Scobey, 109.
Warrenton Junction, Va., 68.
Washington, Augustine, 113.
Washington and Lee University, 75, 122, 124, 125, 145, 148.
Washington, George, 50, 111, 112, 114, 124.
Watkins, Joseph P., 117, 118.
Watson, P. A., 45.
Weems, Parson, 112.
Weldon and Petersburg, 63.
West, Edward A., 254.
Western Maryland, 42.
Western Pacific, 20, 239.
Western Railroad Company, 45.
Westinghouse, George, 143.
Weymouth, Miss, 126.
Wheeler, General Joe, 36.
Wincheck, General Foreman, 167.
Wingo, Chief Charlie, 202, 213.
Wigmore, Steve, 98.

Willard, A. E., 221.
Williams, A. D., 259.
Williams, Lloyd W., 125.
Williamson, Bob, 217.
Williamson, West Va., 200, 339.
Willoughby, Madame, 153.
Wilson, Woodrow, 284, 292, 296.
Wilson, L. F., 337.
Winchester and Potomac, 55.
Wood, Jasper, 184.
Wood, Leonard, 109.
Wright, W. W., 70.

Wyoming Central, 160.
Wyman, Frank, 161, 167, 180, 189, 257.

Y

Young, Brigham, 160, 240, 241, 246.
Young, Brigham, Jr., 242.
Young, J. H., 297, 302.
Young, John W., 160.

Z

Zuni, Va., 141.

No. 6